LAND IS THE CRY!

Land Is the Cry!

Warren Angus Ferris, Pioneer Texas Surveyor
and Founder of Dallas County

Susanne Starling

Texas State Historical Association

Austin

Copyright © 1998 by the Texas State Historical Association, Austin, Texas. All rights reserved.
Printed in the United States of America.

Library of Congress Cataloging-in-Publication Data:

Starling, Susanne

      Land is the cry!: Warren Angus Ferris, pioneer Texas surveyor and Founder of
Dallas County/ Susanne Starling.

        p.   cm.

        Includes bibliographical references (p.   ) and index.

        ISBN 0-87611-161-4 (alk. paper)

        1. Ferris, Warren Angus, 1810-1873.   2. Pioneers—Texas—Biography.
3. Surveyors—Texas—Dallas County—Biography.   4. Frontier and pioneer life—Texas.
5. Dallas (Tex.)—History.   6. Texas—History—Republic, 1836–1846. 7. Trappers—Rocky
Mountains—Biography.   I. Title.

        F390.F42S73   1998

        978'.02'092

        [B]—DC21

                                         98-31394

                                              CIP

5 4 3 2 1   98 99 00 01 02

Published by the Texas State Historical Association in cooperation with the Center for Studies
in Texas History at the University of Texas at Austin.

Book design by William V. Bishel. Dustjacket design by David Timmons

∞ The paper used in this book meets the minimum requirements of the American National
Standard for Permanence of Paper for Printed Library Materials, z39.48—1984.

This book was made possible in part by grants from the Summerfield G. Roberts Foundation, Dallas,
and the Dallas County Sesquicentennial Celebration Committee.

DALLAS   COUNTY   SESQUICENTENNIAL

CELEBRATION   COMMITTEE

FRONTISPIECE: Early surveying instruments used during the Republic of Texas include a Gurley
"peepsight" compass with its walnut storage box, drafting instruments in a sharkskin case,
pocket compasses, and A. B. Lawrence's *Texas in 1840, or the Emigrant's Guide to the New
Republic* (1840). Instruments from the collection of the Star of the Republic Museum,
Washington, Texas. *Photograph by Lynn A. Herrmann, Fredericksburg, Texas.*

Contents

List of Illustrations

ACKNOWLEDGMENTS

Books are never written in a vacuum. My grateful appreciation goes to those persons whose encouragement over the past decade led to the publication of this book. Friends Jacqueline Burden, Kelly Patterson, Mary Lynn Hartman, and Mary Jo Majors thoughtfully read the manuscript and offered helpful suggestions. Professors at the University of North Texas, Hugh Ayer, the late Jim Pearson, William H. Wilson, and Randolph B. "Mike" Campbell, aided in its publication. Dallas-area historians A. C. Greene, Mike Hazel, Sam Ratcliff, Frances James, Elizabeth Enstam, and the late Max McCullough encouraged me at crucial times; while computer whizzes David Preston, Bill Webb, and Francis Shaner helped me over or around seemingly insurmountable obstacles on the word processor.

Greg Smith and Nell Been Davis, Ferris descendents; Imogene McCausland, widow of Walter McCausland; and Linda M. Lebsack, secretary to the late Fred A. Rosenstock; were important sources of information. They and Texas historians Archie P. McDondald, Paul Lack, Robert M. Utley, and Fred Tarpley answered my queries. A big thanks goes to surveyors Robert West (now deceased), Dan Hampton, Ken Gold, and the North East Texas Chapter of the Texas Society of Professional Surveyors who helped me understand their work. Countless librarians and archivists, including Marcelle Hull, Gerald Saxon, Joan Dobson, Gaylon Polatti, Marjorie Bays, Linda Nickles, Dennis Rowley, Scott Duval, David Farmer, Dawn Letson, Kay Bost, and Catherine Mason, along with Tom Wells, Susan Corrigan, and Kit Goodwin, aided my research.

Finally, my appreciation to John Crain and the Summerlee Foundation for financial support, and to my editors, George B. Ward and William V. Bishel, as well as the anonymous readers for the Texas State Historical Association, who tried to save me from error.

PREFACE

WARREN ANGUS FERRIS, a New York Yankee, deserves to be remembered as "Father of Dallas County." Except for a twist of fate, Dallas, Texas, would have been named "Warwick" by its two founders, surveyor Ferris and Mississippi land speculator William P. King. Historian A. C. Greene calls Warren Ferris the most "unappreciated figure in Dallas history." Ferris has more than local significance, for his gripping story encompasses three arenas: the Niagara frontier of western New York, the fur-trading country of the Rocky Mountains, and northeast Texas under the Republic.

Ferris merited fame even before he came to Texas in 1837. While working as a trapper and fur trader in the Rocky Mountains for six years, Ferris kept a diary of his adventures. This journal, *Life in the Rocky Mountains*, accompanied by a map which he drew from memory, provides a unique and valuable picture of trapper and Indian life during the fiercely competitive early 1830s. Ferris also gave the public its first written description of Yellowstone's amazing geysers and other natural phenomena.[1] His writings fueled westward expansion, responding to America's insatiable curiosity about the frontier.

Although he reveled in the sights and adventures of the Rocky Mountain West, Ferris viewed the fur trade as a business by which he could accumulate enough money to become a landowner. His personal ambition and drive allowed him to advance rapidly from company employee to independent trader. William H. Goetzmann's landmark essay, "The Mountain Man as Jacksonian Man," takes note of Warren Ferris as an example of the "expectant capitalist" operating on the American frontier.[2]

Following his brother Charles D. Ferris to Texas the year after the Texas Revolution, Warren Ferris became official surveyor for Nacogdoches County, which then included much of northeast Texas west to the Trinity River. Although Charles returned to Buffalo, Warren Ferris spent thirty-five of his eventful sixty-two years in Texas.

---

1. W. Turrentine Jackson, "Texas Collection," *Southwestern Historical Quarterly*, 43 (Oct., 1939), 249 (cited hereafter as *SHQ*), notes that Warren A. Ferris, a Texas resident, was the first known individual to describe (in writing) the natural phenomena of the Yellowstone region.

2. William H. Goetzmann, "The Mountain Man as Jacksonian Man," *American Quarterly*, 15 (Fall, 1963), 406.

In his pivotal role as surveyor, Ferris was positioned to effect the direction and character of western settlement. Historian Patricia Limerick suggests that, since the Westward Movement was about the acquisition of real estate, the surveyor or land agent might better characterize the era than the gunfighter or sheriff.[3] Possessor of inside information on the prime locations—best water, best soil, best timber—a surveyor like Warren Ferris was set to show a profit for himself, his relatives, and friends.

Surveying at the Three Forks of the Trinity in 1839, Ferris entered the area before John Neely Bryan, the traditionally recognized founder of Dallas, and Ferris's surveys determined the line of future streets and roads that shaped the physical appearance of the county. In 1847, Ferris settled down to farming east of White Rock Creek. Except for brief surveying assignments with the Peters Company and Dallas County, he devoted himself to raising a family, developing agriculture on the Blackland Prairie, and building a community.

Fortunately, this literate and versatile young surveyor was also a prolific letter writer, and much of the family correspondence to and from Buffalo has been preserved. Letters from Ferris, his mother, his brother Charles, and most importantly his half-brother Joshua and half-sister Sarah Lovejoy were located and collected in the 1930s and 1940s. These letters, along with Sarah's copybook and diary, are preserved in the Ferriss/Lovejoy Collection at Brigham Young University in Provo, Utah; it is through this lengthy correspondence (1828–1885) that we may reconstruct the exciting life and times of Warren Ferris.

At first glance, Ferris seems a stereotypical figure of the trans-Mississippi West. The three phases of his career—fur trapper, land surveyor, and pioneer farmer—parallel the evolutionary stages of development described by Frederick Jackson Turner.[4] The westering experience, with all its good and evil elements, molded our national character and is reflected in the life of Warren A. Ferris. Idealism, romance, curiosity, and love of adventure gave way to self-interest, ambition, and greed, which finally mellowed into patience, contentment, and civic responsibility. The restless young wanderer matured into a responsible family man as wild Texas was tamed.

Warren Ferris, however, was a complex man, not easily categorized. His long and varied career reveals the best and worst characteristics of the nineteenth-century frontiersman. A man worthy of the Romantic period,

---

3. Patricia N. Limerick, *Legacy of Conquest: The Unbroken Past of the American West* (New York: W. W. Norton, 1987), 55.

4. Frederick Jackson Turner, "The Significance of the Frontier in American History," The Annual Report of the American Historical Association for 1893, reprinted in Turner's *The Frontier in American History* (New York: H. Holt & Co., 1920), 1–38. Turner's thesis emphasized the successive waves of development, each more complex and sophisticated, which surged across the continent.

he was a flawed hero. His moods and motives often conflicted, producing a tension between ideals and behavior not unusual for his times or ours. Ferris's action-packed life is rich in human drama. His is a story, both interesting and important, full of violent aggression, intrigue and scheming, poignant romance, and bitter family quarrels.

INTRODUCTION

The Modern Search for Warren Ferris

My SEARCH FOR THE ELUSIVE WARREN A. FERRIS began in a freshman history class I was teaching at Eastfield Community College in Dallas, Texas. Sitting at the back of the room that spring of 1981 was a slim, quiet student who announced one day that his ancestor had surveyed Dallas County and that he "had the papers to prove it." Greg Smith presented a scrapbook that had belonged to his grandmother Lucy Pounds Smith, descendant of Warren Angus Ferris; her collection included two of the oldest original letters written from Dallas County.

Research in Buffalo, New York, Provo, Utah, and Austin and Nacogdoches, Texas, revealed that others had sought information on Warren A. Ferris. The earliest inquiry was made in 1900 by Olin D. Wheeler, a St. Paul, Minnesota, journalist who ran across a copy of the *Western Literary Messenger*, an obscure periodical that carried an intriguing early description of Yellowstone geysers. Wheeler used the excerpt in *Wonderland*, a 1901 publication of the Northern Pacific Railroad, and sent inquiries to the Buffalo *Courier* as to the identity of its mystery writer.[1]

A series of simultaneous but, at first, unrelated events in the 1930s led to investigations of Warren Ferris in Texas, New York, and Colorado. These efforts finally merged and continued into the 1960s. A Buffalo stamp collector, Walter McCausland, came into possession of a packet of the Ferris/Lovejoy correspondence in 1936. At first only interested in the stampless covers, McCausland's casual reading of the letters turned to fascination.[2] He acquired the original Warren Ferris map of the fur country, located numerous Ferris descendants, and found additional family letters.

---

1. On September 4, 1900, Wheeler's inquiries were answered by Warren A. Ferris's nephew, George W. Ferris, writing in the Buffalo *Courier*. On Sunday, May 5, 1901, the *Courier* carried a story entitled, "Buffalo's Greatest Explorer" which asserted the importance of Ferris's Rocky Mountain journal. "Probably no other trapper of the time was like young Ferris, educated and of unusual literary ability." Ferriss/Lovejoy Collection, MSS 1505, Box V, Folder 10 (Harold B. Lee Library, Brigham Young University, Provo; cited hereafter as FLC).

2. McCausland related the story of his sleuthing to the Buffalo Stamp Club on Oct. 8, 1937. "Where My Hobby Horse Led Me" described the evening when he, his wife, and sister first pored over the Ferriss/Lovejoy letters, "almost a complete correspondence . . . rich in local color, frequently brilliant in literary style . . . occasionally sparkling with genius." McCausland devoted much of the next fifteen years to travel and correspondence related to Ferris.

As interest in Texas history flourished around the time of the 1936 Texas Centennial, Homer DeGolyer of Dallas spotlighted Ferris as the surveyor of Dallas County. DeGolyer, who was collecting original material on southwestern history, researched county and state records, interviewed Ferris's living descendants in Texas, and located family letters.[3] Professor Harrison A. Trexler of Southern Methodist University interviewed Ferris's neighbors in the Dallas Forest Hills Addition. About the same time, R. B. Blake of Nacogdoches collated significant East Texas history, including materials related to Ferris and his associates.

In Denver, Colorado, bookdealer Fred Rosenstock collected back issues of the *Western Literary Messenger* which had serialized Ferris's journal. He decided to publish the colorful account of Rocky Mountain adventures. Paul C. Phillips, University of Montana historian of the fur trade, was working with Rosenstock when, through a fellow historian, Fred Voelker of St. Louis, they were put in touch with McCausland and DeGolyer. In 1940, through the opportune circumstance of these Buffalo and Texas connections, Rosenstock published *Life in the Rocky Mountains* and a reproduction of the Ferris map of the Yellowstone country.[4] Paul Phillips's excellent introduction not only gave the proper historic setting on the fur trade but also contained important material on the Texas years.

Local Dallas historians W. R. Conger, Ruth Cooper, and Robert Cole worked with Lucy Pounds Smith in the late 1950s to save the Ferris Cemetery and draw well-deserved attention to Warren Ferris as the founder of Dallas County. In 1962, the Dallas Public Library hosted an exhibit on Ferris. Mrs. Smith, Mrs. Mike McKool, Eugene Ferris, and other descendants organized a family association to memorialize their ancestor. By coincidence, also in 1962, the Knox/Albright Art Museum in Buffalo exhibited a collection of the work of Lars Sellstadt, an early Buffalo artist who had married into the Ferris/Lovejoy family and painted their portrait.

In the years after publication of Ferris's journal, McCausland, DeGolyer, Rosenstock, Phillips, and descendants of Ferris exchanged

---

3. DeGolyer, brother of Dallas geologist Everett DeGolyer and president of Southwestern Microfilm, Inc., wrote "Warren A. Ferris, 99 Years Ago," for the Dallas *Morning News*, Nov. 15, 1939. He interviewed Ferris's three living children, Mary Catherine Cannon, Sarah Ellen Greenwood, and Henry Ferris, who became major sources for his writing. Homer DeGolyer Collection (DeGolyer Library, Southern Methodist University, Dallas).

4. In his introduction to the second edition of Warren A. Ferris, *Life in the Rocky Mountains: A Diary of Wanderings on the Sources of the Rivers, Missouri, Columbia, and Colorado, 1830–1835* (2nd ed.; Denver: Old West Publishing Co.,1983), Rosenstock called publication of the Ferris work "one of the great adventures" of his career as a bookdealer and publisher. His forty years prospecting the works of Ferris, a thrill, "sometimes approaching a miracle," were highlighted by the location of ten missing issues of the *Western Literary Messenger* in 1939; his meeting with DeGolyer who had material on Ferris in Texas; and as the book was about to go to press, contact with McCausland who had located the Ferris map.

correspondence and visits. Their mutual interest in Warren A. Ferris created a bond of friendship. McCausland wrote, "I have a warm spot in my heart for old man Ferris and anything connected with his life and work."[5] DeGolyer and McCausland each planned to write a biography of Ferris, but both died, DeGolyer in 1963 and McCausland in 1966, before achieving that goal. Rosenstock purchased the Ferris map from McCausland in 1946, and after her husband's death, Mrs. McCausland sold Rosenstock the private collection of Ferris/Lovejoy letters. Rosenstock hoped to locate the original manuscript of *Life in the Rocky Mountains* and/or a portrait of Warren A. Ferris, which would merit re-publication of the book.[6] In 1983, Rosenstock's Old West Publishing Company printed a second edition, edited this time by LeRoy Hafen of Brigham Young University where the Ferris/Lovejoy Collection is now housed. New information furnished by Dale L. Morgan on Ferris's 1834 connection with the Hudson's Bay Company merited this second printing.

While researching the life and times of Warren A. Ferris in Buffalo, in the Rocky Mountains, and in Texas, I have frequently retraced the trail of these earlier historians. The near-miracle of their collaboration, the dedication of their efforts, and the close personal friendships that evolved among them are impressive. Time is long overdue for proper recognition of Ferris's role in the settlement of the North Texas frontier. It is my hope to complete the work of earlier researchers with publication of the biography of a very human man whose life mirrors the conquest of the American West, from Canada to Mexico.

---

5. McCausland to rancher Jack Doorty who resided in "Ferrisland" near Kalispell, Montana, Apr. 15, 1941. FLC, Box V, Folder 6.

6. Unfortunately, neither a photograph of Warren A. Ferris nor his manuscript have been located. His surviving descendants gave verbal descriptions of Ferris to Walter McCausland (Jan. 25, 1959, and Apr. 20, 1951, ibid, Box VI, Folder 8, and Box IX, Folder 3), stating that he closely resembled his son Charley. The Ferris manuscript "Life in the Rocky Mountains" was in a black trunk supposedly lost when a fire destroyed the home of his son Robert.

Part One

☆

Mountain Man

ON THE NIAGARA FRONTIER

W ARREN ANGUS FERRIS was born the day after Christmas, 1810, in Glens Falls, New York, the son of Angus and Sarah Gray Ferriss. His father was a descendant of Zachariah Ferriss, an early New England settler who participated in King Philip's War (1675–1676) against the Massachusetts Indians and died in an expedition against Port Royal in Queen Anne's War (1710). Over the next five generations, the Ferrisses inched their way westward, joining a host of Yankees migrating into lands unsettled by whites. The second Zachariah Ferriss (as it was then spelled) settled in Connecticut where he, his wife, and four of their eight children converted to the Society of Friends. One of these, son Benjamin Ferriss, became a noted speaker at Quaker Hill, New York; he and his family were among the few of the "friendly persuasion" who supported the American Revolution. Benjamin's grandson, the first Warren Ferriss, moved his family to Glens Falls where two of his grandsons married daughters of Benjamin Wing, a prominent Quaker.[1]

Of the early Ferriss family and their cousins the Wings, a descendant, Ferris Greenslet, wrote in her family history, *Under the Bridge*:

> A generation before the Greenslets had taken fish off the North Shore and run into trouble in Salem, a numerous clan of Wings, Quakers, non-combatants and astonishingly prolific, landed at Sandwich in the inner elbow of Cape Cod. With them, intermingled in business and marriage, came a family of Ferrises, less prolific, more belligerent, and exemplifying in every generation the self-evident truth that adventures are for the adventurous. . . . As time went on, the Ferrises flourished less than the Wings, who attended the Friends' meeting house and kept their eye on the business ball, while the Ferris men read Tom Paine and Byron, played the flute, went shooting and fishing even on Sunday, but seldom to church. . . . When the budget failed to balance, when they didn't have cash in the pocket to buy what they wanted, fishing Ferrises would sell off a little land and proceed as before. They became a kindly, humorous, imaginative, sporting, not very thrifty tribe.[2]

---

1. Sarah Louise Ferris Austin, Warren Ferris's niece, compiled "The Ferris Ancestry" (1876), documenting seven lines of descent from passengers of the Mayflower. (Manuscript in Grosvenor Library, Buffalo, New York; Microfilm copy, MF 79.60, DeGolyer Collection).

2. Quoted in Walter McCausland, "Life of Warren Angus Ferris," unpublished manuscript (1959), 4–5 (Buffalo and Erie County Historical Society Library, Buffalo, New York; cited hereafter as BHS).

It was a penetrating evaluation of "the fishing Ferrises" that seemed to hold true over the generations.

Angus Ferriss was born in Glens Falls, New York, in 1787, the year of the writing of the new Federal Constitution. In 1810 he married Sarah Gray at Queensbury, a little village between Lake George and Glens Falls. Sarah, daughter of Jabesh and Ruth Norton Gray, also traced her ancestry to early New Englanders. "Sally," as she was called, was three years older than Angus. Their first child, Warren Angus Ferris, named for his father and grandfather, was with the young couple when they joined the westward migration in 1812. At Pittsfield, thirty miles south of Utica, they paused for the birth of their second son, Charles Drake Ferris, on December 5.[3] (Warren and Charles Ferris later chose to drop the second "s" in their surname.)

When Angus Ferriss reached Buffalo on New York's western frontier, he judged business opportunities to be slight so he pushed on to the settlement at Erie, Pennsylvania. Hostilities with the British in Canada soon erupted into war; Oliver Hazard Perry worked feverishly to build a flotilla of American gunboats at the Lake Erie port. Quick to seize opportunity, Angus Ferriss purchased two small ships for freighting military supplies. His hopes for financial success were dashed when he fell ill, and on September 10, 1813, the day of Perry's decisive naval victory over the British at Put-in-Bay, Angus Ferriss died, his life cut short while he was still in his twenties.[4]

After her husband's death Sally Ferriss returned to Buffalo where she met Joshua Lovejoy, a successful merchant who suffered heavy personal and financial losses in the War of 1812. He was in his forties, fifteen years older than she, and had a teenage son, Henry Lovejoy. Like the Ferrisses, the Lovejoys had moved west in the early 1800s, from the Finger Lakes region to Avon on the Genesee River, and, in 1811, to Buffalo where Joshua engaged in commerce on Lake Erie. When war was declared in June 1812, the British seized one of Lovejoy's ships. Later his warehouse at Black Rock was burned by invading British troops. His losses ran into the thousands of dollars, but his personal loss was even greater.[5]

Buffalo village, so vulnerable to attack from Canada, was lulled into a false sense of security after Gen. Peter B. Porter's men repulsed a British attack at Black Rock Ferry in July 1813. Lovejoy and his son participated in this battle, twelve-year-old Henry bringing home a British cannonball

3. Reference to family Bible owned by W. H. Britton Jr., grandson of Joshua F. Lovejoy, Nell Been Davis Collection (Center for American History, University of Texas, Austin; cited hereafter as CAH). These papers were preserved by Sarah Ellen Ferris Cannon, youngest surviving daughter of W. A. Ferris and Nell Been Davis, Ferris's great-granddaughter.

4. McCausland, "Life of Warren Angus Ferris," 5.

5. Ibid., 7.

as a souvenir of the victory. However, the trouble was not over; in December, the British, outraged at the burning of Newark (Niagara) and Queenstown, Ontario, again advanced on American settlements. Gen. George McClure abandoned Fort George and drew his troops back to Batavia, New York, leaving the Niagara Frontier exposed to British attack.

Most of Buffalo's residents fled before the British advance. Militiamen, including Joshua Lovejoy, attempted a defense at Black Rock, but after a brief skirmish on December 30 the militia fell back, allowing the British and their Indian allies to sweep unopposed into Buffalo village. Some twenty defenders manned a single cannon at Main and Niagara Streets; overloaded in haste, the cannon blew off its chassis. Those villagers who remained fled in panic as the cry went up, "Run, boys, run. The Indians are coming!" Young Henry Lovejoy was with his mother that fateful winter morning. Since he had fought against the British, Sarah Lovejoy ordered her son to flee; but she determined to stay and defend their home. At his mother's insistence, Henry escaped into the woods to join the flood of refugees in a pell-mell flight up the eastern road that led to safety.[6]

The Indians moved up Washington Street, torching the wooden houses as they came. Balls of fire shot into the sky like meteors in the cold morning air. Martha St. John, who lived across the street and survived the attack, saw an Indian enter the Lovejoy home and rip the curtains from the window. When Mrs. Lovejoy struck his hand with a carving knife, the Indian raised his tomahawk, killed the plucky woman with one crushing blow to the head, and proceeded to fire the house. As British troops entered the village, Mrs. St. John and her daughters dragged Sarah Lovejoy's body from the flames. Later that day, New Year's Eve, they placed her corpse on a bed in the partially burned house. Tears were shed at the sight of the tall woman, dressed in a black silk dress, her long dark hair hanging down through the rope bedcords to the floor. Two days later, the Indians came back to set a funeral pyre that cremated Mrs. Lovejoy's body inside her own home. As the charred village still smoldered, Lovejoy, his son, and other refugees returned to a scene of desolation. What once had been a pleasant woodland village was but smoking ruins. Joshua and Henry Lovejoy gathered Sarah's bones into a handkerchief for burial.[7]

It was a personal tragedy never to be forgotten by those who experienced it, but life went on and a new beginning was made. Only a few months later, in April 1814, the Buffalo *Gazette* reported: "Buffalo village

---

6. The burning of Buffalo and death of Sarah Lovejoy are well documented in "Recollections of the Burning of Buffalo," *Publications of the Buffalo Historical Society*, I (1927), 311–336, with an eyewitness account from Margaret St. John Skinner, 337–406. See also H. Perry Smith (ed.), *History of the City of Buffalo and Erie County* (2 vols.; Syracuse: D. Mason Co., 1884), I, 154–156, II, 60.

7. Ibid.

. . . is rising again."[8] The sound of saw and hammer told of reconstruction underway. By June, Buffalo boasted twenty-three houses and forty crude huts, four general stores, and three taverns. Gen. Winfield Scott established his headquarters there, a reassuring signal to the returning settlers. Sally Ferriss found a frontier village rising from the ashes of war when she arrived in 1814. Life was hard for a widow with two infant sons, but Sally was young and energetic; she opened a sewing and millenery shop in her home. She was also attractive, and marriageable women were few. Her vivacious spirit, her sparkling blue eyes and well-shaped mouth set in an oval face, and her proud, determined chin caught the eye of widower Joshua Lovejoy.[9] On August 13, 1815, the couple was married by Judge Oliver Forward.[10]

Thus it was that the two Ferris boys, Warren and Charles, grew up in an agreeable Niagara frontier village that bustled with activity. Their cottage on Tupper St. near Main was one of a cluster of wooden structures on a bluff or "terrace" overlooking elder swamps with Lake Erie beyond. At the foot of Main was Buffalo Creek, from which the village took its name. To the west across the narrow Niagara River and its awesome falls lay Canada. To the north and east was a vast woodland with abundant supply of lumber, furs, and game. The streams and lake furnished fish aplenty. Warren Ferris learned early to hunt, fish, and trap. Squirrel, deer, duck and turkey, bass, pike, or lake trout supplemented the family larder.

Fifty years later, Henry Lovejoy recalled the pristine beauty of the Buffalo surroundings in his youth:

> save a few scattered hamlets . . . one unbroken and primeval forest cast its shadows over and around its whole extent; relieved only by a little ray of light, where the entrance to Buffalo Creek revealed to the eye a glimpse of the broad expanse of Erie's waters. . . . At that time no vessel's prow had ever disturbed the peaceful waters . . . naught but the Indian's canoe and the batteau of the . . . voyageur, as in his yearly round in search of fur. . . . At that time Buffalo Creek . . . a quiet and lonely spot, where fishing and fowling could be enjoyed to their full extent.[11]

About four miles up Buffalo Creek was a populous village of friendly Senecas, the "keepers of the western gate" of the Iroquois Confederacy. Here began Warren Ferris's fascination with Indian culture. The men and boys of Buffalo often joined in Indian celebrations like the strawberry

8. McCausland, "Life of Warren Angus Ferris," 8.

9. Ibid., 6. The description perhaps is based on the Sellstadt portrait of Sally Ferris.

10. Buffalo *Gazette*, Aug. 15, 1815.

11. Henry Lovejoy, "Reminiscence of Buffalo (1810)," a paper read before the Buffalo Historical Society, May 3, 1864 (BHS Manuscript Collection).

dance, the green corn festival, and the mystic sacrifice of the white dog. Warren and Charles Ferris, tagging behind their older stepbrother Henry, observed Indians lounging on the streets of Buffalo, silently smoking their pipes, soaking up the sun, watching the white man's activity. The boys learned to recognize colorful Indian stalwarts like Red Jacket, noted for his oratorical skill in maintaining the rights of his people. In June, when they collected their annuities, Indians outnumbered whites in Buffalo. Tribesmen from as far away as Ohio and Pennsylvania gathered on a grassy slope to compete in foot races and ball games, amazing the Ferris boys with their speed and agility.[12] Skill in hunting and fishing and knowledge of Indians would prove invaluable to Warren Ferris in later years.

During the years of Ferris's childhood, Buffalo experienced a fresh wave of settlers. New roads hastened westward migration, and there was even talk of an overland canal connecting Lake Erie with the Hudson River which might make Buffalo a major inland port. However, the economic hopes of Buffalo village were dashed when, in 1816, an unseasonable June frost nipped local crops. Farmers wore coats to work in the fields and kept hearthfires burning all summer. The time that went down as "The Year Without a Summer" brought food shortages and inflation, which caused hardship for many, including the Ferris/Lovejoy family. Now there were six to feed and clothe as Joshua Ferris Lovejoy was born June 18, 1816. Henry Lovejoy became a breadwinner at age sixteen, teaching school at Cold Spring. Sally brought in some money with her sewing and millinery work, but her husband had little success in pressing his claim for war losses. He wrote, "I would be willing to accept land for my claim if the treasury would be willing to pay me that way." Lovejoy borrowed money from his brother Jonathan in New York City and asked him to find an opening for Henry. In 1817, Henry visited his mother's brother, James Johnson, in York (Toronto), Upper Canada, where young Lovejoy ran a writing school and continued his own studies. Happily, the spring of 1817 brought warmer weather and improved business. An influx of settlers from New England occupied new homes built of brick from the local kiln.[13]

Sally Lovejoy must have anguished about raising three impressionable young boys in the crude frontier town vividly described by an unidentified critic:

> The habits of the villagers were what might be expected . . . among a people thrown together from so many different sources . . . leading a rude, eager, frontier life. Away from restraints, unacquainted with each other, not knowing how long they might remain together, without fortunes, many of them without families, in a community where

---

12. Ibid.
13. McCausland, "Life of Warren Angus Ferris," 10–11.

public opinion had yet to be formed, where laws and schools and customs were yet to be established, it is not strange that the people were
unscrupulous, careless and gross.

Profanity was rife on every hand. Society was held at taverns and
gaming tables. The Sabbath was a day for pleasure or of toil, as choice
or convenience required. . . . The children were without competent
schools or general instruction. . . . They met at every turn a company
of obscene idlers, or saw by the wayside a group of besotted Indians.[14]

Cultural progress was soon to come to the Niagara frontier. To meet the
spiritual needs of the rough community, a Congregational and
Presbyterian Church was organized, receiving its first pastor in 1816.
Since there was no building, services were held in the schoolhouse, a tavern, or a private home. When the Sunday School opened in August 1817,
Sally Lovejoy enrolled her two youngsters.[15] The Ferris boys probably
found Sunday School tame, but frontier Buffalo rarely lacked exciting
diversion.

As early as 1807, the citizens of Buffalo gave attention to the education
of their children. The fire of 1813 destroyed the schoolhouse at Pearl and
Swan Streets, but it was one of the first structures rebuilt. Amos
Callendar taught there in 1815, and, by 1818, when the Ferris boys were
of school age, he had been joined by Mr. Pease and the Reverend Babcock.
In 1822, a new school opened on the west side of Main Street between
Mohawk and Genesee Streets with Millard Fillmore as its youthful
teacher.[16] Sally Lovejoy's youngest son Joshua attended Buffalo's first private high school, Western Literary and Scientific Academy. Although
Warren Ferris stated that he enjoyed little formal education,[17] his few
years of schooling were likely supplemented with reading and discussion
at home. The Ferris/Lovejoy correspondence reveals a family well read,
with a flair for history and literature, an interest in the arts and sciences,
skill in mathematics and ability in languages.[18]

During the summer of 1824, Joshua Lovejoy became so ill that he and
son Henry, then twenty-four, set out for Saratoga Springs to take the
curative waters. When the treatment proved ineffectual, they went on to

14. Quoted in ibid., 12. Unfortunately, McCausland did not footnote his work,
making confirmation of sources, beyond the Ferris/Lovejoy letters, difficult. This
quote is not attributable, but McCausland, who did extensive research in newspaper, manuscript files, and other holdings of the Buffalo Historical Society, is usually reliable.

15. Ibid., 13. Church records show Warren (age six) and Charles (age four)
enrolled Aug. 3, 1817. Their names do not appear after 1819.

16. McCausland, "Life of Warren Angus Ferris," 24. Some of the locals thought
highly of Fillmore, who was new to town in 1822, and said he might rise to be a
justice of the peace or even serve in the Assembly in Albany.

17. Warren Ferris's letter to Angelina Cook of Paris, Illinois, Oct. 5, 1845, Davis
Collection.

18. McCausland, "Life of Warren Angus Ferris," 23–24.

Jonathan Lovejoy's home in New York City. Henry wrote to his stepmother that Joshua had received every care but suffered an incurable illness and grew weaker each day. Three days later, he added a postscript: "Last night at twenty minutes before eleven, apparently easy and free from pain, he breathed his last."[19]

A widow again at age thirty-nine, Sally Lovejoy faced the daunting responsibility of supporting her family of five. Warren was not yet fourteen, his brother Charles two years younger; an infant child, Ruth Norton Lovejoy, had died in 1822, less than two years of age; of the three living children by her second marriage, Joshua was eight, Sarah six, and Louisa one. The mother was thrifty and skilled as a seamstress, so she managed to hold the family together. When Joshua Lovejoy's war claims finally were settled, Sally invested with her stepson Henry in a five-acre lot on the south side of Seneca Street, west of Chicago Street, stretching to Little Buffalo Creek. By the new family home on Seneca, at the eastern edge of the village, they had a small garden, a cow pasture, and a field planted in corn and potatoes. Adjacent was Erastus Granger's woodlot and across the street was Kipp's Rope Walk.[20] Here Warren and Charles Ferris spent their formative teenage years.

During the memorable year 1825, Buffalonians moved from one exciting event to the next. On the blustery morning of June 4, an impatient throng awaited the arrival of General Lafayette who was on a 5,000-mile tour of the United States. After delay caused by heavy winds, the general debarked from a lake steamer at midday, accompanied by dignitaries and the Buffalo band who met him in Dunkirk. Loud huzzahs and a military salute greeted Lafayette on his arrival, and he was escorted to Benjamin Rathbun's Eagle Hotel where a platform had been raised.

Sally Lovejoy, mother of the Ferris boys, attended the public reception which followed the welcoming speeches. She wore a white silk dress made of two breadths of material, so tight she could hardly walk, as was the fashion of the day.[21] Dressed in such grand style, Sally was a living advertisement for her skill as a seamstress. Later the children heard how their mother shook hands with Lafayette, who greeted the crowd before hurrying on to Niagara to see the falls.[22]

---

19. Ibid., 15.

20. Handdrawn map of Buffalo property and surroundings, perhaps by Henry Lovejoy. FLC, Box VII, Folder 3.

21. Walter McCausland, "An Early Buffalo Journalist," a paper presented to The Literary Clinic of Buffalo, N.Y., May 8, 1944, 3, ibid. Box VIII, Folder 4, and BHS. Sally Ferris Lovejoy lived to age seventy-nine and frequently recalled her attendance at the Lafayette reception to her children and grandchildren. Her dress was perhaps of the Empire style, popularized in the court of Napoleon and fashionable in America in the 1820's.

22. McCausland, "Life of Warren Angus Ferris," 16–17.

Three locals did not join in the welcome for Lafayette; Isaac, Israel, and Nelson Thayer were convicted of a brutal murder and sentenced to be hanged on Friday, June 17. Morbid curiosity brought thousands of spectators to witness the event. When the hangman's ropes were placed around their necks, the Thayer brothers gave out an eerie wailing cry which was taken up by the crowd. A swish of a sword cut the ropes, and three bodies dangled in space. As the Thayers were cut down, the crowd silently dispersed. It was Buffalo's last public execution.[23]

Somewhat more wholesome was the ceremony to dedicate the "cornerstone" of the Jewish City of Refuge, to be built on Grand Island. At dawn on September 2, 1825, artillery woke the citizens of Buffalo; it was the traditional signal for important events. The day featured a giant parade with a grand marshal, bands, and military companies in full dress, dignitaries of New York, Masons and Knights Templar, and finally Mordecai M. Noah himself, originator of this dream of Ararat. Noah called for a worldwide census of Jews and a tax on each to defray expenses for emigration to the asylum of Grand Island. Ararat would be a homeland not only for Jews but also a refuge for Indians, whom Noah considered descendants of the Lost Tribes of Israel. The idealistic scheme never got much farther than the September ceremony, and finally the cornerstone was placed in a Buffalo museum as mute testimony to this unlikely project.[24]

A more practical dream was realized with the successful completion of the Erie Canal. The 363-mile-long overland canal, a superb engineering feat, connected Lake Erie with the Hudson River and the Atlantic Ocean, thereby stimulating westward development and making New York City a world-class port. The canal was built in sections; each opened as completed, some as early as 1817. In October 1825, the final and most difficult link from Lockport across the Niagara Escarpment to Buffalo was completed. When the guard rails opened, water rose to its appointed level. The canal was only four feet deep, but that was deep enough to float a loaded barge and change history.

Gov. Dewitt Clinton and a host of dignitaries came for the canal's official opening on October 26. It was a clear, crisp autumn day. Led by the village band and militia companies, a parade included workmen who had built the canal: diggers, axmen, masons, and carpenters. During the congratulatory speeches, Jesse Hawley of Lockport, whose essays had first sparked interest in an overland canal, declared that New York had "made

23. Ibid., 18–19. Also detailing events of 1825 are George Condon, *Stars in the Water: The Story of the Erie Canal* (Garden City, N.Y.: Doubleday, 1974), 7, and Richard C. Brown and Bob Watson, *Buffalo: Lake City in Niagara Land* (Buffalo: Windsor Publications, 1981), 38.

24. McCausland, "Life of Warren Angus Ferris," 19–21.

the longest canal, in the least time, with the least experience, for the least money, and of the greatest utility in the world."[25]

As the Buffalo ceremony reached a climax, dignitaries boarded the festooned barge, *Seneca Chief*, which carried two kegs of "the purest waters of Lake Erie" to be emptied into the Atlantic Ocean in symbolic joining of the waters. Another barge bore animals, rare birds, fishes, and insects of western New York, including a pair of eagles, a pair of fawns, a fox, two young bears, even two Seneca Indian boys. Pulled by four gray horses, the first boat majestically moved along the towpath. Suddenly, a thirty-two-pound cannon fired a crashing volley, setting off a cannon "telegraph" across the state. The shot was heard at Tonawanda where another cannoneer fired away so that the gunners at Lockport heard the roar and fired, and so on from village to village all the way to New York City. It took one hour and twenty minutes for the cannon relay to reach New York and set up a return relay of cannon fire to Buffalo. It seemed just about everyone in New York heard the cannonade that day; some, senses heightened by the excitement, claimed they heard four volleys.[26]

Two young, impressionable boys, Warren and Charles Ferris, lived in the throbbing frontier village of Buffalo during these exciting events of 1825. Parades and speeches, dignitaries and famous personages, cannon fire and martial music, violence and death shaped their youth. The wider world reached Buffalo and beckoned her young men to seek adventure.

The Erie Canal boosted Buffalo's growth tremendously and gave the town an air of transience. From 1812, the hamlet of 200 grew slowly until 1820 when there were slightly over 2,000 residents. After the canal opening in 1825, population boomed. By 1840, there were 18,000; by 1850, 42,000; and, on the brink of Civil War in 1860, 100,000 Buffalonians. Many only hesitated on the Niagara frontier before they plunged into the beckoning land of the interior. A sense of impermanence was aptly illustrated by Jake Beale's answer to Buffalo's perpetual housing shortage. A bargetown of derelict canal boats on the waterfront, "Bealesville" was an eyesore until the 1840s when it was destroyed by a ferocious lakestorm. The blessings of rapid growth were mixed.[27]

Pamphleteer Gideon Ball judged Buffalo in 1825 to "exhibit a bustle and hurry of business not unlike a seaport" but her houses were still mostly wood and scattered, her streets unlit except for a few oil lamps on Main Street. In summer, Niagara Street, "crossed and hollowed by running

---

25. Condon, *Stars in the Water*, 7.

26. Ibid., 5–8; McCausland, "Life of Warren Angus Ferris," 21–23. Rochester newspaper editor Thurlow Weed arranged to position special cannons at strategic points along the route, the same guns used by Commodore Perry's fleet on Lake Erie during the War of 1812.

27. Condon, *Stars in the Water*, 298.

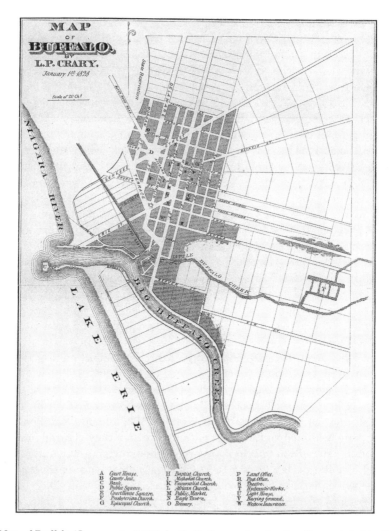

Map of Buffalo (January 1, 1828), by L. P. Crary, showing locations related to the Ferris/Lovejoy Story, including Seneca, Eagle, Swan, Canal, and Main Streets, and Little Buffalo Creek. *Courtesy the Map Collection, Buffalo and Erie County Historical Society, Buffalo, New York.*

streams, was sometimes impassible to man or beast." Buffalo boasted four clergymen, seventeen lawyers, nine doctors, three printers, and two bookbinders. An early census also listed eleven houses of "public entertainment," one rope walk, three tanneries, one brewery, one livery stable, a post office, library, Masonic hall, theater, three churches, and six schools, two private and four common.[28]

Ball failed to describe the raw, seamy aspect of the city that accompanied the rapid growth fostered by the Erie Canal. Buffalo was perhaps the most exciting western outpost of its day, pulsing with lusty action. The Canal District on lower Main Street was a natural battleground for mutually antagonistic lake sailors and canal bargemen; and Canal Street was notorious for its saloons, dance halls, gambling dens, and brothels.[29]

Three years after the thrilling events of 1825, in the fall of 1828, seventeen-year-old Warren Angus Ferris left home to seek his fortune in the West. Although family tradition has it that Sally's public rebuke of her son's incessant pipesmoking played a part in his decision,[30] it was as likely his own sense of adventure that took him west. An avid reader, Ferris devoured tales of John Colter, who had been with Meriwether Lewis and William Clark, and Hugh Glass, mauled by a Rocky Mountain grizzly.[31] The financial straits of his family were also influential. Already Henry Lovejoy had left home to make his own way. Ferris probably reasoned that his departure would ease his mother's financial burden. Sally Lovejoy perhaps also breathed a sigh of relief; for although her son would face unknown danger, it could scarcely be worse than the known evil he might encounter along Canal Street's two torrid miles of trouble. Whatever the factors in his decision, the restless young man headed west.

Warren Ferris first made his way south to Pittsburgh where he was employed by a merchant for three months until the man went out of business; then he worked briefly in a dry goods store before he took mid-April passage on a steamboat down the Ohio River. In his first letter home to his mother on November 29, 1829, Ferris said of his time in Pittsburgh, "The reason of my leaving there I shall not at present give but will only say that I left there on good terms with all I knew."[32] Later, writing to Joshua Lovejoy, he detailed his days in Pittsburgh. Perhaps trying to

---

28. Gideon J. Ball, "Buffalo in 1825," based on the town's first census taken by the state of New York in June 1825. Reprinted in *Publications of the Buffalo Historical Society*, I (1929); Frank Mogavero, "Buffalo in Year 1825," *Niagara Frontier*, VII (Spring, 1960), 44–48.

29. Condon, *Stars in the Water*, 259–261; Brown and Watson, *Buffalo*, 58–59.

30. This information is based on Homer DeGolyer's interview with Sarah Ellen Ferris Cannon. Cited in DeGoyler, "Conquest of the Three Forks," undated, unpublished manuscript, sent to Dr. LeRoy Hafen in 1974 by Mrs. Everett DeGolyer, FLC, Box VIII, Folders 2, 3. Another version of this work is on microfilm in the DeGolyer Collection, MF 79.60.

31. Ferris, *Life in the Rocky Mountains*, 84, mentions that he had read of Colter and Glass.

32. Warren Ferris to Sarah Ferris Lovejoy, Nov. 29, 1829. Quoted in McCausland, "Lives of the Lovejoys," a talk presented to the Buffalo Stamp Club, Oct. 8, 1937 (BHS). Ferris stated that he had written in July 1829 but was afraid the family had not received his letter.

inspire his wayward half-brother to greater diligence, Ferris claimed that he started with but "one Clean Shirt and 12$ in cash . . . a bold resolution to do something at once." Admitting inexperience and plain good luck, Ferris claimed his "zeal & attention" brought him jobs and recommendations until a springtime "irresistible desire to see more of the world" led him to leave Pittsburgh for Cincinnati.[33]

Despite his youth, Warren Angus Ferris appeared singularly suited to a life of adventure in the West. He was equipped with a hardy physique, ambition, and a strong sense of perseverance; "a Stranger will succeed anywhere if he has a faculty of interesting Strangers in his behalf," he wrote.[34] His letters reveal keen curiosity, a sharp eye for detail, a lively sense of humor, and a flair for poetic language. Overwhelmed by the beauty of the Ohio River as viewed from the steamer, Ferris shared his feelings with his mother:

> I cannot describe the delightful sensations I had whilst running down the Majestic Ohio at the rate of 15 miles an hour. The weather was continually serene and the prospects before us constantly new, the beauties of the forests now opening to view, and the verdant hills rising from one graduation to another until they o'er-shadowed the wide Ohio, were sufficient to animate any heart.[35]

On arrival in Cincinnati, the handsome "Philadelphia of the West," Ferris wandered about sightseeing, at first confident that he could find work at any time he wished. Later he recalled to Joshua that his purse "grew slim" and a prolonged search for "a situation" made him regret ever leaving Pittsburgh.[36]

Finally, Ferris landed a job selling magazine subscriptions for the weekly *Western Tiller.* Furnished a horse, he was sent out into rural Ohio along the Miami River. He jawed with farmers, claimed he saw corn grown twenty feet high, and gained a good deal of knowledge about agriculture. But, soon restless to see more of the West, young Ferris took passage on the steamboat *Pioneer* for Louisville. Although he was appalled by the tawdry cheapness of life in the river towns, Warren Ferris relished their excitement, absorbing every exotic sight and sound. Louisville he found "remarkable for its famous canal & disipation [sic] of its inhabitants, its cockfighting & gambling."[37] Jobs there were scarce so he

---

33. Warren Ferris to Joshua F. Lovejoy, Feb. 7, 1836. FLC, Box II, Folder 4.

34. Warren Ferris to Sarah Ferris Lovejoy, letter of Nov. 29, 1829. Ferris's mother is referred to as "Sally" Lovejoy to avoid confusion with her daughter Sarah.

35. Ibid.

36. Warren Ferris to Joshua Lovejoy, letter of Feb. 7, 1836.

37. McCausland, "Lives of the Lovejoys," 5–6. McCausland quotes from a fuller version of this first letter by Warren Angus Ferris than any that the author has been able to locate.

shipped almost immediately on the *Cleopatra* for St. Louis, arriving with his funds exhausted in June 1829.

Ferris spent his last few pennies on some decent clothing, then walked the streets of St. Louis looking for work. An employment agent he hired for $1.50 was only able to tell him there were no jobs, but did help him rent a room where he opened a "mathematical and English school." Like most arrangements of the day, it was a subscription school. His income was dependent on the number of students he could attract and what parents were willing to pay. He was in business, in debt, and at the mercy of the parents that fall of 1829. With cynical good humor, he described his school in a letter to his half-brother Joshua. On the first morning, Ferris arranged benches and made every preparation for the "cultivation of cabbage headed urchins." When the first arrival asked, "Ith thith Koolhouthe [is this the schoolhouse]?" and "Why you hant got no Kollars [scholars]?," Ferris urged patience. Soon "all sorts of little devils" graced his hall. Their teacher observed, "had their parents been as punctual in paying . . . as they [the scholars] were in attending . . . all would have been to my humor."[38] When the term ended, he closed his classroom and found other employment.

Later Ferris confessed that his failure as a school teacher was due to his own bad temper. The parents refused to pay tuition after he "cursed a little Devil for some trifling misdemeanor" and the next day "the Hon. teacher was found entirely deserted."[39] Judging himself ill-suited to teaching, Warren Ferris took employment with Lewis L. Peeder, a riverfront merchant.

His lengthy letter to his mother in the fall of 1829 projected a trip farther west to the prairies of Missouri. Ferris captured snapshot impressions of St. Louis, the river town that was the gateway to the West:

> The population of this place is composed principally of French . . . who are generally absolute strangers to the social virtues and remarkable for laziness and debauching. I have seen a man here murdered in cold blood—The labour here is performed by slaves principally—the most grand and terrific scene I have witnessed is the burning of the prairies which in a dark night is very interesting and strikes the beholder with a pleasing sensation—that terrible disease the liver complaint and the consumption so fatal to the Northern "fair" is wholly unknown here. Of all the luscious fruits I have ever tasted, the pawpaw, perculiar [sic] to this country, excels them all. The persimmon is another fruit I had never tasted before I came here.—The mode of punishing trivial offenses is by whipping publicly or putting in the Stocks—For want of room I shall be unable to give you more of this country at present. . . .[40]

---

38. Warren Ferris to Joshua F. Lovejoy, letter of Feb. 7, 1836.

39. Letter to Joshua F. Lovejoy, Aug. 20, 1840, Smith Papers, original in possession of Leland Smith, son of Lucy Mae Pounds Smith, of Mesquite, Texas (copy at Dallas Historical Society, Fair Park Hall of State; cited hereafter as DHS).

40. Warren Ferris to Sarah Ferris Lovejoy, Nov. 29, 1829.

Business was unstable in frontier St. Louis. Ferris's merchant employer failed, and he skipped town owing his creditors, including Warren. Ferris was again on the streets searching for employment. His dream of seeing the Missouri prairies materialized when he learned that Pierre Chouteau Jr. of the American Fur Company was organizing an expedition to the Rocky Mountains. The prospect of danger only made the undertaking more appealing to the bold youth.

The Chouteau family wielded power in St. Louis for over a century. Through intermarriages the Creole Louisianans, up from New Orleans, formed a tight clan of social and business prominence. Contrary to young Ferris's description of slothful Frenchmen, Pierre Chouteau Jr. looked and acted every bit the aristocrat—tall and erect, with black hair and eyes, smartly dressed, fluent in French and English, as at home in a New York City board room as a western trading post.[41] He evidenced the family traits of shrewdness, lust for money and power, and resolute ruthlessness, but even the Chouteaus took lessons in cutthroat competition from John Jacob Astor.

Frustrated in his earlier efforts to dominate the Pacific fur trade and delayed by the War of 1812, Astor's American Fur Company was ready to make its move into the Rocky Mountains. By employing Chouteau to head his Western Department, Astor gained contacts with French Canadian traders along the Upper Missouri River. The Erie Canal brought cheap transportation to the Great Lakes, opening the vast American interior to eastern and world markets. In 1827, Astor acquired Kenneth McKenzie's Columbia Fur Company whose trading post Fort Union on the Upper Missouri might be reached by steamboat. Astor carefully positioned his company to challenge the dominance of the Hudson's Bay Company in the Pacific Northwest, to break the "Blackfoot Wall" of Indian hostility which, encouraged by the British, had prevented American penetration of the Yellowstone Country.

William H. Ashley's Rocky Mountain Fur Company was Astor's initial competition. In the 1820s, Ashley recruited enterprising young Americans like Jedediah Smith, Thomas Fitzpatrick, William Sublette, Jim Bridger, and James Clyman to penetrate the mountains. He substituted white trappers for less-reliable Indians and initiated the "rendezvous," a trade fair located in the richest fur area. Here mountain men gathered annually, sold their pelts, and were resupplied to continue the hunt. By 1830, Ashley's alumni, organized into a loose partnership known as "The Rocky Mountain Fur Company," controlled the interior trade. These master mountain men knew the terrain, the beaver, and the Indians; but up

---

41. Janet LeCompte, "Pierre Chouteau, Jr.," in *Mountain Men and Fur Traders of the Far West,* ed. LeRoy R. Hafen (Lincoln: University of Nebraska Press, 1965). Eighteen biographical sketches are drawn from the ten-volume work of the same title.

against Astor's political savvy, financial resources, and knowledge of the world fur market, their days were numbered.

Warren Angus Ferris stepped into the Rocky Mountain fur trade with no knowledge of these political machinations, at a moment of fierce competition for control of the lucrative beaver market. In February 1830, he was one of a party of forty-five Americans and Canadians which headed up the Missouri River bound for the fur country.

2

TRAPPING THE YELLOWSTONE COUNTRY

ON FEBRUARY 16, 1830, the first western expedition of the American Fur Company filed away from the warehouse in St. Louis. It was a party of thirty men, mostly French Canadians, with their horses and pack mules. The sound of their merry laughter echoed in the cold morning air. At the outset, these daring young men, motivated by love of adventure and hope of profit,[1] gave little thought to the dangers, hardships, and disappointments that lay ahead.

Our knowledge of Warren Angus Ferris's adventures over the next five years rests largely on his diary and on a few reminiscences that appeared in the Dallas *Herald* in the early 1870s. Ferris developed his diary into a manuscript, "Life in the Rocky Mountains," which was published serially in the *Western Literary Messenger* (1842–1844). The journal, with its vivid descriptions of Rocky Mountain geography, was enhanced by a map that Ferris drew from memory to illustrate the area he traversed.

The adventurers traveled along the north shore of the Missouri, by the river settlements of St. Charles and Franklin, halting at isolated farmhouses to take on supplies and fatten their livestock in preparation for the hard days ahead. Nineteen-year-old Warren Ferris found that he enjoyed sleeping outdoors and eating the hearty camp fare. At Arrow Rock Ferry where they crossed the river, the expedition was joined by fifteen more Canadians. Now the party cut across country. Following Lewis and Clark's route, which avoided the river loop, they proceeded due west to Fort Osage, just below the mouth of the Kansas River near present-day Independence, Missouri. There on the edge of the vast expanse of the Great Plains, they lingered for two weeks, waiting for Indian trade goods to arrive by wagon from St. Louis. Outfitted with guns, ammunition, knives, camping gear, and six traps per man, the brigade now sported tobacco, bolts of brightly colored cloth, blankets, rouge, glass beads, mirrors, and all sorts of trinkets, called "foofaraw," to trade with the Indians. A hundred pack animals carried the equipment and trade goods.

Humor was evident in Ferris's description of pranks aimed at greenhorns like himself. The old hands loved to curl the hair of youngsters with

---

1. Goetzmann, "The Mountain Man as Jacksonian Man," 405–406, cites Ferris's ambiguous motives in joining the western expedition: "Curiosity, a love of wild adventure, and perhaps also a hope of profit," to demonstrate that the mountain men shared the American dream of upward mobility.

lurid tales of encounters with bears and Blackfeet. "We easily came to a good understanding," Ferris wrote. "They told as extravagant yarns as they pleased, and we believed as little as we liked."[2] Ferris sympathized with frustrated mule drivers when the pack animals "seized every opportunity to give . . . vexation . . . tossing their packs (which were lashed on) into a mud-hole, or turning them by a practiced juggle from their backs to between their legs."[3] It was an impromptu rodeo.

Past the military outpost Ft. Leavenworth, overlooking the Missouri River, the expedition reached the Black Snake Hills where Joseph Robidoux operated his trading post. Robidoux, a veteran fur trader, was a sometime associate of Pierre Chouteau. Now a party of forty-five, led by experienced traders Andrew Drips, Joseph Robidoux, and Lucien Fontenelle, they left the last white settlement behind them as they made for Council Bluffs where Lewis and Clark had gathered with the Indians in 1804. En route, Ferris noted the abundance of deer, elk, and prairie hens. Later, he described the graceful antelope ("poetry in motion"), the patient buffalo, pesky "moschetos," flies, sandburrs, and prickly pear cactus thorns. Each day brought some unexpected new excitement; the men lassoed and broke wild horses and fought a dangerous accidental fire that almost destroyed their gear.

They halted to rest and gather supplies at the fur-trading houses at Bellevue and Council Bluffs.[4] Springtime along the Missouri River at Bellevue was a pleasant interlude. The days were sunny, the nights fragrantly cool. Willows and cottonwoods provided welcome shade. The wide river valley was lush; the hills beyond densely forested. It was hard to imagine that behind those bluffs lay thousands of miles of treeless prairie. In preparation for their coming ordeal, the brigade organized into a tightly knit, disciplined body capable of passage across the Great Plains.

Ferris detailed the routine for pitching night camp. Horses, cattle, and mules were picketed in the center of the tents behind breastworks of baggage, guarded by sentries taking two-hour watches. After supper, the men relaxed around the campfire, puffing their pipes and "yarning" until eight o'clock when their talk was interrupted by the cry, "turn out the first guard."[5]

In May, out on the plains, the trappers followed the Platte River westward toward the Rockies, and Warren Ferris saw his first party of mounted Indians, "fine ferocious looking fellows" with whom the party dealt

2. Ferris, *Life in the Rocky Mountains*, 84.
3. Ibid., 86.
4. Lucien Fontenelle operated the Bellevue trading post while the Council Bluff post was the headquarters of Jean Pierre Cabanne, Chouteau's brother-in-law. These trading houses, established by the Missouri Fur Company in the early 1820's, were protected by Fort Atkinson, a ruin by 1830.
5. Ferris, *Life in the Rocky Mountains*, 96.

warily. The Indians were a buffalo-hunting party. On May 14, Ferris saw his first bison (a "stately old chap") and two days later a small herd. That night the party dined on buffalo steak, a welcome change from their diet of boiled corn. Next day, the young adventurer viewed thousands of shaggy bison. "Far as the eye could reach the prairie was literally covered." While he had heard tales of the plains blackened by the masses of buffalo, Ferris was awed by the sight "our language wants words to describe."[6]

On the North Platte in late May, 500 miles west of Council Bluffs, the fur traders encountered a large party of Sioux Indians bearing American flags. Ferris described their dashing appearance: Many wore "scarlet coats, trimmed with gold and silver lace, leggins & mocasins [sic] richly . . . ornamented, and gay caps of feathers."[7] Parleying in the rain, the Indians demanded trade goods. Trigger fingers rested close to firearms before the tense interview was concluded peacefully. A careful student of all he experienced, Ferris also described the first Indian lodge he saw: thirteen straight pine poles which formed a conical frame, covered with dressed buffalo skins, to the height of seven feet.[8] This lodge actually was a tomb; inside were the maimed bodies of two Cheyenne warriors, lying scalpless on a raised platform with their weapons beside them.

In June they crossed the North Platte in bull-hide canoes and camped at the foot of the Laramie Range where they were alert to possible attack by Arapaho and Gros Ventre Indians. Ferris realized that, despite their dark beauty, the ominous hills were a danger to white men, a "place of refuge and concealment for marauding Indians."[9] The trappers skirted the mountains and dropped down to the Sweetwater River.

Ferris's expedition followed a famous trail westward across the treeless plains. Maj. Stephen H. Long's 1820 military expedition and William Ashley's fur trappers had taken the path before them. What came to be known as the "Great Platte River Road" was the primary route of westward expansion, later to be traveled by Mormons fleeing Illinois, wagon trains bound for Oregon, goldseekers headed for California, and fleet Pony Express riders.[10] The trappers stuck to the shorter route on the north side of the river, the Northern or Council Bluff Road. Ferris provided the first written account of this great migration trunkline.

---

6. Ibid., 100–101.

7. Ibid., 102.

8. Ibid., 106–107.

9. Ibid., 108n. "Bull boats" featured hides sewn over a willow framework, caulked with tallow and ashes. Ferris refers to the "Black Hills," probably the Laramie or Medicine Bow Range, noted as the home of hostile Indians.

10. Merrill J. Mattes, *The Great Platte River Road* (Lincoln: University of Nebraska Press, 1969), notes Ferris's early descriptions of landmarks along the route and offers excellent maps.

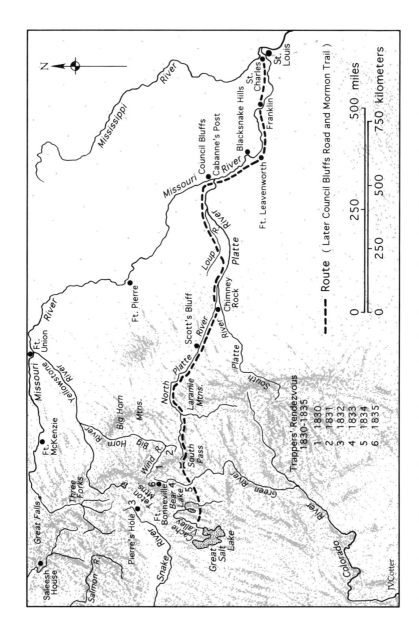

Route taken by Warren A. Ferris and the American Fur Company Brigade (1830), indicating landmarks and rendezvous sites (1830–1835). *Map by John V. Cotter.*

The landmarks of the famous route that Ferris named and described in his journal and later in reminiscences for the Dallas *Herald* included Chimney Rock, an impressive, solitary shaft rising from the level plain; Scott's Bluff, so named for a young trapper abandoned there to die; and Independence Rock, which shaded an early Fourth of July celebration.[11] Ferris's party followed the Sweetwater River to the foothills of the Wind River Mountains, traversing the Rockies through the South Pass[12] and descending to Ham's Fork of the Green River at a point near present Kemmerer, Wyoming.

Along the Sweetwater, Ferris described a "cache," the trapper method of concealing supplies. A round hole some three feet deep was dug high up on a stream bank. Sticks lined the widened hole to keep the cached supplies high and dry. Covered first with worthless hides and then stones and earth beat down as hard as possible, disguised by tufts of grass, the goods would keep for years without damage.

Warren Ferris explained the situation as he entered the fur country. "There are," he reported, "about three hundred men, who compose the roving, hunting parties of these regions."[13] About half of these were Canadians and half-breeds who spoke French. There were also a few Mexicans from the Rio del Norte who spoke Spanish and were darker than Indians. The remainder were Americans. Each year a few of the old-timers left the mountains and were replaced by less experienced newcomers so that the number remained about the same.

Trappers were cast by their garb as well as their duties. Most wore buckskin suits with fringe called "whangs" which could be torn off to mend almost anything. In the mountains, more experienced men could be distinguished from beginners by their suits; old-timers' garb was worn and greasy from feasts of wild game, with scanty fringe.[14] The mountain men were divided approximately equally into campkeepers, who performed all the duties of cooking, dressing beaver, packing and guarding horses, and defending the camp; and trappers who made excursions out from the camp. Trappers were further divided into two classes: those hired by a company to hunt for stipulated salaries and those called "Free Men" who had their own traps and horses and were free agents trading with whomever they pleased.

---

11. Ferris, *Life in the Rocky Mountains*, 103–104, 110, 117n., 118n. He calls Chimney Rock "Nose Mountain" or "the Chimney"; he added the explanation for the name of "Rock Independence," for the incident of a party celebrating the holiday in its shade occurred three months after his passing the site, in July 1830. Another description of these landmarks was given in Ferris's December 28, 1872, article for the Dallas *Herald*.

12. Although Ferris does not use the term "South Pass," his description indicates the party used this route to cross the Continental Divide.

13. Ferris, *Life in the Rocky Mountains*, 360–361.

14. Nell Been Davis, "A Fur Trapper," speech given to the Bastrop (Texas) Historical Society, Jan. 28, 1966, Davis Collection.

On reaching the mountains, the leaders of Ferris's party sent out scouts seeking independent trappers with whom they hoped to do business. Their search was fruitless, for, as the American Fur Company representatives could not know, their rivals, Jedediah Smith and William Sublette, had rendezvoused with "Free Men" on the Wind River some 140 miles to the east. Scouting with Andrew Drips, Ferris and three others traveled west via Sublette's Crossing to the Bear River and Cache Valley near present-day Logan, Utah. Cache Valley, which was to play a prominent part in their wanderings, was a favorite site of early rendezvous.[15] Since it was July and rendezvous time, they hoped to locate trappers there. Young Ferris breathlessly described the panoramic view from a lofty summit, "bleak snow-clad pyramidic peaks of granite . . . in all directions jutting into the clouds" and below the agreeable prospect of Little Lake (Bear Lake) and "a delightful valley . . . spotted with groves of aspen and cotton wood, and beds of willows of ample extent."[16] Such were the locales where fur trappers loved to congregate, but this valley was deserted. Disappointed, the scouts returned to the main party on the Bear River, their search for the elusive "Free Men" unsuccessful.

Always curious of Indian customs, Ferris took the opportunity to visit a Shoshone (Snake) village, containing about 150 lodges and about 400 warriors and their families. The trappers carried clubs to beat off the numerous dogs which greeted them with barks and nips at their legs. Crowds of children followed the whites through the camp. Industrious Indian women busily dressed skins, cut meat into strips for drying, gathered fuel, cooked, or engaged in other domestic pursuits. Ferris observed that Shoshone men were either asleep in their lodges, guarding the horses, gambling, or leisurely "strutting" about the camp.[17] On more than one occasion, Ferris wrote of the Indian penchant for "pilfering." Items about the trappers' camp had a way of disappearing, appropriated skillfully by these "untaught sons of the forest." It seemed that, to the Indians, theft was a virtue and a high art; dishonor lay in being caught.[18]

Now the trappers, having cached supplies, split into three parties and set off in search of beaver. American Fur Company brigade leaders were experienced river traders, but knew not the first thing about mountain

---

15. Cache Valley was the site of rendezvous in 1826, 1827, 1828, and 1831. Watered by the Bear River, the valley lies between Bear Lake and the Great Salt Lake.

16. Ferris, *Life in the Rocky Mountains*, 121–122.

17. Ibid., 125, 359. Ferris judged these Indians the most treacherous, cunning, and vindictive in the mountains.

18. Ibid., 125–126. Although trappers were more tolerant of Indians than most white men, they did not understand the value placed by Indians on generosity. Ferris, for instance, judged the Eutaws not thieves, but beggars. When they asked for Ferris's coat, blanket, or pistols and were refused, the Eutaws commented, "That man's heart is very small." Ibid., 387.

lore. They hoped to locate Tom Fitzpatrick, Jed Smith, or other more sea-soned trappers of the Rocky Mountain Fur Company and follow them to the best beaver haunts. When this failed, they were on their own for this fall hunt of 1830. Ferris, who traveled with Fontenelle's party to western tributaries of the Green River, saw signs of Indians and brother trappers, but few beaver. He realized, on the occasion of being thrown from a horse and breaking his gun, the hourly danger of the solitary trapper, relying "entirely upon the charity of his comrades, from whom should he be acci-dentally separated, he must either perish miserably, or suffer privations and agonies compared to which death were mercy."[19]

On the Salt River near modern Afton, Wyoming, the party tasted the headwaters of the Columbia River, dined on a fall harvest of berries, located salt licks, and viewed what Ferris called "Boiling Kettles." Late in October, the trappers went into winter camp with Robidoux, Drips, some of the Free Men, and a detachment of the rival Rocky Mountain Fur Company. Ferris described the arrival at winter camp in Cache Valley: "We exchanged salutes, and hastened to grasp the honest hands of our hardy old comrades, glad to meet and mingle with them again after a long absence, and listen to their adventures, or recount our own."[20] Despite bitter rivalry, men of competing companies, including the Hudson's Bay men, often hunted and wintered together, for they shared common hard-ships and dangers.

Around Christmas 1830, Ferris and others crossed the "Big Lake," sometimes also called "Salt Lake" because of the saline quality of its waters. In his journal, Ferris repeated the tale of the first circumnaviga-tion of the Great Salt Lake in 1826 and gave an estimate of its dimen-sions, a hundred miles long by seventy to eighty broad. Years later Warren Ferris vehemently objected to a move to name the Great Lake "Lake Bonnyville" merely to gratify the "silly conceit of a Captain Bonnyville [sic]." Ferris argued that Benjamin L. E. Bonneville neither "discovered, or explored it, nor has he done any thing else to entitle him to the honour of giving it his name."[21]

Winter 1830–1831 was the worst of Ferris's experience. Earlier he had complained of a monotonous diet of bacon and cornbread, but before that first winter was over he would have thought such food fit for a king. The

---

19. Ibid., 127.

20. Ibid., 133.

21. Ibid., 142; Dallas *Herald*, Dec. 1, 1866?, clipping in Davis Collection. Bonneville traded with Indians on the Green River between 1832 and 1835. Washington Irving, his Boswell, credited him with significant discoveries, but Warren Ferris allowed Bonneville only a "very fertile imagination." Like most mountain men of the time, Ferris viewed Bonneville with scorn. He asserted: "Major Bonneville made no discoveries. He only traversed the beaten track where thousands passed before him." Ferris had personal reasons for resenting both Bonneville and Irving.

snow was unusually heavy. Game was scarce. When wild geese appeared in early April, the hunters decided to break winter camp. They left snow-bound Cache Valley and proceeded slowly up the Bear River, near starving half the time. Ferris recalled the ordeal:

> Our horses were in the most miserable condition, and we reduced to mere skeletons. Our gums became so sore from eating tough bull meat, that we were forced to swallow it without chewing; and to complete our misery, many of us were nearly deprived of sight from inflammation of the eyes, brought on by the reflection of the sunbeams on the snow.[22]

The brigade's condition worsened when Shoshones stole horses and looted caches. Warren Ferris gave a glowing tribute to the Horn Chief, a friendly Shoshone, who forced his warriors to return the loot. He also credited the Horn Chief with saving the trappers from massacre the preceding autumn. The chief was, according to Ferris, "as remarkable for his uprightness and candour as they [his people] are noted for treachery and dishonesty."[23]

Three Flathead Indians appeared in the spring camp, bringing word from Hudson's Bay Company trappers that the snow was melting on the Snake River. The American Fur Company men decided to go there for fresh horses. They cached their furs and plodded northeast through heavy snowdrifts, trying to herd buffalo ahead of them to make a road. Their horses crashed through the melting snow and ice, foundering so that the hunters had to cut poles and carry baggage two miles through the drifts. The next day, single file, they marched six miles and back to beat down a path for their horses. In this manner, it took nine days to traverse sixty miles. Ferris described with relief the descent via the Porteneuf River to the camp of Hudson's Bay agent John Work. "Our toils were past, our hardships were over . . . even our animals seemed inspired with fresh life and vigour, for they moved off at a gallop, of their own accord, evidently delighted to find their feet once more on *terra firma*."[24] Resupplied and rested, they began the spring hunt on the Snake River. It was May 1831; the expedition had been gone from civilization a year.

Ferris's brigade leaders continued the practice of shadowing the more experienced Rocky Mountain Fur Company trappers. The 1831 hunt ranged from the headwaters of the Columbia River on the western slope, across the

---

22. Ferris, *Life in the Rocky Mountains*, 146.

23. Ibid., 143.

24. Ibid., 149. After the initial welcome, a quarrel ensued and the American Fur Company party left hurriedly, narrowly avoiding a clash with their competitors. John Work's expedition was the last of the Hudson's Bay Company to that area; the Snake Country was deemed a "fur desert," beaver too scarce to warrant the expense of further trapping. John S. Galbraith, *Hudson's Bay Company as Imperial Factor, 1821–1869* (Berkeley: University of California Press, 1957), 101–102.

Continental Divide, via Lemhi Pass, to the headwaters of the Missouri River on the eastern slope of the Rockies. Beaver trapping was good on Henry's Fork of the Snake River,[25] where the party was taking as many as seventy a day, skinning the hides, and boiling the large fat tails for eating. Ferris described the spectacular "Trois Tetons," lofty mountain landmarks of the region. June in the Tetons provided magnificent scenery with wildflower displays softening the extraordinary raw beauty of the rugged landscape.

During 1831, Ferris's party made contact with Flathead Indians who had been in the trading sphere of the Hudson's Bay Company but were migrating south to avoid their traditional enemy, the Blackfeet. With hostile Blackfeet on the prowl constantly threatening solitary hunters, it was best to travel in large groups or in the company of the friendly Flatheads.

Warren Ferris was charmed by the Flathead Indians, who took their name from an alleged early practice of deforming the head during infancy, a custom they probably never observed. Christianized by Iroquois who accompanied British traders, the Flatheads avoided warfare except in self-defense, a pious stance that put them at the mercy of the aggressive Blackfeet who outnumbered them twenty to one. Ferris held the Flatheads in high regard, judging them courageous, prudent, and honest; they were the only tribe in the Rocky Mountains that had never killed or robbed a white man.[26] Since his brigade leaders were eager to woo the Flathead trade from their British rivals, Ferris was to spend much of his trapping and trading career among these genial Indians and to enjoy considerable success in his dealings with them.

Gambling was one vice not prohibited by Flathead religious views, and Ferris described at length the games of chance, dart throwing, horseracing, and other sports enjoyed by both men and women. A favorite game was "Hand," played with small bones: "These bones they shift from hand to hand, for a few moments with great dexterity, and then hold their closed hands, stretched apart, for their respective opponents to guess in which the true bone is concealed."[27]

In June 1831, Fontenelle and Drips with fifty men, including Indians, departed for Cache Valley, there to rendezvous with Rocky Mountain Fur Company men under agreement to return to St. Louis together.[28] Ferris

---

25. Not to be confused with Henry's Fork of the Green River, Henry's Fork of the Snake was near Pierre's Hole and the site of early Fort Henry, named for Maj. Andrew Henry.

26. Ibid., 162. Ferris's glowing tribute to the Flathead Indians extended to their women who were "chaste & modest." "Many of them," according to Ferris, "would be considered as pretty anywhere." Dallas *Herald*, Jan. 11, 1873, clipping in Davis Collection. It is not known whether he had relations with any of the Indian women, but they were present in the winter camps.

27. Ferris, *Life in the Rocky Mountains*, 167.

28. Three Nez Perce and one Flathead Indian traveled to St. Louis with Drips and Fontenelle that fall. On a quest to gain knowledge of the white man's "Book"

and the rest of the party, in the company of the remaining Flatheads, set out for the Salmon River.[29] The Indians directed them to the western slopes of the mountains, promising many animals, but the trappers were disappointed to find elk, not beaver. The Rockies were overcrowded with trappers, and game was scarce. No buffalo were seen on the western slopes. The men retraced their path, the hunt a failure.

Ferris's party crisscrossed the mountains through Lemhi Pass, by Horse Prairie, down into the Big Hole Valley. Following the path of Lewis and Clark, they trapped that summer at the Three Forks of the Missouri River.[30] Here the hunters were alert to the least sign or unusual occurrence, for they were in Blackfoot country. Moccasin tracks, distant horsemen, the smoke of a far-off fire, none of these were trifling matters, for, as Ferris explained, "Every man carries . . . his life in his hand, and it is only by the most watchful precaution . . . that he can hope to preserve it."[31] The hunter's wisdom, studious eye to the smallest detail, would serve Ferris well in later years as a surveyor on the Texas frontier.

As the trappers departed the Jefferson River, back across the mountains to Clark's Fork of the Columbia River in mid-September 1831, Ferris gave a vivid description of the colorful Flathead party accompanying them. It was a riot of color and sound and action. Three thousand horses of every size and color, with trappings almost as varied as their appearance; a thousand souls from "squalling infancy to decrepid [sic] age," fantastically dressed in scarlet coats, multicolored blankets, buffalo robes painted with "hideous little figures, resembling grasshoppers quite as much as men for which they were intended," and sheep-skin dresses garnished with porcupine quills, beads, hawk bells, and human hair.

"Imagine," Ferris wrote, "this motley collection of human figures . . . with long black locks gently waving in the wind, their faces painted with vermillion, and yellow ochre." "Listen," he urged, "to the rattle of the numberless lodgepoles [trailed] by pack horses, to the various noises of children screaming, women scolding, and dogs howling. . . ." Groups of Indian boys playfully dashed about at full speed; at a distance, a hundred horsemen pursued a herd of antelope; and, in every direction, crowds of hungry dogs chased timid rabbits. Amid the bustle and confusion, sunlight flashed on hundreds of gleaming gun-barrels. The beautiful level

---

(the Bible) and the power to be derived from the "Holy Spirit," the Indians interviewed William Clark, their Great Father of twenty-five years earlier. This spiritual journey, reported in church periodicals, inspired later Protestant missionary efforts.

29. Perhaps this was the occasion of a salmon fishing expedition with the Flathead Indians which Ferris described in the Dallas *Herald*, Dec. 14, 1872, clipping in Davis Collection. Ferris shot the spawning salmon, but the Indian boys beat him three to one, using clubs.

30. Ferris was trapping all summer so did not attend the rendezvous of 1831.

31. Ferris, *Life in the Rocky Mountains*, 175.

prairie and dark blue snow-capped mountains framed the pageantry of their splendid march.[32]

The fall of 1831 was spent awaiting resupply from St. Louis. Andrew Drips was expected to arrive with supplies but was delayed so, in September, Ferris's party joined rival Rocky Mountain Fur Company men in winter quarters on the Salmon River where they had been resupplied by Henry Fraeb. The camp was "a confused scene of rioting and debauchery for several days, after which however, the kegs of alcohol were bunged, and all became tranquil."[33] Almost every trapper who entered the camp told of a close brush with death at the hands of hostile Blackfoot warriors. The situation worsened in 1832 due to irresponsible actions of Kenneth McKenzie, American Fur Company representative on the Upper Missouri, who sold guns and ammunition to the Blackfeet.[34]

In February and March, Ferris and his fellows were on the Snake River, having parted with the Rocky Mountain Fur Company men. Near Cache Valley, they joined the resupplied brigade of William H. Vanderburgh, which had been fitted out at McKenzie's Fort Union. Ferris held great admiration for Vanderburgh, a West Point man and outstanding mountain leader. In late April, Drips finally appeared with fresh supplies from St. Louis. About the same time Warren Ferris had a close shave with a grizzly. Alone on a stream bank, he was charged by a "formidable grizzly bear." Instinctively, he cocked his gun, intending to discharge it in the bear's open mouth should it rear to clasp him. "To my great joy," Ferris wrote, "he passed a few feet from me, and disappeared in the neighboring thickets."[35]

Young Warren Ferris was promoted to clerk in 1832 and given a responsible mission, to visit his beloved Flathead Indians and bring them to summer rendezvous. When he reached the Indian camp, Ferris found that McKenzie's sale of guns to the Blackfeet had taken a terrible toll. In a two-day battle in May 1832, the Flatheads lost twelve men killed and several others severely wounded, besides the loss of 1,000 horses. Their implacable enemy was bent on annihilating the Flatheads who courageously defended their camp. Bearing their wounded on litters, the

---

32. Ibid., 182.

33. Ibid., 198.

34. McKenzie, operating out of Fort Union on the Upper Missouri River, also sold the Indians liquor. After the sale of whiskey to Indians was banned in the spring of 1832, authorities seized 1,400 gallons bound up river on the steamboat *Yellow Stone*. Later, McKenzie was caught operating a still at Fort Union where he claimed to be experimenting with native berries. He was subsequently fired.

35. Ferris, *Life in the Rocky Mountains*, 212. Ferris also told of sharing a cave overnight with a hibernating grizzly; see Dallas *Herald*, Dec. 21, 1872, clipping in Davis Collection. He devoted a whole essay to the dangerous beast in the *Western Literary Messenger*, May 18, 1844.

Indians withdrew and, with Ferris's party, made for Pierre's Hole where the summer rendezvous was to be held.

Pierre's Hole, just west of the Tetons, was chosen as the site for general barter and resupply.[36] The annual summer rendezvous had become a momentous frontier event. Indians and trappers brought in their furs to meet company traders who brought pack trains laden with trinkets, necessities, coffee, tobacco, gunpowder, lead, guns, traps, and whiskey. The year 1832 was a bonanza year for furs; competition between companies kept wages high, so money flowed as readily as the liquor. Since the price paid for trade goods was greatly inflated, trappers were soon parted from their earnings. Resuppliers culled the real profit, but the mountain men had a high old time. Sadly, Ferris and his colleagues were forced to stand by and watch their rivals do a brisk trade because Fontenelle was late with American Fur Company trade goods. When Bill Sublette and Robert Campbell brought in the Rocky Mountain Fur Company goods from St. Louis, they had traveling with them a newcomer to the trade, Boston ice merchant Nathaniel Wyeth. Tom Fitzpatrick, enroute to the July rendezvous, had eluded a war party of Gros Ventre Indians. Afoot after losing his horse, he wore out his moccasins and made others of his hat. A mere skeleton, he staggered into camp to report that the Blackfeet and their allies, the Gros Ventre, were swarming.

Ferris arrived at the rendezvous in time to witness an important encounter with hostile Indians. On July 17, 1832, a party of white hunters and friendly Indians were attacked by a migrating village of Gros Ventre who fell back to a "fort" thrown up in a cottonwood grove.[37] The trappers fired on the fortified Indians all day and, at nightfall, concocted a plan to burn them out; but their Indian allies objected, on the grounds that while the enemy would be destroyed, the plunder would be lost. This disagreement on strategy led to the hunters' withdrawal, and during the night the Gros Ventre slipped away. Nine trappers were killed; numerous others, including Andrew Drips and William Sublette, were wounded in the engagement that came to be known as the "Battle of Pierre's Hole," perhaps the most celebrated Indian encounter in the annals of mountain men. The trappers had fired so many bullets that they had to spend the next day digging lead out of the trees for re-use.[38]

---

36. Pierre's Hole boasted lush meadows for forage, was well watered and shaded by cottonwood trees. David Lavender, *The Rockies* (New York: Harper and Row, 1968), 90, calls it one of the "loveliest spots in the mountains;" and John U. Terrell, *Furs By Astor* (New York: William Morrow Co., 1963), 431, a "valley of rare beauty."

37. According to several eyewitness accounts of this famous encounter, the trouble started when a Flathead chief fired on a Gros Ventre peace parley. The Gros Ventre were allies of the Blackfeet.

38. Warren Ferris gave his eyewitness accounts of the 1832 rendezvous and subsequent battle both in his journal (222–223) and the Dallas *Herald*, Jan. 25, 1873, clipping in Davis Collection.

In early August, disappointed that Fontenelle still had not arrived with supplies, Drips and Vanderburgh determined to move east toward the Green River.[39] They crossed into Jackson Hole at the eastern foot of the Tetons and then descended to the Green River where they intercepted Fontenelle, fifty men, and an equal number of pack horses. Exchanging supplies for the furs they had collected that spring, the two brigades parted. Fontenelle returned to St. Louis; Vanderburgh and Drips headed north to dog the trail of the Rocky Mountain Fur Company brigades on the headwaters of the Missouri River.

Warren Ferris, age twenty-two, having shown himself a resourceful young man as clerk, continued to lead small trapping groups, deliver messages, and cache and recover supplies.[40] In August 1832, he was ordered to bring the Flathead Indians to Horse Prairie for trading. With two companions, Ferris searched the Snake River plains and along the Salmon River. Concluding that the Indians had already passed over the mountains, they gave up the pursuit and hurried to rejoin the main company. After a difficult crossing of the Continental Divide, they came into the Big Hole valley to meet Drips and Vanderburgh on September 1, 1832. In his journal, Ferris described the arduous mountain crossing. Steep slopes and intertwined fallen trees forced the men to leap their horses across obstacles or backtrack to find safer passage. Once when an avalanche of huge rocks, trees, and snow presented a barrier impassable for horses or men, they followed the sharp edge of a narrow ridge between two dark canyons which yawned in immeasurable depth beneath their feet on either side.[41]

Reunited, the main party stalked the Rocky Mountain Fur Company hunters, hoping to be led to the best beaver country. As Ferris put it, "we immediately followed, determined to overtake them and by this means share a part of the game, which is usually found in advance of a company, but *never* behind."[42] For their part, Tom Fitzpatrick, Jim Bridger, and others of the rival company leaders were sick of being trailed through the mountains. At the 1832 rendezvous, they decided to lead their competition into Blackfoot Country, lose them, and leave them to fend for themselves.

Brigades under Drips and Vanderburgh caught up with the opposition near the Three Forks of the Missouri, where the Jefferson, Madison, and Gallatin Rivers converge, in the heart of Blackfoot country. Scouting parties reported some game, Blackfoot signs, but few beaver. Drips was

---

39. Fontenelle was delayed at Fort Pierre, waiting for twenty recruits aboard the *Yellow Stone*, which was becalmed downstream. Fort Pierre, a cottonwood stockade at the mouth of the Bad River, was named for Chouteau and is the site of present Pierre, South Dakota.

40. Ferris's article in the Dallas *Herald*, Nov. 20, 1872, clipping in Davis Collection, explained the responsibilities involved in retrieving the cached supplies.

41. Ferris, *Life in the Rocky Mountains*, 229–230.

alarmed by the Indian signs and took his brigade and headed south. But Vanderburgh's party, which included Ferris, continued its stay in Blackfoot territory, moving along the Philanthropy (now Ruby) River and finding numerous beaver and buffalo. "[Black]Foot-Indians were seen lurking about the thickets," Ferris noted, "evidently watching an opportunity to kill some of our trappers, who being aware of their design, always go out in parties of several together."[43]

On October 14, 1832, Ferris and six others, including Vanderburgh, set out from the encampment to investigate an Indian alarm brought in by hunters. They rode into a deadly ambush near present-day Alder Gulch, Montana. The scouting party crossed a deep gully, ever alert, carefully scrutinizing a grove of trees, watching each wavering twig and rustling bough to catch a glimpse of their enemy. Suddenly, at least twenty shots burst upon them from the gully; as if by magic, more than a hundred warriors appeared both in front and on either side of them at the terrifying distance (later measured) of thirty steps.

Caught in a deadly crossfire with bullets whistled at pointblank range, the trappers dashed for cover. Vanderburgh, whose horse was shot dead under him, calmly leveled his pistol at the foe and shouted for his men to stand firm. It was too late. Ferris was struck in the left shoulder but managed to stay horsed and fled. Vanderburgh, seeing himself surrounded and cut off from escape, continued to fire his pistol at the charging Indians until a volley of bullets cut him down.[44]

Wounded, leaderless, and frightened, the trappers nearly panicked and separated, but after further consideration they stuck together for mutual defense. Ferris was treated by one of the men who dressed his shoulder wound with salve. The hunters then retreated to a nearby Flathead village. With his arm in a sling, Ferris mended rapidly, although he would favor his left side for the rest of his life. Friendly Indians later found and buried the bones of William Vanderburgh; the Blackfeet had brutally stripped the flesh from his body. It is not known whether Ferris blamed himself for failure to go to Vanderburgh's relief. The attack was so sudden, the gunfire so withering, and the odds so great that a rescue surely seemed impossible, even suicidal. Ferris, who thought he was mortally wounded, admitted, "I felt little like returning." Later he wrote a tribute to his much admired commander:

> Thus fell William Henry Vanderburgh . . . at the time he perished, under thirty years of age. Bold, daring, and fearless, yet cautious, deliberate, and prudent: uniting the apparent opposite qualities, of

---

42. Ibid., 233.

43. Ibid., 237.

44. Ibid., 242–243. Ferris described this same incident in an article he wrote for a Dallas newspaper in the early 1860s. The article was reprinted in the *Rising Star* (Eastland County, Texas), copy in Davis Collection.

courage and coolness, a soldier and a scholar, he died universally
beloved and regretted by all who knew him.[45]

Late that fall, the remnants of Vanderburgh's brigade moved to
Bonneville's log huts on the Little Salmon River to winter with the Rocky
Mountain Fur Company men. The year 1832 ended at a low point. The
companies had ruined each other's fall hunt, engaged in unnecessary
Indian fights, and wasted resources. Yet in winter camp everyone was
friendly, satisfied to join in poking fun at newcomer Benjamin Bonneville.
Bonneville, on leave from the U.S. Army, entered the mountains in 1832
and was generally regarded by the mountain men as a pretentious ama-
teur.[46] Ferris, not much impressed with Bonneville's crude temporary
shelters, joined Joe Walker, one of Bonneville's brigade leaders, and Tom
Fitzpatrick to travel south to winter with Drips's party on the Snake
River.

New Year's Day 1833 was spent feasting, drinking, and dancing.
During January, winter camp relocated three times, seeking better forage
for the animals. Long snowbound days were passed mending clothes and
traps, playing cards, and "yarning." When the weather was fair, the restless trappers amused themselves with athletic contests, riding, shooting,
and wrestling. There were visits between the three camps (Bonneville's,
the American Fur Company, and the Rocky Mountain Fur Company) and
exchanges of news and gossip. Hunters left the camp at daylight and
returned in time for breakfast, laden with meat of various kinds as game
was plentiful in the region.

All awaited the melting of the snow; when the geese returned late in
March, Ferris joined Drips's brigade, which moved up the Lewis River to
begin the spring hunt. The weather continued cold and raw into April.
Crossing the mountains into the Salt River valley where Ferris had earlier seen the "Boiling Kettles," they again encountered Bonneville's men,
and Ferris revisited the bone-scattered battlefield at Pierre's Hole.

Benjamin Bonneville's well-located fort on the Green River[47] was the site
for the summer rendezvous. The 1833 gathering was a large one, featuring

---

45. Ferris, *Life in the Rocky Mountains*, 243.

46. Bernard DeVoto, *Across the Wide Missouri* (Boston: Houghton, Mifflin Co.,
1947), and William H. Goetzmann, *Exploration and Empire: The Explorer and the
Scientist in the Winning of the American West* (New York: Alfred A. Knopf, 1966),
reevaluate Bonneville's contribution to western exploration. Not successful as a fur
trader, Bonneville perhaps had other objectives. DeVoto suggests that he was an
intelligence agent of the U.S. Army who tested a wagon road into the mountains,
probed Hudson's Bay Company outposts, located a fort in a strategic position along
major overland routes, and sent Joseph Walker to map a route to California.

47. Ferris, *Life in the Rocky Mountains*, 274, 281n. gives one of the best descriptions of this fort and its setting, calling it "Bonnyville's Folly" or "Fort Nonsense,"
since so much effort was put into construction so soon abandoned. Ferris rarely
missed an opportunity to disparage Bonneville.

representatives of all the mountain fur companies, many small outfits, and large numbers of Indians. Nat Wyeth was back, a little wiser, trying to interest Bonneville, who was nearly bankrupt, in a merger of resources. Again, Sublette and Campbell beat Fontenelle to the rendezvous, and accompanying the Rocky Mountain Fur Company supply train was a Scottish soldier/sportsman, William Drummond Stewart.[48] Some fifty or sixty lodges of Shoshones encamped about the fort, exchanging pelts for powder, lead, knives, and trinkets.

As hunters drifted in, they brought tales of Joe Walker's successful hunt, of William O. Fallon's trip to Taos for supplies,[49] of one man's brush with a grizzly, of others who suffered bites from rabid wolves. Four hunters appeared at camp naked and sunburned after having capsized their raft on the Lewis River, losing all their gear and clothing. During the three weeks of the summer rendezvous, the trappers craved release from such constant danger: they feasted, sang, danced, bragged, brawled, guzzled raw alcohol mixed with Green River water, traded favors with Indian women, and competed in riding and shooting contests.

News from St. Louis told of Andrew Jackson's reelection and his fight against the Bank of the United States. Word of home led Warren Ferris to a rare expression of homesickness. He describes a poignant dream of "home, mother, sisters, brothers . . . the lovely streets of my native village . . . the well remembered haunts of my childhood . . . the friendly hands of the companions of my youth." "I awoke," he said, "to the unwelcome conviction of absence from home, and the certainty of comparative solitude, in the Rocky Mountains."[50]

The 1833 Green River rendezvous marked a turning point in the history of the fur trade. The price of beaver fell to $3.50 a pelt in St. Louis; buffalo robes were more valuable.[51] Cutthroat competition and bitter rivalry had taken a heavy toll. The Rocky Mountain Fur Company was forced to admit that the American Fur Company was in the mountains to stay; no use to try to lose them or lead them into ambush. By mutual agreement, the rivals divided the beaver country: American Fur Company brigades would hunt the Flathead and Teton country, the valley of the Great Salt

---

48. Stewart attended every rendezvous from 1833 to 1838. His interest was in organizing hunting parties and gaining experience for writing novels. In 1837, "Sir" William Stewart, having inherited his brother's title, made what he felt would be his last trip to the Rockies. He contributed mightily to Western history by bringing Baltimore artist, Alfred Jacob Miller, to capture the Green River rendezvous in sketches and notes. Miller's spontaneous drawings of the Indians, trappers, and physical landscape provide priceless glimpses of mountain life. Stewart's adventures, illustrated by Miller's paintings, are the subject of DeVoto's *Across the Wide Missouri*.

49. Ferris, *Life in the Rocky Mountains*, 281n. Not to be confused with Benjamin O'Fallon, U.S. Indian agent on the Upper Missouri River in the 1820s.

50. Ferris, *Life in the Rocky Mountains*, 279.

51. Lavender, *The Rockies*, 91.

Lake, and along the the Snake and Salmon Rivers; the Rocky Mountain
Fur Company trappers would operate along the Green and Yellowstone
Rivers, and the Three Forks of the Missouri.

In late July 1833,[52] Warren Ferris and Robert Newell led a party of
thirteen on a third trading mission to the Flathead Indians. Ferris had
gained a reputation for keen dealing with the Flatheads; he saw this
expedition as an opportunity to cement his influence with that tribe. His
lyrical description from the heights of Teton Pass looking back toward
Jackson Hole, evidences his high spirits:

> Gazing down . . . from our elevated position . . . one of the most beauti-
> ful scenes imaginable, was presented to our view. . . . quite filled with
> large bright clouds, resembling immense banks of snow, piled on each
> other in massy numbers, of the purest white . . . mingling in one vast
> embrace their shadowy substance.—Sublime creations! emblems apt
> of the first glittering imaginings of human life! like them redolent in
> happiness, and smiling in the fancied tranquil security of repose. . . .
> Alike evanescent are the dreamy anticipations of youth. . . . Turning
> with reluctance to things of a more terrestrial nature we pursued our
> way down to Pierre's Hole.[53]

In mid-August, Ferris's expedition reached Flathead lodges on the
Bitterroot River in present western Montana. Here they were welcomed
in the traditional Flathead manner. The Indian men shook hands and
made short prayers; women brought baskets of fruit and provisions; the
chief and his retinue came to smoke a pipe with Ferris and inquire of his
business. Ferris had no interpreter but managed, through sign language,
to inform the chief of his object to trade. After politely listening in silence,
the old chief in the name of his people thanked Ferris for coming so far,
through a dangerous country, to bring them munitions and tobacco, articles of which they were in much want. He promised to encourage his
young men to hunt and trade with the American Fur Company men and
aid them in all possible ways.[54] The trappers learned that the Flatheads
had suffered more at the hands of their enemy, the Blackfeet, who massa-
cred thirty of them in the past spring. It seemed the Blackfeet were making good on their threat to exterminate their sworn enemy. Ferris's party
traded glass beads for beaver pelts and provisions, then accompanied the
tribe eastward on a buffalo hunt.

The journal account skips until late October when the hunters were at
Henry's Fork of the Snake River, trying to make connection with Drips. Ferris,
ever curious, sometimes played the amateur naturalist, contemplating the

52. Ferris's journal skips to July 20, 1833; the complete manuscript has never
been located so we cannot know what was omitted. The disconcerting omissions,
which increase in 1834–35, probably occurred when the serialized version was edited for the *Western Literary Messenger*.

53. Ferris, *Life in the Rocky Mountains*, 283–284.

54. Ibid., 286–287.

natural phenomenon he encountered in the Far West. After describing undulating mountains of sand west of present-day St. Anthony, Idaho, Ferris judged they might be the deposit of an ancient ocean or perhaps the result of volcanic action obvious in the area.

During October 1833, parties of hunters gathered at the Three Forks of the Missouri to float their furs downriver to Fort Union. On November 2, Drips arrived with his company after a successful fall beaver hunt. The trappers eagerly exchanged news, swapping tales of hazard and adventure. Both Fitzpatrick's and Bonneville's men had encounters with Crow Indians who had declared war on hunting parties found in their territory. They lost some horses and pelts to the Indians, but, despite difficulties, a good number of hides remained to be shipped to St. Louis via steamboats that were plying the Missouri River up as far as Fort Union.

Warren Ferris decided to winter with the Flatheads. In the company of François Pillet (Payette), a half-breed Indian, he made a dangerous but successful march north and reached the Flathead lodges in late November. There they met Francis Ermatinger, an agent of the Hudson's Bay Company. Payette and Ermatinger influenced Ferris to join the rival British firm; when Ermatinger set out by canoe for Fort Colville on the Columbia River, he carried a proposal to chief trader Archibald McDonald that "A. Ferris" be hired as a sub-trader and furnished Hudson's Bay Company goods. Such a shift of loyalty was appealing to Ferris since the price and availability of British trade goods on the Columbia River was much lower than that of American goods shipped up the Missouri. Thus, in the winter of 1833–1834, Warren A. Ferris became an independent trader, working with Hudson's Bay employee Nicholas Montour.[55]

Through Ferris, the British company extended its reach southeast to the Green River trappers. In a letter of March 6, 1834, McDonald commented on Ermatinger's favorable impression of Ferris "as a fit person to be entrusted with the management and distribution of property."[56] The contract with the Hudson's Bay Company stipulated that Montour and Ferris trade with the Snake Indians and not the Flatheads, who were already in the British sphere. All furs and pelts traded were to be yielded to the Company at the Flathead trading post where they would be transported to Fort Colville and thence to Forts Walla Walla, Spokane, and Vancouver.

The British, beginning in 1833, decided to supplement their fur trade in the Pacific Northwest by dealing with the ever more numerous American independent trappers in the mountains. To this end, Ermatinger sought

---

55. Ibid., 305, 308, 332n. Ferris's journal does not make this arrangement clear, but his new situation was clarified in 1969 when letters were discovered by historian Dale L. Morgan in the publications of the Hudson's Bay Record Society of London, IV, 1941, 142. Ferris's status as an independent trader, peddling Hudson's Bay Company goods, is also clarified in Lois H. McDonald, (ed.), *Fur Trade Letters of Francis Ermatinger* (Glendale, Calif.: A. H. Clark Co., 1980), 170, 175–176, 183.

56. Ferris, *Life in the Rocky Mountains*, 306.

entry to the American summer rendezvous.[57] Hudson's Bay Company agents also wanted to cut American influence among the Flathead Indians. Hiring Warren Ferris away from his American Fur Company employers was a clever move to accomplish these goals.

Ferris spent the early portion of the winter with Payette's Indian family along a small stream in a pretty valley. He hunted on snowshoes every day and made progress in learning the Indian language. At Christmas, he celebrated the holiday, his twenty-third birthday, and the new partnership in Montour's log cabin where he reported, "we drank a variety of appropriate toasts, suited to the occasion, and our enlarged and elevated sentiments, respecting universal benevolence and prosperity, while our hearts were warmed, our prejudices banished."[58] Apparently Ferris felt no compunction about his change of allegiance; rather, he took the view of a hardened realist, convinced that business was business. He and Montour toasted "the next favorable opportunity offered for taking advantage of the ignorance and necessity of the Indians, in *honorable* barter." Ferris philosophized on the slipperiness of business ethics:

> Alas, for poor human nature! *Truth* is too abstract and difficult to be comprehended—*Justice* too holy and intricate to practice—*Honor* too lofty and profound to be governed by—and all too obsolete and unfashionable to direct—*in the vulgar concerns of trade.* . . . [S]elfishness and intrigue is but another name for frailty. . . . Such, at least, I have found the *world*.[59]

Through his experience, Warren Ferris had learned it was the free agent who enjoyed the greatest financial advantage. While some mountain men were satisfied with plenty to eat, some grog, tobacco, a few horses, and Indian wives, others grumbled that they were in constant debt to the American Fur Company, which "used them up."[60] Ferris never intended to be exploited. With an eye on the future, he was determined to accumulate money for the purchase of land of his own. Describing his progress in the fur trade to his half-brother Joshua, Ferris stated that in his second year in the mountains he made only $300 and the next year he was no richer. After promotion to clerk of the American Fur Company in 1833, Ferris wrote, "I had $600 and two fine horses of my own." As an agent of the Hudson's Bay Company during 1834 and 1835, Ferris tripled his savings. He had $1,800 at his command.[61]

---

57. DeVoto, *Across the Wide Missouri*, 108. Ermatinger contacted Nathaniel Wyeth about attending the 1833 rendezvous. Wyeth, while visiting Vancouver that year, gave the British information about the American companies in the mountains.

58. Ferris, *Life in the Rocky Mountains*, 309.

59. Ibid., 309–310.

60. DeVoto, *Across the Wide Missouri*, 383.

61. Warren Ferris to Joshua F. Lovejoy, Feb. 7, 1836. FLC, Box I, Folder 16.

In April 1834, Ferris left the Flathead trading post[62] aboard a barge
loaded with a ton of merchandise and manned by four stout French
Canadians who either paddled or poled the craft. At Horse Prairie he met
Montour and Ermatinger. The goods were loaded on pack horses for the
mountain crossing. On the Arrowstone River (now Clark's Fork of the
Columbia), Ferris found his old partner Newell and got word of Drips and
Fontenelle, all now his trading rivals. Having rested their mounts, Ferris
and Montour set out looking for American independent trappers to the
southeast. On May 17, 1834, they "ascended a bold hill and came in view
of the plains of the Snake River, and the 'Trois Titons.'"[63]

Ferris's curiosity on this crossing was piqued by tales heard at the 1832
Pierre's Hole rendezvous, tales of remarkable boiling springs on the
sources of the Madison River. This time he determined to examine for
himself the marvels described to him by at least twenty mountain men.
Taking with him two Indians, Ferris rode some sixty miles out of his way
and after two days reached the vicinity of the springs. At dusk, after a
cup of coffee, they lay down to sleep; but Ferris reported that "the contin-
ual roar of the springs" prevented slumber and made him impatient to
examine its source. When he arose in the morning, he was astounded by
the clouds of vapor that hung over the springs like dense fog and by the
frequent explosions of varying degree that assaulted his ears. When the
full reality of the springs burst upon his view, he judged that "the half
had not been told" of their spectacle and novelty. "The largest of these
wonderful fountains," he marveled, "projects a column of boiling water . . .
to the height of more than one hundred and fifty feet . . . accompanied
with a tremendous noise . . . at intervals of about two hours."[64] Thus
Warren A. Ferris penned the first detailed, eyewitness description of
Yellowstone's geysers, an account so fantastic it was generally disbelieved
back east until, years later, photographers captured the marvels.

Rejoining Montour at Pierre's Hole in late May, Ferris took his British
trade goods to the 1834 summer rendezvous. The first part of the rendezvous was held on the Green River; the second and main gathering at
Ham's Fork some twenty-five miles west. Small parties of trappers drifted
in from various sections of the fur country, relating their customary tales

62. Flathead Post or Salish House on Clark's Fork of the Columbia, just below
Thompson Falls.

63. Ferris, *Life in the Rocky Mountains*, 326.

64. Ibid., 327–328. The *Western Literary Messenger* for July 13, 1842 contained
an article entitled "Rocky Mountain Geysers." Since Ferris's account was far more
detailed than an anonymous one published in *Niles Register* (Baltimore), Oct. 6,
1827, Olin D. Wheeler recognized its primacy, calling it the "first known description of the geysers of the Yellowstone country" (Buffalo *Courier*, Sept. 4, 1900). W.
Turrentine Jackson wrote that a Texan, Warren Angus Ferris, was the "first
known individual to describe the natural phenomenon of the Yellowstone region."
Jackson, "Texas Collection," *SHQ*, 43 (Oct., 1939), 249.

of harrowing escapes. Ferris learned from Andrew Drips that his old commander Fontenelle was trapping in the Eutaw (Ute) country.

New faces at the 1834 rendezvous reflected accelerated changes coming to the mountain wilderness: present were sightseers, scientists, and missionaries bound for stations with the Flatheads and Nez Perce. Nat Wyeth and William Drummond Stewart were back, but there were also botanist Thomas Nuttall, ornithologist John Kirk Townsend, and diarist William M. Anderson. Elderly Indian chieftains received their customary watered whiskey and inferior tobacco. Rev. Jason Lee, the Methodist missionary, was appalled at the drinking, brawling, gambling, and trade in Indian women. The bales of furs were small; rumor had it that Astor was selling out and the Rocky Mountain Fur Company was going under.[65]

Ferris's account jumps from May to August 1834, but Canadian sources reveal that he traded his goods and paid his debts to the Hudson's Bay Company. John McLoughlin, Chief Trader at Fort Vancouver, reported to London, September 10, 1835: "Mr. Francis Ermatinger went . . . to the American Rendezvous [of 1834], and got paid the advances he had made last year to Mr. Faries [Ferris] of the American party."[66] Ferris continued to be supplied by the Hudson's Bay Company, as revealed by his continued association with Ermatinger and Montour. During his final months in the Rockies, Warren Ferris became acquainted with the customs of the Ute Indians and the geography of present-day Utah and Colorado, thus rounding out his comprehensive knowledge of the Rocky Mountain West.

The rendezvous of 1834 was the last for the Rocky Mountain Fur Company, which was dissolved that summer. They succumbed to the ruthless competition and superior resources of the American Fur Company. It was a Pyrrhic victory, however, for the beaver were hunted out. The fur harvest had fallen from 2,000 beaver in 1832 to around 200 by 1835. More than that, demand had fallen. Fickle fashion was changing. Silk hats rather than beaver ones were the latest style in Europe. In the spring of 1834, ailing J. J. Astor sold his fur company to Ramsay Crooks (Northern Department) and Pierre Chouteau Jr. (Western Department).

Ferris was alarmed by the changes he saw wrought in the mountains. Each year beaver and buffalo became more scarce. One of the first to express conservationist views, he deplored the slaughter of millions of buffalo for sport and hides. Many concerned hunters predicted their extinction. Ferris also observed that the curse of whiskey furnished in trade for buffalo and beaver pelts had turned the Indians moody, melancholy, mean, and abusive. "They are melting away," he wrote, "before the curse of the white man's friendship."[67]

65. Dale Morgan's description in Ferris, *Life in the Rocky Mountains*, 365n., based on journals of William M. Anderson and Nathaniel Wyeth.

66. Ibid., 365–366n.

67. Ibid., 363.

In the summer of 1835, Ferris received the first letters from home in five years.[68] He learned that his mother was having difficulty settling her husband's estate with her stepson Henry Lovejoy. Ferris had invested his assets in preparation for future trading expeditions; but, when he received the urgent letters from home, he "sacrificed his prospects"[69] and left the mountains. On October 9, 1835, Warren Ferris returned to Bellevue on the Missouri River; en route he passed by Fort Leavenworth where he watched Col. Henry M. Dodge review U.S. troops. At Boonville, Missouri, Ferris sold his horse and equipment, raised $800, and took a steamboat to St. Louis, arriving on November 15 after an absence of nearly six years. From there, he traveled to Buffalo.

He had been mostly happy in his Rocky Mountain adventure. When the days were warm and pleasant, when he was well-armed and mounted, when the companionship was good and the chase exciting, Ferris was in his element. "Gloriously bounding over the plains," he recalled, "*then* I was really, rationally happy."[70] Solitude, danger, and savagery were behind him as he headed home to Buffalo and his family. Warren Ferris, who had left Buffalo as an untested youth not yet eighteen, returned a mature man of twenty-four who had seen sights and survived experiences unbelievable to most of his fellow Americans.

---

68. It is not clear from his journal that Ferris attended the 1835 rendezvous on the Green River. Probably he was there. He stated that in July 1835 he received seven or eight letters from his family, forwarded from St. Louis by Chouteau. Warren Ferris to Joshua F. Lovejoy, Feb. 7, 1836. FLC, Box I, Folder 2. Probably these letters came with the resupply brigade, and Ferris used the rendezvous as an opportunity to liquidate his assets.

69. Ibid.

70. Ferris, *Life in the Rocky Mountains*, 365.

3

HOMECOMING

WARREN FERRIS RETURNED to a thriving boomtown when he came home to Buffalo, New York, in the fall of 1835. Pleasant houses and gardens lined Exchange and Seneca Streets, but the town was still miserably lighted and had no sewage system, and few boardwalks. Niagara Street was a sea of mud in spring and summer. Pigs and cattle roamed free by day but were penned at night for fear the Indians might steal them.[1]

Completion of the Erie Canal made Buffalo a funnel for westward migration, through which passed thousands of hardy adventurers to board the lake steamers for Michigan or travel overland via Pittsburgh to the Ohio Valley and beyond. Aggressive developers coveted Seneca land and engaged in frenzied building to meet Buffalo's perpetual housing shortage. Land prices skyrocketed. "Real estate," said the Buffalo *Daily Star* of December 30, 1835, "seems to be the only article which commands money."[2] People signed notes for friends to borrow cash to buy land, which they could then use as collateral to buy more land and build houses. Unfortunately, the Ferris/Lovejoy family was unable to take advantage of the booming land market as their choice five acres were tied up in a prolonged lawsuit between Sally Lovejoy and her stepson Henry Lovejoy. It was this dispute over division of the property that brought Warren Ferris home from the mountains.

Figuring mightily in the Ferris/Lovejoy fortunes was Buffalo entrepreneur Benjamin Rathbun, owner of the Eagle Hotel and Tavern on Main Street and kingpin of local real estate. Buffalo in 1835 was largely "Rathbun-built." In that year alone, Rathbun built ninety-nine structures, including fifty-two stores, thirty-two dwellings, and the Eagle Street Theater.[3] He ran the post lines; built stagecoaches, railroad cars, and pleasure carriages; owned a saw mill and dry goods, hardware, and grocery stores. Rathbun was constructing a railroad to his new hotel at Niagara Falls. In 1831 the ambitious developer organized the Bank of Buffalo to issue notes sufficient to finance the building boom. His was one of a flurry of such private banks springing up on the frontier. Over 3,000 persons, one out of every four wage earners in Buffalo, were on Rathbun's payroll.

---

1. Lucy W. Hawes, "Buffalo Fifty Years Ago," a paper read before the Buffalo Historical Society, Apr. 27, 1886, 3–4, copy in BHS.

2. Quoted by McCausland, "Early Buffalo Journalist," 6, FLC, Box VIII, Folder 4.

3. McCausland, "Lives of the Lovejoys," 11.

The visionary promoter with his square face, firm lower jaw, black cut-away coat, and black tie was well known to everyone in town. Although he rarely spoke or smiled, his self-possessed demeanor inspired trust and confidence.[4] However, beneath Rathbun's cool exterior was the turmoil of his desperate search for capital to stave off creditors, especially New York City lenders with their high interest rates. The day-to-day operations of Rathbun's financial empire were left to his brother Lyman. Together the Rathbuns were involved in risky ventures based on mysterious financing which put the Buffalo economy, so outwardly healthy, on a shaky foundation.[5]

Warren Ferris knew nothing of Rathbun's affairs when he arrived home in December 1835. He was concerned only with the financial difficulties of his own family. To his chagrin, Ferris found his mother and half-sisters Sarah and Louisa at home alone. Joshua Lovejoy, his younger half-brother, was in Michigan working for a cousin; and Charles Ferris, in what must have appeared to Warren an incredibly irresponsible move, had left for Texas where a revolution against Mexican rule was in the offing. During the Christmas of his twenty-fifth birthday, Warren Ferris was brought up to date on the family's affairs during his absence.

While Ferris had been tracking beaver in the Rocky Mountains, his brother Charles, age nineteen, helped support his mother and two half-sisters.[6] Charles Ferris was employed as a clerk at the Buffalo post office, but his correspondence reveals wide interests. He was honing the skills of a reporter which he one day would parlay into a journalistic career. In June 1832, Charles wrote to Joshua of the cholera epidemic in Quebec, judging that Buffalo would "not escape its ravages," a prophecy that came true later that month when the city was struck by the devastating illness.[7] In the same letter, Ferris commented to his younger sibling on world affairs, noting the defeat of the Reform Bill in England and unsettled affairs in France, Greece, Belgium, and "poor Poland." In chatty letters to

---

4. Samuel M. Welch, *Home History: Recollections of Buffalo Fifty Years Since* (Buffalo: Peter Paul & Brothers, 1891), 197–199.

5. Virginia Hubbard, "The Buffalo Economy; 1836–1843," an undated, unpublished thesis gives a good picture of the Buffalo economic situation in 1835 and 1836 (BHS).

6. In a lengthy letter to Joshua, Nov. 20, 1836 (FLC, Box II, Folder 4), Charles spoke of his mother's self-denial and courage in the struggle to support her children. "How she has born [sic] up under circumstances of such extreme destitution for twelve long years, without help, without a friend or advisor, and little other means than the labour of her hands for the joint support of herself and her family of little ones, I must confess I am at a loss to determine." Ferris noted that the family received no assistance from Henry Lovejoy, though he was the guardian of the younger children.

7. McCausland, "Early Buffalo Journalist," 4. Welch in his *Home History*, 264–269, describes the death carts that patrolled the Buffalo streets during the humid summers of 1832 and 1834, and the experimental treatment for cholera which prescribed a bag of camphor worn about the neck.

Joshua, Ferris described noted visitors to Buffalo such as Daniel Webster, Henry Clay, and the Indian leader Black Hawk. Another letter revealed Charles Ferris as a social critic and shrewd judge of character when he commented on an itinerant revivalist, one Burchard, who by theatrics sought to convince his listeners that "folly is wisdom and the exercise of reason, crime." Charles assured Joshua that Buffalo was much the same despite the clergyman's exhortations, "as much praying and as much cursing as usual, as many godly and moral lectures and yet as much iniquity as ever."[8]

Young Joshua Ferris Lovejoy had, for his part, been sent to Michigan to work for a Quaker cousin Nelson H. Wing, merchant and founder of Dexter village near Ann Arbor. In 1832, fifteen-year-old Joshua boarded a steamer and crossed the lake to Michigan Territory to earn his own way and relieve the family of another mouth to feed. Except for the respite of summer visits, Joshua chafed under the direction of his older cousin. Detroit, Lovejoy observed, was the "center of rogues in America but the girls are handsome."[9] His letters to his mother, Charles, and younger sisters reveal Joshua to be clever, sensitive, self-centered, and incurably romantic. Lord Byron was his hero. Josh, a favorite with his mother and sisters, was a trial to Charles who urged him to be on his good behavior and stick with Wing for at least a year: "Be careful not by any ill-advised act to compromise your reputation or allow base for slander at your age."[10] Yet Lovejoy borrowed money in advance of his salary and fell into debt to Wing whose employ he later quit. He clerked in a store, waited tables, tended bar, and bemoaned his poverty. With young friends in Detroit, Ypsilanti, and Dexter, he participated in a secret fraternity of their own invention, the SUFN or "Staff of Union Fear Naughts," of which Josh was chaplain, addressed as "Elder Finney." He dabbled in Democratic Party politics and plots to free Canada, attended seasonal balls and parties, participated in a literary society, wrote poetry home to Sarah and Louisa, chased the girls, and ran up debts. Josh was a thoroughly charming rascal who longed for the easy wealth that would certainly follow settlement of the lawsuit with Henry Lovejoy.

Meanwhile the suit over whether Henry would receive one or two of the five Buffalo acres dragged on in court. The family financial situation was so desperate that they could not pay taxes or even interest due on taxes. Sally's brother-in-law, Jonathan Lovejoy of New York City, stepped forward to prevent foreclosure and save the property by paying two years interest due. In return, Jonathan Lovejoy held a $2,000 mortgage on the land.[11]

---

8. McCausland, "Early Buffalo Journalist," 5.

9. Joshua Lovejoy to Charles Ferris, Feb. 1, 1832. FLC,Box I, Folder 6.

10. Charles Ferris to Joshua Lovejoy, July 9, 1833. ibid., Box I, Folder 4.

11. Joshua Lovejoy to Henry Lovejoy, Dec. 31, 1837, ibid., Box II, Folder 9; Box III, Folder 23.

Sally Lovejoy, always the protective mother, wrote Joshua in December 1833 that Charles was about to marry and asked that Josh discourage what she considered an unwise step. Several weeks later Lovejoy penned a letter most revealing of the family thought patterns. To Charles he wrote:

> I would not see you joined to the best lady in the U.S. unless she was rich. . . . Pause before you take this desperate leap, think . . . upon its Consequence. Think on the desolate Condition of your mother—on the unprotected State of your Sisters, portionless, without friends, without means to procure an education, what must Become of them? . . . think, reason, don't be blinded. We have no powerful friends; we have to depend on ourselves.[12]

Despite this brotherly advice, Charles Ferris married Hester Ann Bivins of Clarence, New York, on May 5, 1834; the newlyweds came to live with Sally and the girls on Seneca Street. While Joshua was home for the wedding, Ferris proposed he take a job at the Buffalo post office, but Josh returned to Michigan instead where in July he received a letter from his fourteen-year-old sister. According to Louisa, Ferris visited a fortune teller who predicted that their lawsuit against Henry Lovejoy would be successful and that his brother (Warren) a great way off was on his way home.[13] Perhaps reassured by this optimistic forecast, Charles Ferris blithely decided to strike out for Texas.

In the fall of 1835, agents of Anglo settlers in Texas were active in New York, raising money and recruiting volunteers to fight the Mexican dictator Santa Anna. They offered large grants of free land as inducement to soldiers of fortune willing to join the Texians in opposition to Mexican injustices.[14] Volunteers from the United States made haste for Texas, fearing the conflict would be over before they could get there. Charles Ferris resigned from the post office, left his pregnant wife Hester with his mother, and, bearing letters of introduction to Sam Houston and Lorenzo de Zavala, headed for Texas on November 18, 1835.

Nineteen-year-old Sarah Lovejoy gave her version of Charles's departure in a January 1836 letter to Josh. She reported that Charles had gone South to "become a Patriot . . . to aid and assist the Texians in their glorious struggle between Liberty and Santa Anna and to gain Honour and a high name and . . . to be rewarded with Land in Texas."[15]

Warren Ferris intimated a quite different reason for his brother's sudden departure:

---

12. Joshua Lovejoy to Charles Ferris, Feb. 1, 1834, ibid., Box I, Folder 7.

13. Quoted in McCausland, "Lives of the Lovejoys," 8.

14. A handbill, "Volunteers to Texas," issued in New Orleans, April 23, 1836, offered 320 acres of Texas land to recruits for three months service, 640 acres for six months service, and 1280 acres to volunteers for the duration of the war. Microfilm MF79.60, DeGoyler Collection.

15. Sarah Lovejoy to Joshua Lovejoy, Jan. 24, 1836, FLC, Box II, Folder 3. In a letter to her cousin in February, Sarah suggested yet another reason for Ferris's

Charles has been guilty of a caper common to young men of his age but which has ruined him in this Buffalo village and he has been compelled to seek fortune by uniting himself to a volunteer company who left New Orleans for Matagorda on the first of January—to aid the Texians—in their struggle for Liberty.[16]

I was . . . sorry that Charles has gone to Texas—his calculations were to gain honour and harvest laurels (I mean land) at the expense of Hardship Perils and perhaps life (an excellent prospect) . . . The reason of Charles leaving Buffalo was some unfortunate scrape with a girl that nobody knows.[17]

Whatever Charles Ferris's motives in leaving, Warren, who had anticipated a brief visit in Buffalo and quick return to the mountains, found himself responsible for a family of women in financial crisis, and faced an unlimited stay. Evidently frustrated, he complained to the half-brother he hardly knew, "I am now involved in a series of Perplexities arising from dificulties [sic] with which I am but partially acquainted . . . and can do nothing of consequence without your assistance."[18] This same letter, commanding Joshua Lovejoy to come home, revealed Ferris's personal dream for use of the money once the court case was settled and the Buffalo property could be sold. He included the entire Ferris/Lovejoy family in his hopes:

to purchase a plantation in the western part of the State of Missouri with which I am perfectly acquainted . . . to build a commodious house to decorate the fields with grain . . . to form a park and Grace it with Buffalo, Antelopes and Deer . . . with such an establishment we might enjoy all the comforts of a happy fireside.[19]

In February 1836, Warren Ferris chastised Joshua for the delay in responding to his letter and noted that the suit with Henry Lovejoy would have to be postponed until summer when Josh and Charles could return to Buffalo. Ferris apprised Joshua of family news, advised him to "Be constant Attentive, economical, and above all throw vanity to the devil," and informed him that while waiting in Buffalo he was writing a journal recounting his adventures in the Rocky Mountains. "I have written about 300 pages letter sized sheets and have 100 more to write."

Ferris devoted himself to developing material from his diary, an account of activities and observations from February 1830 to November

Texas venture, saying that he had ruined his health working for the post office and hoped to restore his physical vigor in Texas. Sarah Lovejoy to Angeline Gray, Feb. 20, 1836, ibid., Box II, Folder 4.

16. Warren Ferris to Joshua Lovejoy, Jan. 1836, ibid., Box II, Folder 4. Exact date unknown but apparently after receipt of Charles Ferris's Jan. 1, 1836, letter from New Orleans.

17. Warren Ferris to Joshua Lovejoy, Feb. 7, 1836, *FLC*, Box I, Folder 4. Such an explanation must have seemed ironic to Joshua Lovejoy after all of Charles Ferris's unsolicited advice on maintaining a good reputation.

18. Warren Ferris to Joshua Lovejoy, Jan. 1836, FLC, Box II, Folder 4.

19. Ibid.

1835. "Life in the Rocky Mountains: A Diary of Wanderings on the Sources of the Rivers Missouri, Columbia, and Colorado" proved to be a treasure house of lore on the life of the trappers. It was the first extensive fur trader's diary and the only day-to-day account ever produced.[20] From memory Ferris drew a map showing the mountains, valleys, rivers, and landmarks of the beaver country. This map, fourteen by twenty inches, was highly detailed, and, considering Ferris's lack of precise instruments, it was a remarkably accurate portrayal of the area he visited.[21]

Sally Lovejoy wrote Joshua in March 1836 concerning Warren Ferris's disappointment that he arrived home only to find his brothers gone. She said that he was threatening to go back to the mountains as soon as the journal and map were prepared for publication. Ferris's mother judged that her son's account of the fur trade would "be seen with great interest."[22] She also reported that Henry Lovejoy was making frequent visits to their home and seemed eager to settle the case out of court, but on his own terms.[23]

Gradually word filtered back to Buffalo of Charles Ferris's exploits in what had become open rebellion against Mexico. His first letter home, written from New Orleans on New Year's Day 1836, said that he planned to sail with other volunteers for Matagorda on the Texas coast. A February letter told the family of his safe arrival in Texas. He had traveled inland from Matagorda Bay to San Felipe de Austin, a village of five stores and some thirty houses on the Brazos River. San Felipe was the central Anglo town and the seat of the rebel government. Ferris reported that he found the Texas climate healthy and the people confident.[24] At the time of his writing, Ferris was at Dimitt's Point (LaVaca Bay), headed, he said, to join the main Texas army at San Antonio. Ferris told his family

---

20. LeRoy R. Hafen, editor of the second edition of *Life in the Rocky Mountains*, discusses the primacy and importance of Ferris's work over six earlier accounts by or from mountain men. Hafen (ed.), in Ferris, *Life in the Rocky Mountains*, 17–19.

21. Ibid., 21–24, 28n. Here Hafen emphasizes the value of the Ferris map which is the earliest, most complete original fur trapper's map extant. (It is reproduced as a foldout map in the back of this book.) Though unsigned, the writing on the map is clearly that of Warren A. Ferris. Paul C. Phillips judged, "No other map of the early nineteenth century can compare with it in comprehensive accuracy." Preserved by the Lovejoy family in Buffalo, the map was purchased by Walter McCausland in the late 1930s and later sold to Brigham Young University in whose archives it now is housed.

22. Sally Lovejoy to Joshua Lovejoy, Mar. 27, 1836, FLC, Box I, supplementary material.

23. Ibid. In 1835, Henry Lovejoy was a candidate for Buffalo alderman, receiving the least votes of four candidates. Possibly he felt his reputation was damaged by the bitter, prolonged lawsuit with his stepmother.

24. Texians were overconfident after victories at Gonzales and San Antonio in 1835. Few believed that Santa Anna would invade Texas to discipline their actions.

that he held the rank of colonel and was aide de camp to acting Gov. James W. Robinson, charged with overseeing of stores.[25]

The situation in Texas in February 1836 was much more serious than Ferris painted it in his reassuring letter to Buffalo. Three Mexican armies under command of General Santa Anna advanced into Texas in mid-February. Meanwhile the Texas government was paralyzed by internal disputes, and the army was disorganized and undisciplined. Volunteers, fresh from the United States, were often disorderly, drunk, or brawling; they insisted on voting on everything, including whether or not to obey orders.[26] Despite the confusion, the morale of the rowdy volunteers was high. They were eager for a fight.

In early 1836 commander Sam Houston concentrated his troops at Refugio and Goliad, ordering San Antonio to be abandoned and those troops to withdraw to Gonzales to defend a line along the Guadalupe River. Independence had not yet been declared but was favored by Gov. Henry Smith, Houston, and a growing number of Texians. Opponents of independence[27] advocated cooperation with Mexican liberals in a civil war against Santa Anna; this faction controlled the governor's council and included Lt. Gov. James W. Robinson. They supported a scheme to occupy the rambunctious army with an expedition against Matamoros on the Rio Grande. By such a bold move, they argued, Santa Anna's Mexican opposition would be encouraged and his demise assured.[28] Smith and Houston

---

25. Ferris's Jan. 1, 1836, letter is referred to in Sarah Lovejoy's letterbook on Jan. 24, 1836, FLC, Box II, Folder 3. Charles Ferris's letter of Feb. 21, 1836, was on a torn sheet of a pocket notebook, ibid., Box I, Folder 2. Sally Lovejoy also refers to its contents in her letters to Joshua Lovejoy, Mar. 27 and Apr. 6, 1836, FLC, Box I, supplement. and Box II, Folder 4. Ferris's rapid rise in the Texas Army is puzzling. Possibly he was elected colonel by a company of volunteers. Numerous "volunteer aide de camp" positions were created to locate and organize transport of supplies. By mid-February 1836, Dimitt's Landing was a depository for government stores landed at Lavaca Bay. Walter Prescott Webb, H. Bailey Carroll, and Eldon Stephen Branda (eds.), *Handbook of Texas* (3 vols.; Austin: Texas State Historical Association, 1952, 1976), I, 503.

26. Paul D. Lack, *The Texas Revolutionary Experience: A Political and Social History, 1835–1836* (College Station: Texas A&M University Press, 1991), 52, 55, 253–256, gives a clear picture of the deep political conflicts that divided Anglo-Texans in the spring of 1836.

27. Margaret S. Henson, "Tory Sentiment in Anglo-Texan Public Opinion, 1832–1836," *SHQ*, XC (July, 1986), 1–34, admirably traces the evolution of the anti-Houston party. Its roots lay in the Peace Party prior to the Texas Revolution. "Old Texians," men of property whose claims rested on Mexican citizenship, were slow to support independence. They first advocated cooperation with Mexican liberals and later opposed Houston's retreat policy, demanding protection of property.

28. Henderson Yoakum, *History of Texas: First Settlement to Annexation* (2 vols., 1855; reprint, Austin: Steck-Vaughn Co., 1935), II, 56. Quotes a letter from Henry Millard of Nacogdoches, Jan. 14, 1836, stating that Frank W. Johnson and 300 men had marched for Matamoros to rendezvous with Mexican leaders supporting the liberal Constitution of 1824.

opposed the strategy, preferring a defensive stance. Bitter factionalism led the Council to impeach Smith, and Robinson became acting governor.

Disgusted with the Council, Sam Houston took leave from the army in February and traveled to East Texas to negotiate a treaty of neutrality with the Cherokee Indians. Houston and fellow negotiator John Forbes agreed to honor Cherokee claims to territory in East Texas that the Indians had occupied for fifteen years;[29] in exchange, the Cherokees promised to remain neutral in disputes between Texas and Mexico. Although the Cherokee Treaty purported to guarantee "safety in rear of the army," folks in the Nacogdoches area kept a suspicious eye on their Indian neighbors.

While Texians argued over strategy, Mexican troops advanced rapidly on San Antonio and Goliad. Instead of heading for San Antonio, Charles Ferris apparently traveled to Goliad where he joined the command of Col. James W. Fannin. On February 28, 1836, Ferris acted as a courier for Fannin, bearing word to the governor of Urrea's capture of Texas forces at San Patricio. General Fannin wrote to Governor Robinson from Fort Defiance (Goliad), "this morning Col. Ferris left this post with a communication from me."[30] Ferris's selection as express rider took him east from Goliad just a month before the tragic massacre of Fannin and his men. It was the first of a series of narrow escapes for young Ferris.

At Washington-on-the-Brazos on March 2, Texas delegates formally declared independence from Mexico, and in mid-March a constitution was adopted. David G. Burnet was elected interim president and Lorenzo de Zavala vice-president of the new Republic of Texas.

Resuming command of the army, Sam Houston mustered the Texians to defend San Antonio. On March 11, he arrived in Gonzales only to learn that the Alamo had fallen. At midnight on March 13, he ordered Gonzales burned and began a slow withdrawal to the Colorado River. Houston hoped to build his army to face the Mexican onslaught but did not foresee the panic that took charge of Texians. On the Colorado at the village of Columbus, word came that Fannin's army at Goliad had been taken captive.[31] Another Mexican force under General Sesma was only two miles

---

29. Cherokee Treaty, Feb. 23, 1836, in Dorman Winfrey (ed.), *Texas Indian Papers (1825–1843)* (5 vols.; Austin: Texas State Library, 1959) I, 14–17. The Cherokees and twelve associated bands were guaranteed title to lands north of the San Antonio Road, west of the Angelina and Sabine Rivers. Any surveys or Anglo claims to land within the Cherokee Reserve were declared null and void.

30. John H. Jenkins (ed.), *The Papers of the Texas Revolution* (10 vols.; Austin: Presidial Press, 1973), IV, #2196.

31. Stephen L. Hardin's *Texas Iliad: A Military History of the Texas Revolution* (Austin: University of Texas Press, 1994), 164–172, gives an excellent summary of Fannin's fatal mistakes. Caught in the open while belatedly evacuating Goliad, Fannin's troops were easy prey for the dreaded Mexican cavalry. On reaching San Felipe, the dismayed Houston learned that Fannin and his 400-man army were executed on Palm Sunday, March 27.

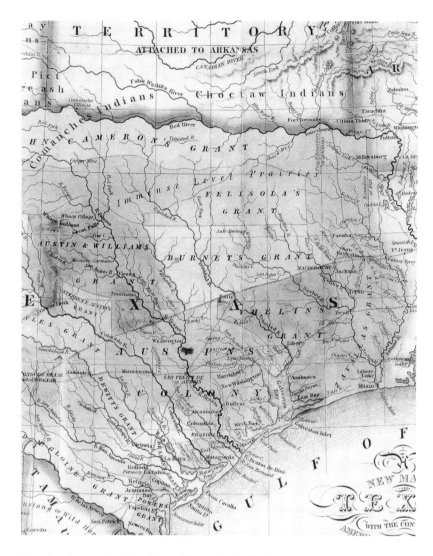

This detail from the *New Map of Texas* by J. H. Young (1836) is an example of a "pocket map" that might be folded and easily carried by an emigrant. It shows Texas as it was when Charles and Warren Ferris arrived. Original $12^3/_4$ x $15^3/_8$ inches. *Courtesy Special Collections Library, University of Texas at Arlington.*

away from Columbus. Terror struck the civilian population. Houston's army melted away as soldiers deserted to search for their families and aid in their evacuation.[32] When the Texas army retreated to San Felipe on

32. Andrew F. Muir (ed.), *Texas in 1837: An Anonymous, Contemporary Narrative* (Austin: University of Texas Press, 1988), 145. The anonymous author

the Brazos River, the government fled to Harrisburg and later to Galveston where they could take ship if necessary. Late spring "northers" and icy rain lashed hundreds of refugees who clogged the muddy roads and piled up at impassable river crossings.[33] Santa Anna, eager to finish the Texas business and get back to deal with his opposition in Mexico, was also slowed by the miserable weather.

At some point during the retreat from the Colorado River to the Brazos, Charles D. Ferris joined the main Texas army and became associated with those critical of Houston's military strategy.[34] Ferris agreed with Moseley Baker, Wylie Martin, and other critics who demanded that Houston make a stand at San Felipe. When the army moved upriver, these intransigent officers were left behind to guard the river crossings. Ferris was with Baker, who bitterly followed orders to burn his home village of San Felipe, then crossed the river to watch enemy troop movements.[35] The main Texas army under Houston camped in the timber of the Brazos River bottom near Jared Groce's plantation (modern Hempstead) where for two weeks Houston drilled his grumbling soldiers. Waiting, he watched to see in which direction Santa Anna would advance. It was a dreadful gamble; having placed his army between the Mexicans and Nacogdoches, Houston left populous sections of the coast, including Harrisburg and the key port at Galveston, exposed to attack by Santa Anna's forces.[36]

---

judged that those "old Texians" who fled with their families wanted to take a stand on the Colorado River and were furious with Houston for exposing their homes to Mexican attack. After seeing their families to safety, they returned—too late for the fight.

33. Fane Downs, "'Tryels and Trubbles': Women in Early Nineteenth-Century Texas," *SHQ*, 90 (July, 1986), 48–54, offers a potent view of the so-called "Runaway Scrape," the month-long flight of Texas families eastward before the invading Mexican armies. See also Yoakum, *History of Texas*, II, 109; Lack, *The Texas Revolutionary Experience*, 222–223; and Hardin, *Texas Iliad*, 163.

34. James W. Robinson served in the Texas Army from March 12 to September 15, 1836. Charles Ferris, with Robinson, joined Houston's army near Columbus on the Colorado River. Webb, Carroll, and Branda (eds.), *Handbook of Texas*, I, 256, II, 490. Probably Ferris met Isaac W. Burton through Robinson, since both Robinson and Burton were from Nacogdoches. Robinson was among those many critics who denounced Houston's failure to fight the Mexican army on the Colorado, calling it not fear but poor military judgment. Hardin, *Texas Iliad*, 187.

35. Houston later denied giving the order to burn one of Texas's most historic villages, the capital of Austin's colony. Hardin, *Texas Iliad*, 186.

36. Houston's recent biographer Randolph B. Campbell in *Sam Houston and the American Southwest* (New York: Harper Collins, 1993), 71, 160, praises his "strategic withdrawal," saying Houston built strength while waiting to strike an effective blow. Campbell portrays Houston the realist and man of caution, always showing good sense and practicality. James W. Pohl, *The Battle of San Jacinto* (Austin:Texas State Historical Association, 1989), 11, suggests that Houston took his army north from San Felipe to avoid entrapment in Santa Anna's three-pronged pincer advance. Hardin, *Texas Iliad*, 189, speculates that Houston withdrew seeking

Sam Houston's personality, as well as his actions, were exasperating to many Texians. No one knew what was in his mind, but many suspected he meant to avoid a fight altogether. His critics railed, but "Old Sam" kept his counsel and, until joined by Thomas J. Rusk on April 4, shared his plans with no one. Outnumbered by the enemy, Houston knew he had a single chance to gain victory. One battle had to do. In the early weeks of April, Houston was as patient as Santa Anna was impetuous.

On April 10, Charles D. Ferris, serving as a scout in Baker's command, reported that the enemy was on the move out of San Felipe. Mexicans broke camp, leaving behind a small guard and some artillery.[37] Santa Anna decided to forget the rebel army and capture its government, thus ending Texian opposition to his rule. Outflanking Wylie Martin's troops, the "Napoleon of the West" crossed the Brazos at Ft. Bend (Richmond), leaving his heavy equipment to be rafted across the swollen stream. With a small contingent, Santa Anna plunged toward Harrisburg. Santa Anna had given Houston the opportunity he had awaited.

Immediately on learning of Santa Anna's river crossing and his move toward Harrisburg, Houston commandeered the steamboat *Yellow Stone*[38] to ferry his troops to the east bank of the Brazos River.[39] On April 15, after a two-day march, the army reached a fork in the road. One road led east to the Trinity River crossing and safety in the United States; the other led south to Harrisburg and Santa Anna's army. Charles Ferris, Isaac W. Burton, Moseley Baker and others threatened mutiny[40] if Houston took the road eastward, but already their commander had made the decision to join combat.[41]

---

the cover of the East Texas forests, perhaps hoping to engage in battle close to the U.S. border, giving General Gaines's troops across the Sabine River an excuse to intervene.

37. Jenkins, *The Papers of the Texas Revolution*, V, #2690.

38. Interestingly, this was the same boat used by the Astor fur interests on the Upper Missouri River, carrying supplies to Fort Union in 1832 and 1833. In 1836, the vessel was purchased by Texans and played a valuable role in the revolution. See Donald Jackson's *Voyages of the Steamboat Yellow Stone* (New York: Ticknor & Fields, 1985).

39. On April 12, Santa Anna moved on Harrisburg; on April 13, Houston crossed the Brazos; on April 14, Moseley Baker and Charles Ferris rejoined the main army. According to Pohl, *The Battle of San Jacinto*, 22, Baker was ordered to Liberty to aid in evacuation of refugees but returned to the army in time for the battle.

40. Charles Ferris was critical of Houston in a *Western Literary Messenger* article, Jan. 11, 1843. As reported in Warren Ferris's account of the "Horse Marines," Dallas *Herald*, Oct. 14, 1871: "During the inglorious retreat of General Houston, eastward from the Colorado, about a dozen choice spirits, among whom were Major Isaac W. Burton and Charles D. Ferris, being utterly opposed to the retreating policy of the Commander-in-Chief, resolved to take the opposite end of the road." The timing of this confrontation is confused, but Charles Ferris's anti-Houston stance is clear. Hardin, *Texas Iliad*, 288–289, judges that Sam Houston's numerous critics cannnot simply be dismissed as "spiteful subordinates." Most veterans of San Jacinto and some of Texas's most revered heroes condemned Houston's reluctance to take the offensive.

41. According to John H. Jenkins and Kenneth Kesselus in *Edward Burleson: Texas Frontier Leader* (Austin: Jenkins Publishing Co., 1990), 103–105, Houston

Houston ordered a forced march to Harrisburg (now Houston, Texas). Reinforcements, including a company of East Texas men,[42] finally arrived; and the Texians were armed with the "Twin Sisters," two six-pound cannon donated by the city of Cincinnati, Ohio. Although still outnumbered by reinforced Mexican forces, Sam Houston wrote on the eve of battle: "This morning we are in preparation to meet Santa Anna. It is the only chance of saving Texas. . . . We go to conquer. . . . I leave the results in the hands of a wise God." Houston chose the battlefield where Buffalo Bayou and the San Jacinto River empty into upper Galveston Bay. Here thick oak groves and swampy marshes provided cover for his riflemen who were lethal in the woods. To the amazement of the Mexicans, however, the Texians charged into the open.[43] The decisive battle, joined on the afternoon of April 21, 1836, lasted only eighteen minutes. Vengeful Texians fell on the Mexican camp during siesta, threw them into a rout, and engaged in a killing frenzy that continued until dusk.

The Ferris/Lovejoy family in Buffalo joined in celebation of the miraculous victory over Santa Anna. Joshua Lovejoy received a letter from his mother dated June 5, 1836, saying that the family had not heard from Charles Ferris since the battle of April 21, but, since his name was not listed among those killed or wounded, she believed he must be safe.[44] With great relief Sarah Lovejoy informed Josh on June 27, 1836:

> The last letter we had from Charles was dated the twenty second of April the day after the battle of San Jacinto and Santa Anna's capture. He was then well delighted with the country and in good spirits—he had thought their next movement would be to San Antonio to endeavour to retake it. . . . Horace Chamberlain is in Texas and was with Charles April 23 when he wrote home he said that Charles had a narrow escape in the battle of the 21st—in the heat of the engagement a Mexican at a distance of five paces fired his musket at him which he avoided but his horse was frightened at the report and threw him, however for once good luck was his. He alighted on his feet, and the Mexican rushed upon him with his bayonet, but Charles was too quick for him and saved his own life, with the loss of part of his rifle.[45]

---

was not at the head of the Army when they reached the crossroads; the Army itself took the turn to the right and San Jacinto. Hardin, *Texas Iliad*, 192, agrees that the Army, not Houston, made the decision to fight.

42. George L. Crocket, *Two Centuries of East Texas: A History of San Augustine County and Surrounding Territory from 1685 to the Present Time* (Dallas: Southwest Press, 1932), 183. Probably forty men under William Kimbro followed the main army as a rear guard and fought under Sidney Sherman on Apr. 21.

43. Hardin, *Texas Iliad*, 201–202.

44. Sally Lovejoy to Joshua Lovejoy, June 5, 1836. FLC, Box I, Folder 14.

45. Quoted in McCausland, "Early Buffalo Journalist," 7. Apparently Sarah's account is based on details in Horace Chamberlain's letter to his father. Chamberlain's report, along with a sketch of San Jacinto, was printed in the Buffalo *Daily Commercial Advertiser*, June 15, 1836. (BHS newspaper file).

Whether Charles Ferris was actually at the battle of San Jacinto is still a mystery. His name appears on no list of San Jacinto veterans, and he never received the 640-acre donation due participants in the battle.[46] The Ferris family always believed Charles fought at San Jacinto. Sarah's diary entry, April 21, 1837, noted: "One year ago this moment and Charles was in the furious battle of San Jacinto."[47] Seven years later, Charles Ferris, editing the *Western Literary Messenger*, included a tribute to the courage of Col. Juan Almonte, Santa Anna's aide at San Jacinto, and referred to himself as "a witness to this heroic act of gallantry."[48] The strongest circumstantial evidence rests on the story printed in the Buffalo *Daily Commercial Advertiser* on June 15, 1836. The New York paper, attempting to satiate public hunger for news from Texas, printed a lengthy report based on a sixteen-page letter from Horace Chamberlain to his father. Chamberlain, another Buffalo volunteer in Texas, claimed to have seen Charles Ferris two days after the battle, at which time he learned of Ferris's exploits. Ferris was scouting for Moseley Baker on April 10 so was probably with Baker when he rejoined Houston's main force prior to the battle. A final piece of indirect evidence is James W. Robinson's letter of introduction in behalf of Ferris. Addressed to Thomas J. Rusk and dated May 9, 1836, three weeks after the battle of San Jacinto, the letter recommended Charles Ferris and referred to his "tried valor."[49]

Ferris carried Robinson's letter to Rusk, commander of the Texas army after Houston was wounded at San Jacinto. Referring to Colonel Ferris, Robinson wrote:

> he proposes raising a company of Cavalry, and as he understands the sword exercises and other duties of the corps of Cavalry and is a young man of classic education and morals, habit and tried valor, I think he will be an ornament to the Army.[50]

Rusk was in Victoria, monitoring the withdrawal of 7,000 Mexican troops still in Texas. Santa Anna, held prisoner at Velasco, signed a treaty recognizing Texas independence and ordering withdrawal of Mexican forces to below the Nueces River, but Texians feared renewed hostilities. On May 29, Rusk ordered Maj. Isaac W. Burton and twenty

---

46. Louis W. Kemp, author of *Heroes of San Jacinto* (1932) and leading authority on the battle, did not at first believe Charles D. Ferris participated, although Kemp admitted his list of soldiers might be incomplete. Walter McCausland's correspondence with Kemp on this point is available, FLC, Box V, 12. McCausland wrote a persuasive argument for Ferris's presence at San Jacinto, "Charles Drake Ferris: Unknown Veteran of San Jacinto," *SHQ*, 63, (Oct., 1959), 290–298.

47. Diary of Sarah Lovejoy, FLC, Box III, Folder 5.

48. Quoted in McCausland, "Early Buffalo Journalist," 7.

49. Robinson to Rusk, May 9, 1836, Thomas J. Rusk Papers (CAH). Copy in FLC, Box V, Folder 8.

50. Ibid.

well-armed, mounted rangers, including Charles Ferris,[51] to patrol the
Texas coast between Victoria and Refugio. Burton, a resident of
Nacogdoches and veteran of San Jacinto, was assigned to block resupply
of the Mexican Army. On June 3, Burton and his men ambushed a small
landing party at Copano Bay; then boarded and captured the vessel
Watchman, laden with provisions for the Mexican Army. Two weeks later,
Burton's men used the captured ship as a decoy to entrap two other ves-
sels, the *Comanche* and the *Fanny Butler.*[52]

Charles Ferris shared in these daring actions and in the celebration
when the ships and much needed supplies, valued at $25,000, were deliv-
ered to Velasco (or Brazoria). Warren Ferris, in an account written in
1871, stated that the townspeople hoisted Burton on their shoulders and
carried him to the hotel where they toasted his rangers as the "Horse
Marines" of the Texas Revolution.[53] Charles Ferris used the prize money
awarded to finance his furlough home. He returned to Buffalo an accredit-
ed agent of the new Texas government, empowered to accept donations in
its cause.[54]

Warren Ferris eagerly awaited his younger brother's return to Buffalo
in the fall of 1836. Charles would come home a hero, bearing claim to
5,400 acres of Texas land for his military service. Sarah Lovejoy wrote
that a thousand and one stories were circulating in Buffalo about Ferris's
Texas adventures. "Texas will be his home," she wrote, "—whether it is
ours or not, this trial [with Henry Lovejoy] will decide."[55] But Charles
Ferris's homecoming was overshadowed by the biggest story to hit Buffalo
since the opening of the Erie Canal; Benjamin Rathbun had been arrested
on charges of forgery! The events to follow would play havoc with the fortunes of the Ferris/Lovejoy family.

On August 3, 1836, Benjamin Rathbun's empire collapsed, his house of
cards brought down by charges from rival bankers. In July, Rathbun was
confronted with a forged note in the name of Charles M. Reed. The

---

51. *Muster Rolls of the Texas Revolution* (Austin: Daughters of the Republic of
Texas, 1986), 183 lists "C. D. Feris" among Burton's Rangers. Based on records of
the Texas General Land Office, Austin (cited hereafter GLO).

52. *Telegraph and Texas Register* (Columbia), Aug. 2, 1836, printed Major
Burton's account of his daring land/sea exploits. See also orders from Rusk to
Burton, May 29 and June 3, 1836, in Jenkins (ed.), *The Papers of the Texas
Revolution*, VI, #3199, #3275; and letters regarding his actions, Rusk to Burnet,
June 13, and Ingram to Parker, June 30, 1836, ibid., IX, #3408, #3575.

53. Warren A. Ferris mistakenly placed the incident before the battle of San
Jacinto, but correctly detailed how Burton's men "enticed a boat ashore by means
of a false flag, captured the boat, and manned it with their own party, boarded and
captured the vessel which proved to be loaded with clothing and stores for the
invading army." Dallas *Herald*. Oct. 14, 1871.

54. Jenkins (ed.), *The Papers of the Texas Revolution*, IX, #4332, Governor
Burnet's list of civil officials shows Charles D. Ferris empowered as "an agent to
receive donations for Texas."

55. Sarah Lovejoy to Joshua Lovejoy, Aug. 14, 1836, FLC, Box I, Folder 16.

forgery, kept quiet at first, became public as the extent of criminal activity became clear. In Philadelphia, Nicholas Biddle of the Bank of the United States showed David E. Evans a note bearing his forged signature. Three additional forgeries of $5,000 each were discovered. Rathbun claimed no knowledge of such forged bank notes. Friends advised him to flee to Canada, but on August 3 both Benjamin and Lyman Rathbun were arrested and held in the very jail they had built.[56] Two nephews, Lyman R. Howlett and Rathbun Allen, who were clerks for the company, were sought in connection with the actual forgeries.[57] Both young men fled the city; Howlett disappeared permanently, but Allen was apprehended in Ohio and returned to Buffalo.

Local newspapers, with interests tied to Rathbun, were slow to print the details; but rival Rochester papers fanned public reaction. Rumors flew. Holders of Rathbun's worthless notes might lose as much as half a million dollars. His many construction projects came to a standstill. On August 4 and 5, a mob of unemployed workers stormed the jail where the Rathbuns were held. Buffalo was split into pro and anti-Rathbun factions. The Ferris/Lovejoy family was sympathetic with the promoter, agreeing with those who saw him as a victim of circumstances. The key issue revolved around how much Benjamin Rathbun knew of the sources of his credit and whether, as principal, he was responsible for illegal acts of his associates.[58]

Feeling ran so high that Rathbun's lawyers called for a change of venue, doubting he could receive a fair trial in Buffalo. Released for a week on $60,000 bond to straighten out his affairs, Rathbun signed over his properties which were then inventoried and sold to meet the demand of creditors. An already serious economic crisis in Buffalo was worsened by the impact of President Andrew Jackson's Specie Circular issued in July 1836. Jackson's action, designed to cool speculation, combined with Rathbun's exposure to create loss of confidence, withdrawal of paper notes, and a severe money shortage in Buffalo.

In the fall of 1836 Charles Ferris acquainted himself with his five-week-old son Charley and renewed his relationship with his older brother whom he had not seen in eight years. Enthusiastically, he pored over Warren Ferris's journal of Rocky Mountain adventures, using his considerable literary talents to help with editing. In October the Ferris brothers submitted the journal to Carey, Lea & Blanchard publishers of Philadelphia.[59]

---

56. Stories appeared in the Buffalo *Daily Commercial Advertiser*, Aug. 4, 5, and 12, 1836. (BHS newspaper file).

57. Howlett, a bright teenager who rode a pony about Buffalo as he conducted business for his uncle, was said to be adept at counterfeiting signatures. Welch, *It Is Home History*, 200–201.

58. Roger Whitman, "The Queen's Epic," an undated, unpublished manuscript is an excellent source on the Rathbun affair. (BHS).

59. Family letter to Joshua Lovejoy, Oct. 26, 1836, Davis Collection. Charles Ferris, home in Buffalo, told his half-brother of completion of Warren's journal and

Charles Ferris was eager to return to Texas and busily laid plans to conclude his affairs in Buffalo. He had struck a firm friendship with his commander Isaac W. Burton of Nacogdoches; they planned to enter business together. Warren Ferris was also leaning toward going to Texas with his brother. He was not comfortable with town life in Buffalo, the beaver glory days were clearly over, economic conditions in the United States were not promising, and Texas seemed the land of opportunity. In a long letter to Joshua Lovejoy on November 20, 1836, Charles Ferris described their plans:

> I shall then soon return to Texas and there win wealth and fame or perish in the attempt. . . . I shall be engaged in military operations against either the Mexicans or Indians, and hold the commission of captain in the battalion of rangers . . . to protect the frontiers against Indian depredations. . . . Warren will accompany me to that country.[60]

As always, Ferris admonished his young half-brother to forego frivolous expenses and to care for his mother and sisters who would be left alone in privation until Charles could make good his Texas land claims or until the suit with Henry Lovejoy was settled. He cautioned Josh against putting any imprudent remarks regarding Henry to paper and thereby endangering their case; until termination of the suit, Charles urged "Show restraint, distrust everyone."[61] Ferris promised to return for the family in the summer of 1837 and suggested that Joshua also relocate in Texas, invest in a plantation and some slaves in the South. Charles Ferris's enthusiasm for Texas infected the entire family, even his wife Hester who was clearly unhappy about being abandoned for a second time. Sally Lovejoy sold her dowry property in Glens Falls, New York, to raise money for her sons' return to Texas. It was Sally's last unencumbered asset.[62]

The Ferris brothers' departure from Buffalo was hastened when Lyman Rathbun jumped his $20,000 bail and decided to join them in the trip to Texas. Charles Ferris and Rathbun made a dash on horseback to Pittsburgh; there they separated at the dock, planning to rendezvous downriver at Natchez. Rathbun rode on across country while Ferris took the steamer to Louisville. Warren Ferris followed with the baggage; he was to meet Charles in Louisville. But a posse on Lyman Rathbun's trail

---

his plan to return in a few weeks to Texas. Though the family was desperate for money, Charles cautioned against premature settlement with Henry Lovejoy. He estimated the value of the Buffalo property at $60,000 and urged Josh not to accept the $3000 Henry had offered for his part. Charles Ferris wrote: "I shall counsel no terms with such a man, but war—war—war to the knife, and the knife to the hilt." He also warned Joshua not to borrow money from their "lying New York uncle," a reference to Jonathan Lovejoy.

60. McCausland, "Lives of the Lovejoys", 9–10.

61. Ibid., 10.

62. FLC, Box III, Folder 6.

caught up with the Ferris brothers in Louisville and held them for questioning. Meanwhile, Rathbun escaped to his sister's home in Grand Gulf, Mississippi, then made his way to New Orleans and on to relative safety in the Republic of Texas. The Ferrises were released by the authorities, but were followed on the chance they would lead authorities to Rathbun. Warren Ferris related the story of their wild flight southward in a letter to his half-sister Sarah from New Orleans on December 31, 1836:

> I immediately went to the [Louisville] post office and found a letter from Charles directing me to call at the Louisville Hotel. . . . I immediately went and sure enough found him and our friend Doct Leonard. . . . In the meantime four persons came in pursuit of Rathbun . . . Merrill, Miller, Barton and White. . . . The first of these immediately continued down the river but the others remained to watch Charles and when I arrived . . . they seized my trunks . . . the horses . . . were also seized. At Natchez we went to the post office but found no letter from R consequently we know not where he is.[63]

The Ferrises reached New Orleans aboard the steamboat *Henry Clay* on December 30. They purchased surveying equipment, thinking surveying might offer a practical alternative to military service. Thus Warren Ferris abandoned his plan to return to the mountains and his dream of a family "plantation" on the Missouri. Now his lot was firmly cast with Charles and the new Republic of Texas.

---

63. Typescript of a letter from Warren Ferris to Sarah Lovejoy in care of Horace Chamberlain, Dec. 31, 1836, from New Orleans, ibid., Box I, Folder 3. In this letter, Ferris described his Louisville reunion with trapper friends of Rocky Mountain days. He learned that five or six of his old companions had been killed, Fontenelle, Fitzpatrick and Company had broken up, and Andrew Drips was head of a new American Fur Company expedition.

Part Two

☆

Frontier Surveyor

★ 4 ★

GONE TO TEXAS

CHARLES FERRIS, with his older brother Warren, returned to Texas in early January 1837. Disembarking at Velasco (near modern Freeport, Texas), they traveled up the Brazos River to Columbia in hopes of finding Charles Ferris's former commander, Isaac Burton, who had promised to help him settle in the new Republic of Texas. Columbia (now West Columbia), a small community of only a few hundred people, was temporary capital of the fledgling Republic, and the town swarmed with important men of government and recent arrivals. Excitement was in the air. Each week brought boatloads of ambitious adventurers rushing to Texas to gain wealth or glory; most sought employment in the Army of the Republic.

The sudden, decisive victory over the Mexican Army at San Jacinto did not bring unity to Anglo-Texans. Once the threat of Mexican re-invasion appeared unlikely, Texians relaxed into a quarrelsome pattern. Sam Houston, recovered from wounds suffered at San Jacinto, was now president of a problem-ridden young Republic. Financial difficulties were most pressing; the government was broke and in debt. Politicians jockeyed for power while idle, unpaid soldiers threatened mutiny.[1] Political rivalries were reflected in the army, where commissions were freely granted one day only to be annulled the next. When army commander Felix Huston agitated for invading Mexico, Houston vetoed the plan, replacing Huston and furloughing the troublesome army, except for ranger battalions to protect the frontier from Indian incursions.[2]

Since opportunities in the military appeared to be disappearing, Charles and Warren Ferris decided to take up surveying. Each Texas veteran who emigrated with his family was to receive a Spanish "league and labor" of land, nearly 5,000 acres, and the Ferris brothers could foresee unlimited opportunity for surveyors to locate bounty land owed to the soldiers and headrights claimed by legions of new settlers. Possibly the brothers had some knowledge of the art of surveying from their stepbrother Henry Lovejoy, who became a civil engineer and official surveyor of Buffalo;[3]

1. Lack, *The Texas Revolutionary Experience*, 137, 258.

2. Yoakum, *History of Texas*, II, 209. Stanley Siegel, *A Political History of the Texas Republic: 1836–1845* (Austin: University of Texas Press, 1956), 61, 65–66. In March 1837, Houston furloughed most of the army, offering free transport to New Orleans or land as payment for services. No more volunteers were to be accepted.

3. McCausland, "Lives of the Lovejoys," 2, and Smith, *History of Buffalo*, II, 60. Lovejoy lay out a tract at Black Rock and with Peter Emslie surveyed much of south Buffalo. He was Buffalo city surveyor in 1844–1845.

more likely they were self-taught and bluffing any real experience. While in New Orleans, they purchased the necessary instruments and books to prepare themselves to join Isaac Burton who was already surveying around Nacogdoches.

The man who was to promote Ferris fortunes in Texas was Georgia-born Isaac Watts Burton, a rising figure in Nacogdoches society and politics. At age twenty-seven, after a brief stint at West Point,[4] Burton headed west where, in Louisiana, he met Martin Lacy. Burton married Lacy's daughter and, with the Lacys, emigrated to Nacogdoches. Almost immediately Burton became involved in Texas politics. He played a minor role in the 1832 struggle that resulted in expulsion of Mexican troops from Nacogdoches. Prior to the Texas Revolution, Burton practiced law and did a bit of surveying; it was his ambition to publish a newspaper and enter politics.

Burton's stature in East Texas was due, in part, to the connection with Martin Lacy. In early 1832, Lacy brought his large family and six slaves to Texas where he became a landowner and Indian trader. From a strategic point on the San Antonio Road west of Nacogdoches, [5] he monitored activities of the nearby Cherokee. Lacy's son, William Young Lacy, married the daughter of Peter Ellis Bean, old-time settler and Indian agent of Nacogdoches.[6] Like many established Texians during the revolution, Martin Lacy evaded military service, although he was listed in Michael Costley's ranger company.[7] Lacy did not speak or write Cherokee; in fact, he was illiterate except for the ability to sign his name.[8] Through Bean, Lacy won the trust of the Indians and developed a prosperous trade with the nearby tribes. Nacogdochians chose Lacy's son-in-law, Isaac Burton, veteran of San Jacinto and captain of the "Horse Marines," to represent

---

4. Isaac W. Burton, "Experiences in Texas," in Charles A. Gulick (ed.), *The Papers of Mirabeau B. Lamar, Edited from the Original Papers in the Texas State Library* (6 vols. in 7; Austin: A. C. Baldwin, 1921–1927), III, 287–295 (cited hereafter as Lamar Papers). By his own account, at age seventeen after only one year, Burton left the academy, having proven himself unworthy through "reckless, irresponsible" acts. In Texas, he likely knew fellow Georgians Fannin and Lamar.

5. Lacy's Fort, two miles southwest of modern Alto, Texas, stood on a hill overlooking Mustang Prairie and the point where the San Antonio Road intersected that leading south to Washington-on-the-Brazos.

6. R. B. Blake Collection, 75 vols. (CAH), XXVIII, 374. Peter Ellis Bean's friendship with the Cherokees kept the Indians in check during his eleven-year tenure as agent (1825–1836).

7. Costley, with K. H. Douglass, founded the settlement of Douglass (1835), west of Nacogdoches on the San Antonio Road. Other early settlers in his ranger company included John Jordan and David Crist who later became frontier surveyors. Blake Collection, LIII, 258.

8. Ben H. Procter, *Not Without Honor: The Life of John H. Reagan* (Austin: University of Texas Press, 1962), 21n.

them in the first congress of the Republic.[9] This was Burton's situation when the Ferris brothers landed in Texas.

On arrival in Columbia, Charles Ferris resigned his military commission.[10] Finding that Burton had departed after the adjournment of Congress, he set out to follow his patron 300 miles up-country to Nacogdoches, leaving his brother behind to study the new surveying books and recover from a fever developed en route to Texas. As soon as Warren Ferris regained his strength, he was to join Charles in Nacogdoches where they would engage in business with Burton.

Warren Ferris passed the winter in Columbia, reading his books and trying to recover. He waited two months for word from his brother and, not hearing, determined to strike off on his own to find him. As spring came to Texas, Warren Ferris traveled downriver to Brazoria, then by ship to Galveston Island. He spent several weeks with Maj. I. N. Moreland who was in charge of Mexican prisoners captured at San Jacinto the previous spring. The old customs house where Moreland lived was the only substantial structure on Galveston Island, a desolate sandspit where wild deer roamed.[11] About 100 Mexicans, many of whom were hired out to local planters as laborers,[12] were housed in squalid huts on the low, dreary island. Luckily, Ferris departed and most of the Mexicans were released before a devastating hurricane known as "Racers' Storm" struck Galveston, destroying Moreland's house.

In April, Ferris proceeded up the Trinity River to Liberty where he caught sight of General Cos and other Mexican officers held prisoners there.[13]

---

9. Patsy McDonald Spaw (ed.), *The Texas Senate*, vol. 1, *Republic to Civil War, 1836–1861* (College Station: Texas A&M University Press, 1990), 7, 32, 324n. Burton lost his first bid for the Senate to Robert Irion (Burton claimed Irion narrowly won because of Mexican votes), but served in the lower house of the first congress, first session. He was elected to the senates of the second, third, and fourth congresses (1837–1840).

10. Sarah Lovejoy to Joshua Lovejoy, May 2, 1837. FLC, Box II, Folder 5 (based on Warren Ferris's letter of Apr. 2, 1837). The Buffalo family mistakenly believed that Warren had received a commission in the Texas army when the Buffalo *Daily Commercial Advertiser* (Feb. 22, 1837) carried a report from the *Telegraph and Texas Register* (Columbia) of January 27. Sarah Lovejoy's letter of March 12 (FLC, Box I, Folder 2) referred to the report that "Major W. A. Ferris who left this city for Texas with L. Rathbun is organizing a company of Texas militia." Probably Warren was confused with Willis A. Ferris (no relation) who had come to Texas earlier. Sarah's letter to Joshua Lovejoy, May 9, 1837 reported that Charles Ferris had resigned his commission. Ibid., Box II, Folder 5.

11. Sarah Lovejoy to Joshua Lovejoy, June 6, 1837. FLC, Box I, Folder 5. Based on Warren Ferris's letter of May 5, 1837. Ferris also recounted his Galveston visit in a reminiscence carried in the Dallas *Herald*, Sept. 2, 1871.

12. Muir, *Texas in 1837*, 6, 10. Also, Margaret S. Henson, "Politics and the Treatment of Mexican Prisoners after the Battle of San Jacinto," *SHQ*, 94 (Oct., 1990), 220. According to Henson, John James Audubon visited Galveston in April 1837 and commented on the Mexican prisoners.

13. Warren Ferris, "Reminiscence of 1837," Dallas *Herald*, Sept. 2, 1871.

From this settlement on the Trinity, Ferris plunged northeast into the dense forests of East Texas, the "Big Thicket," a forbidding swampy region where one might easily get lost. On foot, in terrain where a horse was considered essential, Ferris pushed several hundred miles north through the wild region. Survival skills, well learned in the mountains, stood him in good stead on this lonely journey.

Sarah Lovejoy's letters of May 2 and June 6, 1837, written to her brother in Michigan, related Warren Ferris's progress in Texas. She described his dangerous trip, alone except for two dogs, through the wilderness to Nacogdoches where he met only disappointment:

> He left Galveston on the morning of eleventh of April—and arrived at Nacogdoches the twenty-fourth. Here he learned that Charles was there with Major Burton March sixteenth. On the twenty-fifth he [Warren] set out for Mustang Prairie, thirty-five miles to the west— the residence of Squire Lacy—Major Burton's father-in-law. He reached there the next day, and then learned that Charles and Burton were surveying on the Trinity near its mouth, and thus he had passed very near without seeing them. . . . It was a most unfortunate occurrence, for the means which Warren had to attempt that journey were slender indeed.[14]

Ferris described his trip, a harrowing experience for a newcomer to Texas, even a man accustomed to wilderness treks. He reported to his family in Buffalo how at one point his "dogs ran howling back followed by two large and ferocious wolves" who fled at the sight of a human. Later he came upon "a large and magnificent prairie resembling a beautiful green lake, surrounded by bold Pine headlands and intersected by islands and promontories of dark forests." Reconnoitering the scene with his telescope, Ferris spied a large herd of cattle but could discover no herdsmen. A trail led him to a village of some twenty houses, located in the shade of vine-covered trees. Although "fowls were cackling, hogs grunting, cattle lowing and horses neighing," the village was deserted. So many paths intersected the village that Ferris became bewildered and lost his way. The sun disappeared, and lowering clouds threatened rain. Disoriented and exhausted, Ferris sat down in despair; then suddenly he noticed a whisp of smoke in the distance and followed it to the lodge of a lone Shawnee. The Indian welcomed the weary traveler, allowed him to spend the night, and explained that the Shawnee of the deserted village had relocated to the north on the Sabine River.[15]

---

14. Sarah to Joshua, June 6, 1837, FLC, Box I, Folder 17.

15. Ibid., based on Warren Ferris's letters of April 2, May 5, and June 6, the first received from Texas, brought to Buffalo from New Orleans, and hand-delivered to his sister and mother by Flint Ransom. DeGolyer judged that the deserted Shawnee village lay in what is now Angelina County. Shawnee Prairie is near Huntington, Texas, off Highway 69.

Warren Ferris's first Texas letters revealed that none of the family letters were reaching him, so the next communication was carried personal-
ly by Horace Chamberlain who was returning to Texas after a furlough in
Buffalo.[16] Sarah and her mother expressed concern at hazards he faced in
his dreary journey to Nacogdoches. Sarah praised her half-brother's
artistry with a pen: "you place the scene so vividly before one, had I a
painting I should have transferred the scene to canvas, and made a glorious picture." She judged the demanding adventure better to be imagined
than experienced. Ferris's mother wrote that she could not sleep for wor-
rying about the "dangerous journey few men would have attempted
alone." Sally Ferris urged her son to write and tell her "how [you] fare
there and whether you get enuff [sic] to eat. . . . how you like the country
and if you think I had better come there to live."[17]

The family believed the Ferris brothers were together in Nacogdoches,
but such was not the case. With Charles Ferris off surveying, Warren was
alone and ill in this isolated outpost of Anglo-American civilization.
Exposure and privation on the strenuous trip up-country caused a relapse
of his fever. Like every Texas immigrant, Ferris faced an adjustment to
summer heat and humidity. He lost weight, felt lethargic, and experienced chills and fever.

Malaria-like fevers were considered more fearsome to early Texians
than the threat from Indians or Mexicans. Most Texas villages were located on river banks or in low bottom lands, and malaria was associated
with the "bad air" of such swampy areas. The causes were not well under-
stood; everything from bad food, to overexposure to the sun, to "over-
excitement" was blamed. Preventatives included morning coffee, wines,
red pepper, and brandy. Treatment, by poorly qualified frontier doctors,
usually involved "puke, purge, and bleeding" with heavy doses of calomel,
castor oil, and Epsom salts to cause sweating. A fever could not be taken
lightly; "bilious" fever might be fatal in the first two days.[18] Even a light
case would lay a victim low for weeks, as it did Warren Ferris. During an
extended illness, he ran up a debt of several hundred dollars to the
Nacogdoches inn where he took lodging and to Dr. Eldridge G. Harris.[19]

---

16. Chamberlain commanded an artillery regiment on Galveston Island in
December 1836; perhaps he received letters from Ferris in April 1837. Daughters of
the Republic of Texas, *Muster Rolls*, 162–163. According to Blake Collection, III,
146–149, Chamberlain lost his commission as first lieutenant for overstaying his furlough in 1837, but he was not courtmartialed and was later reinstated in the army.

17. Ferris/Lovejoy family to Warren Ferris, June 1837, FLC, Box I, Folder 2.

18. William R. Hogan, *The Texas Republic: A Social and Economic History*
(Norman: University of Oklahoma Press, 1946), 224–226, 232, 236.

19. Eldridge G. Harris, another Georgian, fled to Texas after killing a man while
defending his pharmacy. He served in the Texas army and practiced medicine in
Nacogdoches. Blake Collection, LVI, 207.

In Nacogdoches, Charles Ferris had achieved quick acceptance due to his friendship with Isaac Burton. Ferris agreed to edit Burton's newspaper, the *Texas Chronicle*, and to invest in a surveying partnership with his influential friend. Sarah Lovejoy told Charles's wife Hester, who was in Clarence, New York, with her family, that one member of the posse trailing Lyman Rathbun had followed Charles Ferris to Nacogdoches hoping to be led to Rathbun. The officer gave up the chase and grudgingly admitted that Charles "bore a good reputation" in Texas, "was very well known and very much liked."[20] These compliments were of little use to Warren Ferris, lying abed miserably waiting his brother's return from the surveying expedition to the south.

Charles Ferris returned to Nacogdoches only briefly that summer. While in South Texas, he received letters informing him of developments in Buffalo. The lawsuit with Henry Lovejoy was settled, with the promise of a handsome sum of money Ferris could use to impress Burton. Also there were distressing messages from his wife, who complained of his long absence and infrequent letters. Their baby son Charley had been seriously ill and was too much for her. Hester Ferris demanded, "I want you to come direct and not stop anywhere—if you do not I shall certainly think you care more for others than me."[21]

In August 1837, Charles Ferris returned to Buffalo. Henry Lovejoy had agreed to settle for two of the five acres and a seventy-foot frontage on Seneca Street. He would also assume the $2,000 mortgage held by his uncle. Warren Ferris consented to these terms and urged his brother to subdivide their three acres into small lots and sell them in order to raise the most capital.[22] Charles Ferris promised Burton that he would return to Texas with a substantial stake to invest in their mutual enterprises. It was his plan to settle his affairs quickly, sell the Buffalo lots, gather his family, and return to Texas to claim his bounty land. This plan was to be frustrated by events in Buffalo.

The entire Ferris/Lovejoy clan was eager to be off for Texas. Brother Joshua devoted much time to thoughts of "Texian Times, Texian Climes, and Texian manners."[23] He was working out his debt to cousin Wing, his health was poor, and Michigan, he complained, was deadly dull. In July 1837, Joshua Lovejoy wrote to Warren Ferris of his desire to come to Texas, advising his older half-brother:

> There is a great cry for Texas now. Thousands are migrating to that country in hopes to better their situation. . . . The time for making a

20. Sarah Lovejoy to Hester Ferris, Apr. 12, 1837, FLC, Box I, Folder 10. Sarah urged her sister-in-law not to "judge ill" of Charles for his failure to write.

21. Hester Ferris to Charles Ferris, July 5, 15, 1837, ibid., Box I, Folder 6 (carried to Texas by Horace Chamberlain).

22. Warren Ferris to Charles Ferris, Nov. 26, 1837, ibid, Box I, Folder 4.

23. Joshua Lovejoy to Sarah Lovejoy, Feb. 19, 1837, ibid., Box I, Folder 2.

fortune in Texas is now—in the beginning when the country is new you can select locations such as must be valuable eventually . . . keep your eye on those spots on rivers—and get them in your hands.[24]

Despite his crowded social calendar, Lovejoy was in a gloomy mood. He wallowed in self-pity that wealth had not come his way, bemoaned the "lost romance" of his youth, and craved the "southern sun." Josh confessed in a letter to his sister Sarah, "I was sued last fall for seduction and breach [of] promise."[25] Although the charges, later extended to slander, were withdrawn, Lovejoy's romantic peccadillos threatened his future in Michigan. He notified the "Gents" of his fraternity that he intended to "leave this camp for another clime."[26]

In October 1837, young Lovejoy went home to visit Buffalo. Charles Ferris, also home that fall, shared with Warren his misgivings about their half-brother:

> Joshua . . . arrived here about a week ago, without money and in debt to Wing some two hundred and fifty dollars—he has been I believe an extravagant spendthrift fool, and I suspect in reference to women very dissipated. One would have thought that in all the circumstances of the case [Henry Lovejoy's] he would have been more prudent. I dont [sic] know what the fellow can think or expect.[27]

Such a warning of Josh's dubious character should have impressed Warren Ferris more strongly.

Nineteen-year-old Sarah Lovejoy kept a diary through most of 1837 that reveals the daily life and hopes of the Buffalo family. Increasingly, Sarah expressed the family desire to go to Texas. "Buffalo is fatal to us all," she declared. "When business is settled we . . . embark for Texas for the *new home* of ours . . . our family will yet find a resting place there."[28]

In her frequent brief entries, Ferris's half-sister described her day-to-day activities: sewing, embroidering, trimming hats, reading, writing poetry and letters, attending the Eagle Street Theatre, entertaining guests, playing chess, caring for children. Sarah Lovejoy was not so placid as her outward demeanor might have seemed. Her diary reveals those volatile teenage moods that fluctuate between depths of exaggerated despondency and heights of romantic excitement. Often she thought of impending death. "I believe I am more than half a Quakeress now, in dress sometimes I am and in my manners. I do wonder what I shall ever become if I live. I'm sick of the world and weary of everything." On other

---

24. Joshua Lovejoy to Warren Ferris, July 30, 1837, ibid., Box I, Folder 1.

25. Joshua Lovejoy to Sarah Lovejoy, July 16, 1837. Quoted in McCausland, "Lives of the Lovejoys," 13–14.

26. Joshua Lovejoy's letter of Oct. 10, 1837 to the SUFN General Staff. FLC, Box II, Folder 9.

27. Charles Ferris to Warren Ferris, Oct. 20, 1837, ibid., Box I, Folder 1.

28. Sarah Lovejoy's diary entries, Mar. 8, 17, 1837, ibid., Box II, Folders 3, 5.

occasions she felt "fame might be mine if I were to live and try for it—a bright name in the literary world. I wish I were less sensitive." She inquired of her diary, "Shall I seek happiness in love? in fame?" Sarah admired Flint Ransom, who flattered and teased her unmercifully; but she was even more attracted to her handsome cousin Zebulon Ferris whose intellect, dignity, and courtly manner reminded Sarah of her older brother Charles.[29] Zeb Ferris inspired a love poem:

> Oh God could I but bring *him* to my side
> I would be whatever he could wish
> I would share terror and danger with him
> For him I'd brave peril and death.[30]

She wondered if she could avoid the name "Old Maid,"[31] and longed to be alone with Zebulon. And then, when she most wanted to be gay and entertaining, found herself listless and shy. And these myriad emotions came to bear in a single month![32]

Sarah Lovejoy's diary entry of August 16, 1837, exclaimed, "My brother Charles is *here* in this house as I am alive, straight as he could come from Texas he has—unexpected." Three days later she wrote: "my own brother Charles—*in jail*, arrested, charged with a felony, no bail until Monday. To be examined on what he knows of Lyman Rathbun."[33]

Charles Drake Ferris was accused of abetting a criminal escape. During his week in the Buffalo jail he assured his family and friends that his conscience was clear. Ferris insisted that he was a "citizen of a foreign country [the Republic of Texas]" and needed to return to his official duties there. When he publicly denounced the court's action in detaining him, the district attorney accused him of contempt; but he got off with an apology to the court.[34] During his imprisonment, Ferris wrote a verse of nine stanzas on Goliad, entitled "Fannin or the Massacre of LaBahia," which he submitted anonymously to the *Daily Commercial Advertiser*.[35] On September 1, the Grand Jury indicted Ferris of "conspiracy against the

---

29. Ibid., Apr. 11, 1837.

30. Ibid., July 5, 1837.

31. Charles Ferris shared the view that Sarah might never marry. He wrote to Warren in Texas, "Sarah will be 20 years old in March [1838]. . . . Sarah will I am inclined to think *be a maid* and live with us." Charles to Warren Ferris, Oct. 20, 1837, ibid., Box I, Folder 1.

32. Sarah Lovejoy's diary entries of June 24, July 5, 9, 11, and 19, 1837, ibid., Box II, Folders 3, 5.

33. Ibid., Aug. 19, 1837.

34. McCausland, "Early Buffalo Journalist," 11. Also reported in the *Buffalonian*, May 7, 1838.

35. Charles Ferris's poem appears in Sarah Lovejoy's letterbook, FLC, Box III, Folder 3. Wrongly assuming that a woman had written the emotional piece, the Buffalo paper declined publication, criticizing "her" impiety of language (apparently in reference to the Deity). The rejection is mentioned in McCausland, "Early Buffalo Journalist," 12.

laws." His steadfast friends Flint and Rodolph Ransom made bond so that he was released from jail, but Charles Ferris was bound to remain in Buffalo for the duration of the Rathbun litigation.

Actually, there were three Rathbun trials. The first was held in Batavia, New York, in early 1837 while Charles Ferris was still in Texas. In a statement published by the *Daily Commercial Advertiser*, Rathbun put himself in the best possible light. He claimed no knowledge of forgeries and placed any blame on his brother Lyman who, he claimed, handled the day-to-day affairs of their business ventures.[36] In March, the Buffalo developer boarded a coach of his own stageline for a jolting forty-mile ride along icy roads to Batavia where he arrived seventeen hours later to face charges in a less friendly atmosphere. Although Rathbun Allen was apprehended in Ohio and returned to New York to testify against his uncle, the prosecution's case was weak without the testimony of the fugitive Lyman Rathbun. After fifteen hours of deliberation, the jury reported itself unable to reach a verdict. A mistrial was declared, and Rathbun returned to Erie County.[37]

Benjamin Rathbun enjoyed widespread support in Buffalo where many ordinary people believed he had done no wrong. The community was polarized; the upper classes generally felt Benjamin Rathbun an unprincipled scoundrel while the working class folk saw him as something of a martyr, persecuted by wealthy financial rivals. Sally Lovejoy's millinery business suffered when well-to-do customers boycotted the "family that helped Lyman Rathbun escape." Sarah wrote that in regard to the Rathbun scandal, the "family [is] on wrong side of street—shunned by all but Ransoms."[38]

Rathbun's attorneys hoped to introduce new evidence from "missing witnesses" at his second trial. During the summer of 1837, agents tried to locate Lyman Rathbun who, far away in Texas, might willingly assume responsibility for the forgeries.[39] In the fall of 1837, Charles Ferris returned to Buffalo and was seized by the authorities to give testimony in the controversial case. Feelings ran high in Buffalo; violence lay just below the surface.

Fanning the emotional fires was Tom Nichols, youthful editor of the *Buffalonian*, a newly established sensationalist newspaper.[40] Nichols was greatly admired by Sarah Lovejoy who confessed in a letter to Joshua

---

36. *Daily Commercial Advertiser* (Buffalo), Feb. 21, 1837. See also the Benjamin Rathbun Papers, which include Rathbun's sixty-eight-page "confession" (BHS).

37. Details of the March trial were carried in the *Daily Commercial Advertiser* (Buffalo), Mar. 26, 1837.

38. Sarah Lovejoy to Joshua Lovejoy, Dec. 11, 1836. FLC, Box II, Folder 4.

39. The commission to take Lyman Rathbun's testimony in Texas was reported in *Daily Commercial Advertiser* (Buffalo), July 10, 1837.

40. Welch, *Home History*, 308–309.

that she believed him "the first star of the heavens."[41] Nichols's weekly scandal sheet soon became a daily, with a large circulation of avid readers who followed the Rathbun case with interest.[42] Charles Ferris shared his sister's admiration for flashy Tom Nichols and his spicy newspaper; in late 1837 he went to work for the *Buffalonian* at a salary of $15 a week. By 1838, Ferris was associate editor of the paper, which became the voice of Rathbun supporters. Certain parties were so enraged over their coverage of the case that a mob wrecked the newspaper office and tried to kidnap the editors for a "tar and feather" party. Charles Ferris received a cut over the eye in the fracas.[43] Nichols's scathing attacks on public figures earned him a stint in jail on libel charges, leaving Ferris to run the *Buffalonian*.

There were two Rathbun trials in 1838. Charles Ferris's precise testimony at the trials is not known, but it was his involvement as a witness that prevented his return to Texas and held him in Buffalo during 1838. In July, the Buffalo trial ended with Rathbun's acquittal;[44] but the second trial in Batavia saw the conviction of the self-made millionaire. Young Rathbun Allen, arrested this time in New Orleans and held incommunicado, was the state's star witness. His testimony against his uncle was damning. The defense introduced sworn testimony from Lyman Rathbun, given on May 2, 1838, in San Augustine, Texas.[45] Lyman Rathbun assumed blame for the forgeries, but his admission of guilt rang hollow to the jury. After brief deliberation, on October 3, 1838, the jury sentenced Benjamin Rathbun to five years hard labor at Auburn Prison.

During the lengthy litigation, Charles Ferris continued his journalistic career as "motive spirit" of the *Buffalonian*.[46] After Nichols sold the paper to Charles Stimson in 1839, Ferris became part owner and joint editor; but with Nichols's departure and Rathbun's conviction, the paper lost its "cause celebre" and died a natural death in 1840.[47]

Far away in Texas, as he impatiently awaited his brother's return, Warren Ferris adapted to the vicissitudes and opportunities of the new republic.

41. McCausland, "Lives of the Lovejoys," 16.

42. Guy H. Salisbury, "Early History of the Press of Erie County," read Nov. 30, 1863, before the Buffalo Historical Society. *Publications of Buffalo Historical Society* (34 vols.; Buffalo: Bigelow Bros., 1880), II, 99–217.

43. McCausland, "Early Buffalo Journalist," 13–14.

44. Reported in the *Daily Commercial Advertiser* (Buffalo), July 7, 1838.

45. Ibid. O. H. Willis of San Augustine took Lyman Rathbun's testimony. Rathbun also traveled to Houston, Texas, to give testimony before Judge Birdsall. Warren Ferris to Charles Ferris, July 18, 1838. FLC, Box I, Folder 4. John Birdsall, a New Yorker, Attorney General of Texas in 1838, died the following year of yellow fever, the scourge of early Texians. See Adele B. Looscan, "Life and Service of John Birdsall," *SHQ*, 24 (July, 1922), 44–57.

46. So called by C. F. S. Thomas in an unpublished manuscript of the Buffalo Historical Society, quoted in McCausland, "Early Buffalo Journalist," 14.

47. Salisbury, "Early History of the Press," 208.

Word finally reached Ferris that his manuscript, "Life in the Rocky Mountains," had been rejected by the Philadelphia publishers. Carey, Lee and Blanchard judged that his book "would sell" but felt "compelled owing to . . . numerous engagements in other works, to decline undertaking this."[48] In fact, the Philadelphia company had just accepted for publication Washington Irving's account of Capt. Benjamin Bonneville's adventures in the West. Irving, following publication of his *Sketchbook* (1819), was America's most popular writer, while Warren A. Ferris was unknown. In disappointment, Ferris instructed his brother to withdraw the journal from consideration but to keep it so that he might examine it at some future time.

By September 1837, Warren Ferris's health was so improved that he joined Gen. Thomas J. Rusk's militia in an expedition against Indians. One of fifty-six volunteers, Ferris joined in the pursuit of raiders who had attacked scattered Northeast Texas settlements.[49] Anti-Indian feeling ran strong in Nacogdoches. Despite his early fascination with Indian culture both on the Niagara frontier and in the Rocky Mountain west, Warren Ferris reflected the racist values of his time. While in the fur country, Ferris concluded that, with few exceptions, Indians were "rascally, beggarly, thieves and rogues."[50] His experience in Texas, combined with his strong desire to acquire land, led him to believe they were also an impediment to progress and civilization. In October, through the influence of Vice President Mirabeau B. Lamar and Isaac W. Burton, the Texas Senate refused to ratify the Cherokee Treaty that had been promised by Sam Houston in return for Indian neutrality during the Texas Revolution. Anglo-Texans coveted the rich lands of the Cherokee Reserve and longed for any excuse to evict the Indians. Even "Old Sam's" friends loathed his pro-Indian policy. Claiming that Indian depredations were the work of "United States" renegades out of Arkansas Territory, President Houston resisted military action against the Cherokees. During the fall of 1837, Rusk and Burton spearheaded a drive to bring the militia under local, rather than presidential, control. To most East Texans, Houston's command of the militia was but another example of his usurpation of authority, not unlike his negotiation of the hated treaty that created an independent Indian state within the borders of the Republic. W. A. Ferris aligned himself with the anti-Indian majority and made a reputation as a "ranger." Here was a young man, Nacogdoches folk said, of steady nerve,

---

48. Sarah Lovejoy's letter, Mar. 12, 1837, never reached Ferris so he did not learn of the disappointing rejection until he received her letter of June 7, 1837.

49. DeGolyer, "Conquest of Three Forks," 18, cites Warren Ferris's name on the docket of discharged soldiers, Nacogdoches County Certificate No. 33. Carolyn R. Ericson, *First Settlers of the Republic of Texas* (2 vols.; St. Louis: Ingmire Publications, 1982), II, 72, shows the 640 acres Ferris received for this service.

50. Ferris, Dallas *Herald*, Jan. 4, 1873. His views reflect confidence in Anglo-Saxon superiority and the inevitability of Manifest Destiny.

courage, and dependability. A ranger, having seen the frontier land and faced the Indians, might make a good surveyor.

The Nacogdoches society that Ferris sought to enter in 1837 was a culture in transition. What had been a remote Spanish/Mexican outpost, turbulent center of six revolutionary movements, and home to filibusters and freebooters of several nations was rapidly becoming "Anglicized." A considerable town of some 1,000 persons in the Redland Piney Woods along tributaries of the Angelina River, Nacogdoches owed its prominence mainly to its location along the El Camino Real, or Old San Antonio Road, the principle east-west route of Texas. The Redlands of East Texas with its twin towns of San Augustine and Nacogdoches became the "Gateway to Texas," the major overland entry point for American emigrants out of Arkansas and Louisiana.[51]

During the Mexican years (1821–1836) the Anglo-American population grew tremendously. Nacogdoches, so distant from Mexican authority, always looked east to the French and, after 1803, to the Americans at Natchitoches, Louisiana. Generous Mexican land policies, with grants to empresarios such as Frost Thorn, Hayden Edwards, David G. Burnet, Joseph Vehlein, and Lorenzo de Zavala, encouraged immigration. One had only to swear loyalty to Mexico and accept Catholicism to attain citizenship and claim property. Land titles were, however, less easily acquired. Countless squatters occupied land without legal title.[52] Alarmed by the growing numbers of Anglo-Americans in East Texas, Mexico attempted to restrict immigration and trade from the United States.[53] Their efforts proved futile. Smuggling was rampant as illegal immigrants merely skirted the Mexican customs post. Indeed, in East Texas an unmanageable Anglo population acted as it pleased. Hundreds of "New Texians," including Houston and Rusk, arrived on the eve of the revolution.[54]

Nacogdoches played a leading role in fomenting the rebellion, housing and arming volunteers from the United States. Houston and Rusk organized troops while merchants Frost Thorn and Adolphus Sterne raised

---

51. Redlands, so called for the red clay soil which underlay the area.

52. Under Mexican rule almost no titles were issued; the land office was only briefly opened in 1834–1835. No titles were, of course, issued during the revolution so great pressure was exerted to legalize titles as soon as the war ended.

53. Margaret Swett Henson and Deolece Parmelee, *The Cartwrights of San Augustine: Three Generations of Agricultural Entrepreneurs in Nineteenth-Century Texas* (Austin: Texas State Historical Association, 1993), 32–33, 48–49, discusses Anglo-Texan contempt for Mexican authority, the attempt (with the Law of April 6, 1830) to ban immigration from the United States into the borderlands, anxiety over lack of titles to land, and the impact of these on Matthew Cartwright, who immigrated in 1825 to the San Augustine area.

54. James G. Partain, "History of Nacogdoches and Nacogdoches County" (M.A. thesis, University of Texas at Austin, 1968), 176–185. There were 822 certificates for entrance (not to speak of illegal entry) granted in Nacogdoches between January and December 1835.

funds. Yet many substantial men in the Redlands failed to respond to Houston's desperate call for reinforcements in the spring of 1836, either delaying military service or evading it altogether. When the Texas Army fell back before Santa Anna's advance, hundreds of refugees evacuated the area, fleeing with only the clothes on their backs across the Sabine River to the United States. They feared not so much the Mexican Army as the perceived threat from neighboring Indians; it was rumored that Mexican agents were circulating among the Cherokee and Caddo trying to provoke an attack on white settlements. Redlanders were convinced that only the presence of U.S. troops poised on the Sabine kept the uneasy frontier peace.[55]

Racist attitudes in Nacogdoches extended beyond Indians to include its Mexican citizens. Although Anglos and Mexicans served together in local government, the Mexicans lived in separate villages outside town. They were ranchers and farmers; none owned stores or were in the professions. Outnumbered and overwhelmed by a growing Anglo population, Nacogdochians with Spanish surnames experienced discrimination and rapidly became second-class citizens.

Virginian William F. Gray visited Nacogdoches briefly in February 1836 and reported the town "prettily located" but with shabby housing and without a decent tavern. There was, he said, a "tolerably good society in a few families of Anglo-Americans," but there was little contact between them and the Mexican citizens. The Mexicans, Gray observed, were "swarthy, dirty looking people, much resembling . . . mulattos, but having straight hair." They seemed generally quiet, orderly, cheerful, unthrifty, unambitious, but loving dancing and gambling. Gray also described the Indians who came to Nacogdoches in their fantastic dress to trade skins, venison, and pecans. He echoed local public opinion favoring Indian removal, saying the tribes made unpleasant neighbors and retarded settlement of the country by whites.[56]

Nacogdoches leaders, affluent landowners, merchants, and professionals like Adolphus Sterne, Henry W. Raguet, Thomas J. Rusk, John H.

---

55. Jenkins (ed.), *The Papers of the Texas Revolution*, V, #2804, #2807, Reports of J. Bonnell and Edmund P. Gaines (U.S. Army) on alleged activities of Manuel Flores and warnings issued to the Cherokees and related tribes, Apr. 20, 1836.

56. William F. Gray, *Diary of Col. William Fairfax Gray: From Virginia to Texas, 1835–36 and Second Journey to Texas in 1837* (1909; reprint, Houston: Fletcher Young Publishing Co., 1965), 89–99. Gray, in Texas to locate land for American investors, observed intrigues surrounding the February 1, 1836 election of delegates to the Convention; Nacogdoches men of the "independence" persuasion vied with "constitutional" men for votes, and Gray noted, "much ill-will exists in this little community." He also attended a fancy Anglo-Texan ball at Brown's Tavern—and only regretted he did not get to go to the Mexican fandango or monte house (spirited dancing and gambling).

57. James McReynolds, "Family Life in a Borderland Community" (Ph.D. diss., Texas Tech University, 1978), 239–240.

Starr, Frost Thorn, Charles S. Taylor, and Robert Irion, controlled East Texas politics and wielded power in the Republic. It was a tightly knit oligarchy whose families frequently intermarried.[57] They determined who would advance in Nacogdoches society, and it was on their acceptance that newcomers like Warren Ferris depended.

Ultimate recognition in Nacogdoches society required affiliation with the Masonic Lodge. The elite of the town, indeed of all Texas during the Republic, were Freemasons.[58] Membership in Milam Lodge #2, the second oldest Masonic Lodge in Texas, guaranteed the networking necessary to success for Warren Ferris; and the moving spirit of Nacogdoches Masonry was Adolphus Sterne. It was Sterne, a Knight Templar of the York Rite and 32nd degree Mason of the Scottish Rite, who first requested formation of the Nacogdoches Lodge under the auspices of Louisiana Masons.

Sterne was a German Jew from Cologne who came to Texas via New Orleans. He converted to Catholicism, the religion of his wife, and became a successful merchant. Plans for Texas independence were hatched in the comfortable Sterne home on Lanana Street where he played host to countless important figures. He raised and equipped two companies of New Orleans Greys during the Texas Revolution. Beyond being a successful trader and financier, Sterne practiced law and was a skilled linguist. His talents allowed him to accumulate large landholdings.[59] Any young man who wished to advance in Nacogdoches did well to ingratiate himself with Adolphus Sterne.

Still in debt for his health care and lodging, Warren Ferris wrote to his brother in late 1837 desperately pleading for money. He had lost his trunk, which he had left behind in Columbia, had no horse, and needed additional surveying equipment. Their supposed patron, Isaac Burton, had left Nacogdoches to attend a special session of the second Texas congress. Complaining that Burton ignored his letters, Ferris worried that Horace Chamberlain, recently returned from Buffalo to Houston City, had told Burton of Charles's arrest and financial situation, thereby causing a loss of interest in the Ferris brothers. Charles Ferris was "strictly forbidden" to know Lyman Rathbun's whereabouts, but Warren knew that the fugitive was in nearby San Augustine living under the assumed name of Brewster.[60]

---

58. James D. Carter, *Masonry in Texas* (Waco: Grand Lodge of Texas, 1955), 313, 289. Charter members of the Milam Lodge included Houston, Sterne, and Burton; of the group of forty-one men, only seven failed to achieve prominence in the politics or army of Texas. Carter states that 80 percent of Texas high officials came from the ranks of the Masons.

59. Archie P. McDonald, *Hurrah for Texas: The Diary of Adolphus Sterne (1838–1851)* (Austin: Eakin Press, 1986), preface. The Census of 1840 estimated Sterne's holdings at 16,000 acres.

60. George L. Crocket's manuscript notes of Eph M. Daggett's memoirs, "Recollections of the War of the Moderators and Regulators," 1–8 (copy in San Augustine, Texas, Public Library). Daggett related the story of the "great New

Ferris informed his brother that he intended to go into full-time survey-ing. "I have established a reputation and intend to go it with a business myself," he wrote. Charles Ferris was to bring with him to Texas "a mea-suring tape or two, a five pole chain and 1 of ten Varas and another of 20 Varas" to add to the set of common pocket instruments that Warren had purchased for platting purposes. Although he had yet to make any money at surveying, Ferris eagerly anticipated the opening of the land office in the spring of 1838: "a good business can be done at conveyancing that is as soon as the damb [sic] land office opens." [61]

With some humor, Warren Ferris shed light on life in Nacogdoches with a tale of his recent bad luck:

> I am an unlucky dog, the other day I sold two lots that cost me two days labor for a $150 Horse but before he was delivered the proprietor of the Town was killed in a fray and the bargain fell through. I sent a few days since . . . for the horse you left with Lacy but the gentleman [Lacy] said he had swapped the Horse for a man [a slave] and that the man had ran [sic] away. . . . I don't know which is the dumbest fool, you or me, but I rather think you are.[62]

Charles Ferris, having his own run of bad luck, responded to his broth-er's letter, apologizing for leaving him alone and without funds. "I have been the unhappy cause of much difficulty and discomfort to you though god knows how undesignedly." He pledged, "fortune will yet . . . smile upon us both." Unable to raise money in Buffalo, Charles Ferris found himself helpless to aid his brother or invest in Burton's ventures. He com-plained that Burton had violated the terms of their agreement; Charles was to edit the newspaper and Burton was to survey while they divided the profits on both ventures equally. "I did think that I had found an exception in him from the general mass of mankind . . . that he was one who loved generosity for its own sake. I suppose I have been mistaken." Charles Ferris instructed Warren to get title to his bounty land and give it to Burton to hold as security against debts. "When *I do come* give him to understand it will not be with empty pockets."[63]

York forger" whom he met in Texas in April 1837. According to Daggett, the man who called himself "Simon" Rathbun talked candidly about his brother Benjamin, who had "built Buffalo," and about the forgeries. The Rathbuns, he said, were care-ful to cover their forged notes; but, once when one of their steamboats was detained by fog on Lake Erie, they did not meet their draft and were exposed. He told how he escaped a posse and, traveling with Seth Sheldon, entered Texas via Natchitoches. Going under the name of Brewster, he was operating a ferry on the Sabine River. Eph Daggett, who spent some time in East Texas, migrated west and was a founder of Fort Worth, Texas.

61. Warren Ferris to Charles Ferris, Nov. 26, 1837, FLC, Box I, Folder 4. This letter is unusual in its tone, full of profanity and informal wording, unlike any other of Warren Ferris's correspondence.

62. Ibid., Box I, Folder 4.

63. Charles Ferris to Warren Ferris, Oct. 20, 1837, ibid., Box I, Folder 1.

Clearly Charles Ferris knew the whereabouts of fugitive Lyman
Rathbun, whom he referred to in the correspondence as "L" or "R." He
knew that Seth Sheldon and O. H. Willis, two of those who had fled
Buffalo for Texas, were with Rathbun in the San Augustine area.[64] He
advised his brother to ask Rathbun for money and watch Chamberlain,
their Buffalo acquaintance, who might turn Rathbun over to bounty
hunters for a reward. "I suspect he [Chamberlain] would like to get two
thousand dollars you know how. Keep your eye upon him."

Hardened by bitter experiences and disappointed in men he had trusted, Charles Ferris vowed to pursue his own self-interest, and that of his
family. He wrote:

> interest alone is the foundation of friendship. . . . [Y]ou and me will go
> upon our own hook hereafter, and as soon as I can get things settled
> up here . . . [we will] commence a new era in the history of our lives . .
> . for we will go in for making money entirely. . . . Connected with no
> one but ourselves we will conduct our affairs without assistance of
> others, and let them follow their own as we will ours. . . . Secure land
> we are both entitled to and that is all I care about now. *That* with
> what we will take from here will lay the foundation of fortune.[65]

Despite debts, poor health, and bad luck, Warren Ferris was optimistic
about his future in Texas. After all, he had made a reputation as an
Indian fighter and was becoming known as a willing surveyor. On
December 26, 1837, the day after Christmas and his twenty-seventh
birthday, Ferris wrote home to Buffalo to share news of a special gift, his
appointment by the Texas congress as official surveyor of Nacogdoches
County.[66] It was a political plum. The huge county included thousands of
acres of rich land in northeast Texas, stretching west to the Trinity River
and north to the headwaters of the Sabine River.[67] Ferris was elated at
his good fortune. As surveyor, he would have inside knowledge of the best
land and some power in its distribution and development. Burton had, at
last, made good his promise to the Ferrises.

---

64. Warren Ferris to Charles Ferris, July 18, 1838, ibid., Box I, Folder 4. Warren
reported seeing "R" who was enroute to give testimony before Judge Birdsall in
Houston. The fugitive was in good spirits and happy to see young Ferris's fortunes
so improved. Ferris invited Rathbun to move to Nacogdoches and join him in the
land business.

65. Ibid.

66. Warren Ferris to Charles, Dec. 26, 1837, ibid., Box I, Folder 2.

67. Nacogdoches County in 1837 included all or part of twenty-one present Texas
counties: Anderson, Angelina, Camp, Cherokee, Dallas, Delta, Gregg, Henderson,
Hopkins, Houston, Hunt, Kaufman, Raines, Rockwall, Rusk, Smith, Trinity,
Upshur, Van Zandt, Wood, and of course, Nacogdoches.

"JACK OF DIAMONDS"

W HEN THE TEXAS CONGRESS convened in the fall of 1837, Sen. Isaac Watts Burton of Nacogdoches was positioned to advance associates like Warren Ferris. The Second Congress of the Republic of Texas met in Houston City, a new town promoted by the Allen brothers near the site of old Harrisburg. All was "bustle and animation" and a "spirit of speculation" in the seat of government where people were thrown together from all over the world.[1] In mid-December, the Texas Congress elected officials to administer the affairs of the Republic in its various subdivisions or counties.[2] Senator Burton nominated Warren A. Ferris as official surveyor of Nacogdoches County, a far-flung area that included much of northeast and north central Texas. Ferris held this potentially lucrative post for nearly three years, until he became deputy surveyor in late 1840.

The same Congress provided for a land office to open in Houston early in 1838. Upon being notified of his appointment, Ferris took his oath of office,[3] made bond in the amount of $10,000,[4] selected his deputy surveyors, and eagerly awaited instructions. In the interim, he managed Burton's pro-Lamar newspaper, the *Texas Chronicle*, a job that he held until August when the press was sold and moved to San Augustine.[5]

---

1. Muir, *Texas in 1837*, 27–29. A. C. and J. K. Allen established their town on Buffalo Bayou and named it for the hero of San Jacinto. In early 1837, the rough village had only a few tents and a saloon; by April 1837, there were a several log cabins and *two* saloons. As temporary capital of the republic, the population of Houston City grew rapidly.

2. The controversial Land Bill was passed over Houston's veto on December 14; surveyors were appointed in a Friday night session on December 15; and Congress adjourned on December 19. *Journals of the Senate*, Called Session of Congress, Sept. 25, 1837, and Regular Session, Nov. 6, 1837 (Houston: Niles & Co. Printers, 1838).

3. Located by Nell Davis in the Texas State Archives under "William A. Ferris," the oath read: "I W. A. Ferris do solemnly swear that I will honestly and faithfully discharge the duties of my office as County Surveyor in the county and Republic above written [Nacogdoches, Texas] without favor or partiality so help me God." Dated Jan. 24, 1838.

4. Nacogdoches Co. Clerk's Office, Vol. B, 354. Bond made Feb. 14, 1838, K. H. Douglass, Matthew F. Sims, and Benjamin A. Van Sickle were sureties on his note. Ferris's deputies, including Van Sickle, A. G. Hamilton, William Y. Lacy, and Thomas D. Brooks, also made bond in February. Vol. C, 87–88.

5. An announcement in the *Chronicle*, Feb. 28, 1838, stated that W. A. Ferris would conduct business in Senator Burton's absence. DeGolyer, "Conquest of Three Forks," note to Chap. 3. Marilyn M. Sibley, *Lone Stars and State Gazettes: Texas Newspapers before the Civil War* (College Station: Texas A&M University Press, 1983), 91, 95, 106, 149, states that the *Texas Chronicle* was started by Burton to

Ferris related his situation in Nacogdoches and his preparation for surveying:

> I came to Nacogdoches in '37 had no acquaintance and no money.
> Charles' friend Burton assisted me I conducted his press until it was
> disposed of and through his influence was elected County Surveyor by
> joint vote of Congress. When I came here I was perfectly rusty in sur-
> veying and laying 6 weeks sick I got Gibson's surveying and complete-
> ly mastered it and after receiving the appointment instructed my
> Deputies and by this means mastered Gummers, Flint, Davis & c. at
> which time with my previous knowledge of mathematicks I was an
> accomplished surveyor.[6]

In truth, Ferris was as qualified as most pioneers who claimed to be
surveyors. His grounding in mathematics allowed him to determine varia-
tions of the compass. Many self-taught frontier surveyors, apparently
incapable of the calculations, felt it unnecessary to establish "true north"
as it varied from place to place. After his experience in the Rocky
Mountains, Ferris had a good sense of distance and direction; and, judging from his map of the fur country, he was a skilled draftsman.
Surveying required very little equipment, only a "peep-sight" compass, a
"Jacob-staff" for mounting the compass, and chains which were regulated
to the length of ten varas or 27 feet, $9\frac{1}{2}$ inches.[7] With a bit of knowledge,
minimal equipment, and a great deal of self-confidence, Warren Ferris
deemed himself ready to enter the surveying business.

After the Texas General Land Office opened in January, Land
Commissioner John P. Borden instructed surveyors to establish county
boundaries, map the county, then locate lands to be distributed to veterans and new immigrants. The central duty of the county surveyor was to
create an up-to-date map of each county, showing the old surveys and
connecting them to new ones without gaps between the two. Mapping
Nacogdoches County involved listing original claimants and the quantity
of each claim. Much confusion arose from interpreting boundaries of
Spanish and Mexican grants dating back to the 1790s. In the clamor to
secure title to new lands, conflicts with older grants were inevitable.
Surveyors often were guided by inaccurate, incomplete maps and even

---

promote Lamar's political career and lasted just long enough to get him elected.
Burton reported to Lamar on August 24, 1838, "I have sold my press to [W. W.]
Parker of San Augustine, politics the same [pro-Lamar, anti-Houston]." Lamar
Papers, II, #799. Lamar, a Georgia newspaper editor himself before coming to
Texas in 1835, recognized the key role newspapers played in advancing political
careers. Herbert P. Gambrell, *Mirabeau B. Lamar: Troubadour and Crusader*
(Dallas: Southwest Press, 1934), 44.

6. Warren Ferris to Joshua Lovejoy, May 19, 1840. FLC, Box I, supp.

7. E. P. Arneson, "The Art of Terrestrial Measurement and Its Practice in Texas"
and Virginia Houston, "Surveying in Early Texas," from *One League to Each Wind:
Accounts of Early Surveying in Texas*, ed. Sue Watkins (Austin: Von-
Boeckmann–Jones Printers, 1964), 15, 33.

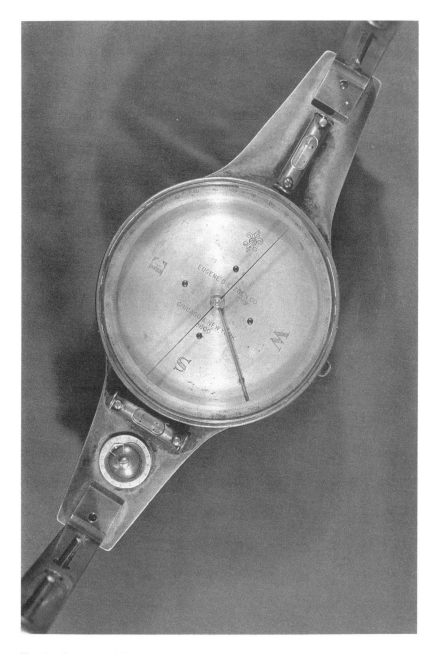

Vernier Compass of the type used by Warren A. Ferris. This compass was used in the 1820s and 1830s and was considered quite precise. *Photograph by Mike Hazel from the original in the O. V. DeSciullo Collection, University of Texas at Arlington.*

more ambiguous instructions. Commissioner Borden noted "the vague manner in which the acts defining the boundries [sic] of the several counties are expressed" and urged cooperation with authorities in adjoining counties in order to reach "some mutual agreement about boundries." Borden directed: "You will proceed as soon as practicable to cause the lines of your county to be run." Ferris was then to furnish surveyors of neighboring counties with maps showing the "true situation."[8]

Difficulties were compounded by the existence of the Cherokee Reserve, claimed by the Cherokee Nation and guaranteed to them by the still unratified treaty of 1836. This choice strip of land, 130 miles long by 60 miles wide, included what is now Smith, Cherokee, Rusk, and Van Zandt Counties. Its rolling, pine-filled hills and sandy, well-watered soil was much coveted by Anglos in East Texas. But Borden cautioned Ferris: "You will be particular not to allow surveys made for individuals on lands within the limits specially reserved by the Government for the Cherokees and other friendly Indians."[9]

Texas land laws reflected transition from Spanish/Mexican land practice to that of Anglo/Southern United States with attendant confusion. Under Mexico, distances were measured by the Spanish league and vara, while grants were made in the "labor," land with water for farming, and the much larger "league," suitable for grazing. Immigrant farmers quickly seized on the idea of becoming stockmen, requesting the "league and labor," which became the standard grant. In 1838, moving to more common English measurements, Borden arbitrarily ruled that a Vara would measure $33\frac{1}{3}$ inches, a Labor (one million square varas) would be 177.1 acres, and a League (25 million square varas) would measure 4,428.4 acres.[10]

Alongside the old Mexican system was now introduced the Anglo-American headright grant which gave each head of family a section of 640 acres, with lesser acreage for single men and widows. Land was Texas's major asset; on its speedy survey and development rested the future of the infant Republic. The Texas Congress, however, could not quite decide whether it wished to sell its public domain to raise money and pay its debts or whether it wished to attract settlers by giving land away. In this setting of ambiguous directives, conflicting laws, and competing claims, Warren Ferris began his surveying career.

The new Texas land laws required that a prospective claimant, on receiving his certificate, engage a surveyor to locate land in an unclaimed

---

8. Instructions, John P. Borden, Commissioner of the General Land Office to W. A. Ferris, June 15, 1838 (GLO).

9. Ibid.

10. The transition caused some confusion. Early frontier surveyors often interpreted the vara or "Spanish yard" as thirty-six feet and measured the league at 4,444 acres.

area and survey it. A fee amounting to one-third the value of the land was paid for a surveyor's field notes,[11] which were then approved by the official county surveyor, presented to the county land board[12] for approval, and finally sent to the General Land Office where a patent or deed would be issued. Years might elapse between granting a certificate and issuing its title. County surveyors and land commissioners held tremendous power in the process.

Although many early Texians were "practical" surveyors, guidebooks advised immigrants to use official surveyors if they wished to validate their claims, so Ferris's business was lively. In the spring of 1838, he divided Nacogdoches County and dispatched his deputies to survey on the Angelina, the Sabine, and Neches Rivers where rich "bottom" land was in great demand.[13] If possible, each block of land was fronted on a stream and then run back for quantity.

Surveyors' guidelines were vague; they were merely told to locate certificates on "unappropriated" land. Typical were Ferris's instructions to deputy Absalom Gibson on February 24, 1838. Expressing confidence in Gibson's ability, Ferris instructed him to determine the boundaries of his territory, note the kinds of timber on the land, and list the names of his chainbearers or assistants. Gibson was told to use a compass of the Rittenhouse construction, to utilize pins of a certain size, and to mark trees with a cross.[14] The Land Office provided a standardized form for field notes.

The main impact of Texas land law was speculation. Because neither veterans of the Texas Revolution who claimed bounty and donation land nor new immigrants claiming headrights were required to live on the land, a brisk trade developed in the sale of certificates and field notes. Speculators hovered like vultures, eager to purchase landscrip (paper redeemable in land) and put together huge tracts for resale. Forgery and fraud were rampant. Land boards, which had to rule on the validity of

---

11. Ericson, *First Settlers*, I, ii.

12. Nacogdoches County's first powerful Board of Land Commissioners included David Rusk, brother of Thomas J. Rusk, Judge William Hart, and Adolphus Sterne. Isaac W. Burton and Martin Lacy served on the board in 1838. DeGolyer, "Conquest of Three Forks," 22.

13. Ibid., 24–25. Ferris's deputies surveyed widely in 1838. Absalom Gibson and James Bradshaw located land southwest of Nacogdoches; William Roark surveyed along the Angelina River below the Old San Antonio Road. Thomas Brooks, a San Jacinto veteran, worked in present Smith and Rusk Counties; B. A. Van Sickle made surveys in what would be Cherokee County; and A. G Hamilton, an English immigrant, worked in present Rusk County Some of these surveys were on lands claimed by the Cherokees. William Y. Lacy, son of Martin Lacy, surveyed west of the Cherokee Reserve in what is now Henderson County, near present Athens, Texas.

14. W. A. Ferris to Absalom Gibson. FLC, Box I, Folder 3. Land Commissioner Borden sent printed instructions to surveyors on January 27 and February 24, 1838.

claims, were swamped with applicants; in two years, 38,000 applicants asked for over fifty million acres of the public domain.[15] Because he questioned their legality, President Houston refused during 1838 to sign many of the patents,[16] an action that drove up the value of the certified copies of field notes.

Warren Ferris reported his good fortune and revealed his personal priorities in a high-spirited letter to his brother Charles. Taking advantage of the rampant "certified copy" fever, he had been getting double fees for his field notes, making $10 to $25 a day. His debts were partially paid, his credit good in any Nacogdoches store, and 100 completed field notes in his desk would bring him $400 at any time he chose. Although as county surveyor Ferris was not allowed to speculate in lands, he placed land near Nacogdoches in his brother's name. A recurrent fever delayed his surveying for two weeks, but Warren Ferris assured Charles, "I am certainly in a situation to coin money and shall not neglect the opportunity."[17]

Both brothers could file for headrights when Charles Ferris returned to Texas; but, in order to get his due, Charles would need to find two witnesses to swear he came to Texas prior to independence.[18] Warren doubted Charles would get all he expected. Speaking of the huge Nacogdoches County area, Warren Ferris reported, "There has been much fraud practised [sic] . . . and hundreds of fraudulent certificates issued . . . a good portion of the public domain will fall into the hands of swindlers." Still, he judged that Texas would not be much harmed as, "Land will rise rapidly in Value and the more owners there are to the Soil the more easily will the National debt be paid by the people."[19]

Warren Ferris urged his family to write all the news from Buffalo and immodestly gave them permission to tell everyone of the importance he had achieved. "I like for some folks to have reason to be envious," he

---

15. Ericson, *First Settlers*, I, introduction, gives a clear description of the vague Texas land laws that provided Borden and Ferris an impossible task and led to fraud and corruption.

16. President Houston detailed his criticisms of the Land Law and reasons for not issuing patents in a message to Congress, May 4, 1838. Amelia W. Williams and Eugene C. Barker (eds.), *The Writings of Sam Houston, 1813–1863* (8 vols.; Austin: University of Texas Press, 1938), II, 212–217. Campbell, *Houston*, 83, points out Houston's predictions of fraud and speculation when he first vetoed the Land Bill in 1837.

17. Warren Ferris to Charles Ferris and family, July 18, 1838, FLC, Box I, Folder 4. This letter reveals the route of Texas mail into the United States from Nacogdoches, via Natchitoches, Louisiana, where it was posted on July 27.

18. Ericson, *First Settlers*, I, introduction, explains three classes of headrights. Eligibility for Texas First Class Headright (A league and labor or 4,605 acres) required claimant be a family man in Texas before March 2, 1836. This deadline was later extended to October 1, 1836. Charles Ferris was in Texas by February 1836, but Warren Ferris did not arrive until January 1837, and therefore was eligible for only a Second Class Headright of 640 acres.

19. Warren Ferris to Charles Ferris, July 18, 1838, FLC, Box I, Folder 4.

admitted. He concluded his optimistic July 1838 letter with a jaunty signature—"Jack of Diamonds."[20]

His status as county surveyor earned Ferris admission into
Nacogdoches society, where he was seen as a responsible and able young
man. He was welcomed in the homes of Nacogdoches leaders such as
Adolphus Sterne and Martin Lacy. In May 1838, Ferris was named
administrator of the estate of Horace Chamberlain who died at Galveston
in February while serving in the Texas Army.[21] In August 1838, Ferris
was selected to assist Mary Harris, widow of Dr. E. G. Harris, in the
administration of his estate.[22] Ultimate recognition that W. A. Ferris was
a "comer" in Nacogdoches was his initiation into the Milam Chapter of the
Masonic Lodge.[23]

At the height of his prosperity in 1838, Ferris purchased land from
Martin Lacy and, in preparation for his family's coming from Buffalo,
planned to have a house built. Sarah Lovejoy gave a description of the
Ferris "home to be" in a letter to her brother Joshua. The house was sited
on a 750-acre tract some thirty-five miles west of Nacogdoches. Part
prairie and part forest, the land had plenty of black walnut trees, a good
mill stream which ran most of the year, and an excellent spring of water
near the buildings. Sarah described a "dogtrot" or double cabin house
with separate kitchen; two cabins, each sixteen by twenty feet, joined by
an eight-foot-wide "Texas hall," porches on the north and south ten feet
wide, the whole covered by substantial roof, and windows without
sashes.[24]

Ferris's new-found prosperity was in direct contrast to the situation in
western New York, hard hit by the Panic of 1837. Before the Ferris/Lovejoy

---

20. Ibid.

21. W. A. Ferris acted on behalf of Chamberlain's family in Buffalo to gain title
to land due for military service. He asserted that Chamberlain "Died while in the
Army of Texas" and was entitled to compensation as captain and a headright as a
single man. In March 1848, Ferris located 1,280 acres in Rusk County for the
Chamberlain family. His service as administrator continued until April 1853.
Blake Collection, III, 146–149; Nacogdoches County Probate Records, A, 168.

22. Nacogdoches County Probate Records, A, 186, and Minutes of the District
Court, A, 34.

23. Archie P. McDonald, *By Early Candlelight: The Story of Old Milam* (Fort
Worth: Masonic Home Press, 1967), Appendix C. Records show W. A. Ferris was
initiated on February 18, 1839. This is despite the fact that minutes of the District
Court, Nacogdoches County, A, 83, 103, show Ferris earlier that month indicted by
the Grand Jury for assault and battery. This offense, usually a fistfight, was not
uncommon and apparently did not work against him. One negative vote would
have barred Ferris from the Lodge.

24. Sarah Lovejoy to Joshua Lovejoy, Oct. 21, 1838, FLC, Box II, Folder 5. The
fanciful house was never built as Charles Ferris advised his brother not to trouble
to do so. Nacogdoches County Deed Records, E, 306, shows a November 27, 1838,
deed from Martin Lacy to Ferris for 738 acres, for which he paid $100. Vol. F, 342
of the county records shows Ferris mortgaging the same land, June 4, 1840, for
$300 to Jackson Todd.

family could liquidate its holdings to join him in Texas, the economic depression worsened. They found themselves "land poor," barely able to pay taxes, and trapped in Buffalo.[25] Charles Ferris marked time studying law and writing for the *Buffalonian*, while Ferris's young half-brother, Joshua Lovejoy, returned to Michigan to wait tables and tend bar. Lovejoy complained of chapped hands too long in dishwater and bemoaned the climate so bad for consumption.[26] His lodge, the "Staff Union Fear Naughts," was involved in the campaign to liberate Canada, a movement in support of William L. MacKenzie and the so-called "Patriot rising" or Upper Canada Rebellion of 1838.[27]

A lengthy letter of May 30, 1839, from Charles Ferris to Warren in Texas fully described the Buffalo situation:

> Times have been so hard here for the last two years that it has been almost impossible to get along, and I have had during that time to support a large family, pay taxes to a considerable amount on the land, and arrange a settlement with Henry which thank Heaven is now nearly concluded.[28]

Charles detailed the terms of settlement whereby Henry Lovejoy received two-fifths of the disputed property for agreeing to pay outstanding court costs and getting their uncle to release the mortgage. He estimated that his mother and sisters would then have clear title to land worth about $30,000 which, if it could be sold, would make them not rich, but independent.

Of the rest of the family, Ferris reported that Joshua at age twenty-three had done himself and his family no good; he was "some five or six hundred dollars in debt in Michigan for the Lord knows what." Sarah, age twenty-one, was "of a literary turn of mind, somewhat talented I think *not* handsome and almost a recluse from society." Ferris felt, "I think I must bring Sarah [to Texas]. . . . Her health is not good. . . . The climate of that country will suit her to a t." Fifteen-year-old Louisa, "pretty, full of spirits, witty and satirical," seemed born for a social life; "She could *queen*

---

25. Joshua Lovejoy to Warren Ferris, Feb. 23, 1838. FLC, Box I, Folder 1. Josh reported that the family could not sell land "at any price."

26. Joshua Lovejoy to his mother, to Charles and the family, Sept. 18, 1837, and Nov. 1, 1838. Joshua wrote that he was in poor health. FLC, Box I, Folder 14.

27. McCausland, "Lives of the Lovejoys," 16, cites Joshua's letter of December 5, 1839, "The Patriots crossed last night. . . . I think however that they are shure [sic] of death—there is a great meeting here tonight for the Patriots—I shall attend—It is of no use—they are (those in Canada) a damned set of craven hearted fools." William L. Mackenzie, former mayor of Toronto, led a band of farmers and mechanics in the autumn of 1837 in an ill-fated attempt to end British rule in Upper Canada. Although Joshua's involvement seems to have been limited to attendance at meetings, the encouragement of U.S. citizens to Canadian rebels contributed to serious tensions between the United States and Britain in 1838–1839.

28. Charles Ferris to Warren Ferris, May 30, 1839. FLC, Box I, Folder 1.

it nobly in Texas," he judged. Charles Ferris proudly described his two sons. His namesake Charley, a "beauty and a wit," was three years old; infant Ned, four months old, was, according to his father, a lively, good-natured youngster.

After news of the family, Ferris ended the long, rambling letter by inquiring as to whether Warren had received a trunk of books and clothes or the newspapers sent from Buffalo by way of O. H. Willis. Finally he implored his brother to go to Natchitoches in person to sign essential legal papers agreeing to the settlement with Henry Lovejoy. "I am anxious to join you there . . . my forced stay here till I get returns from you is the only thing that very much troubles your Brother," Charles Ferris concluded.[29]

Meanwhile, rumors rocked Texas of renewed war with Mexico, possible conflict with the Mexicans in Texas, Indian raids, or any combination of the three. Neither Texas nor Mexico was ready to end hostilities. Fearing reinvasion, some Texians again called for a preemptive strike against Mexico. The lingering fear of collusion between nearby Indians and disgruntled local Mexicans nagged at East Texans especially. Rumors persisted that Mexican agents were moving among the tribes. Most Anglo-Americans viewed Indians with suspicion and regarded Mexicans as an inferior, mongrel race. For their part, Mexican citizens saw their property seized and their rights denied while Indian tribesmen were alarmed by the advance of white surveyors and settlers into their traditional hunting grounds. Mutual distrust might easily erupt into violence.

During this crisis period, the government of Texas was locked in a destructive power struggle. President Sam Houston, determined to pursue a policy of frugality and orderly development, was at odds with the Texas Congress. Sen. Isaac Burton, aligned with Vice President Mirabeau B. Lamar, was ringleader of the clique that opposed Houston. Lamar and his followers wanted expansion, even if it meant extermination of the Indians or confrontation with Mexico.[30]

Houston vetoed the Land Bill in 1837, hoping to delay surveying until ratification of his treaty with the Cherokees could protect Indian land. Burton, chairman of the Committee on Indian Affairs, questioned Cherokee loyalty. He asserted that the Cherokees, with "elevated views of their own importance," planned to unify Indian resistance against the Republic. On October 12, 1837, his committee reported against the treaty and on December 16, the Senate nullified it.[31] Early in 1838, Houston

---

29. Ibid.

30. Campbell, *Sam Houston*, 83, describes the deadlock between Houston and the Texas Congress and the insurmountable financial problems besetting the Republic in late 1838.

31. Ernest William Winkler (ed.), *Secret Journals of the Senate, Republic of Texas, 1836–1845* (Austin: Austin Printing Co., 1911), 74–79.

vetoed Burton's bill "to provide for the protection of the frontier," but Congress passed the Defense Bill, as it had the Land Bill, over Houston's veto.[32] Providing for a volunteer militia, paid directly by Congress, the act allowed the military under the command of General Rusk to operate independent of the executive during the summer and fall of 1838.

The so-called "Mexican Rebellion" erupted outside Nacogdoches on August 4, 1838, when Texians attempted to recover "stolen" horses from a nearby Mexican rancho. Shots were fired, and one Texian was killed. A respected Mexican citizen of Nacogdoches, former alcalde Vicente Cordova, organized the Mexicans to defend their rights. Subsequently it was alleged that Cordova had been in contact with Mexican authorities in Matamoros as early as February 1838, that he styled himself "Commander of Mexican Forces in Texas," and that he had attended a council with the Cherokees and Mexican agents in July 1838.[33] Although he was not privy to this troubling information at the time, General Rusk did not hesitate to call out the Nacogdoches militia. On August 7, Rusk learned that Cordova was camped on the Angelina River with a large number of armed followers, including Indians. Houston, who was visiting in Nacogdoches, issued a proclamation calling for dispersal of the Mexican malcontents. Cordova replied:

> The citizens of Nacogdoches, being tired of the unjust treatment and the usurpation of their rights, cannot do less than state that they are embodied, with arms in their hands, to sustain those rights and those of the nation [Mexico] to which they belong.[34]

Cordova emphasized that his people were determined to defend their rights at the cost of their lives, if necessary; he promised not to bother Anglo families in return for the same promises of good faith from General Rusk. Rusk would deliver no guarantees. Instead, on August 10, he issued an inflammatory denunciation of the "contemptible enemy" who had taken up arms threatening Anglo-American "homes, firesides and liberty." Rusk charged that the "cowards and traitors" compounded their perfidy when they "held illicit commerce with worthless savages." Rusk urged the women and children of Nacogdoches to remain in their homes

---

32. Burton introduced the Senate bill on May 7; it was passed over Houston's veto on May 24, 1838, one day before Congress adjourned. Houston, opposing usurpation of executive power, favored a bill creating a corps of cavalry under his command. Williams and Barker (eds.), *The Writings of Sam Houston*, II, 238–240.

33. Malcolm D. McLean (ed.), *Papers Concerning Robertson's Colony in Texas* (18 vols.; Arlington: University of Texas at Arlington Press, 1990), XVI, 381–382, 544–553, 572, 588, 601–602. McLean collected documents incriminating Cordova as an agent of Mexico, including a letter from Valentin Canalizo, commander at Matamoros, promising Cordova support by Mexican troops in a war against the Texians.

34. From *Red-Lander*, San Augustine, Texas, Sept. 10, 1838. Cited by Yoakum, *History of Texas*, II, 246–247, and DeGolyer, "Conquest of Three Forks," 28.

and trust their safety to those of "stout hearts and strong arms" who would defend them. He called upon the men of the Third Brigade to shoulder arms and "exterminate" the "worthless renegades."[35]

Without further violence, Cordova moved his camp into the Cherokee Reserve; then, when the Cherokees refused to harbor them, Cordova's band traveled farther west to Kickapootown near present Frankston in Anderson County. Although Houston ordered Rusk not to enter the Cherokee Reserve, the Nacogdoches militia advanced to the Indian village at Kickapootown where on a misty October morning they made a surprise attack, destroying the camp and taking prisoners who were later brought to trial at San Augustine.[36] Cordova escaped with a remnant of his men and was next reported to be camped near a Keechi Village at the Three Forks of the Trinity (present Dallas County). An Indian trader characterized their gathering as a "Grand Council of Renegades." About 1,000 Indians of many tribes were said to be powwowing during November 1838 to discuss what could be done about white aggression.[37]

Both Warren Ferris and his patron Isaac Burton enlisted in military service during the Cordova Rebellion, which Burton anticipated as a "fine hanging frolic."[38] During the August excitement, Ferris was a sergeant in the Nacogdoches militia; and, in the expedition against Kickapootown that fall, he was a private in a company of Nacogdoches mounted volunteers.[39] Knowledge of the land made Ferris and his deputy surveyors invaluable to such military expeditions. Indeed, it was often the surveyors who first reported Indian movements on the frontier.

At Kickapootown, Ferris observed General Rusk using his favorite military strategy, luring the enemy from cover with taunts. Rusk hurled insults at the Mexican/Indian camp: "you damned cowardly ___ ___ ___,

---

35. DeGolyer, "Conquest of Three Forks," 28–29, quotes Rusk Papers. John S. (RIP) Ford in his memoirs, *Rip Ford's Texas* (Austin: University of Texas Press, 1963), 18, states that Rusk promoted war with the Cherokees and their eventual expulsion. His position on Indians differed sharply from that of his friend Houston. Ford states (p. 28), "General Rusk used his influence with the people to prejudice them against the Cherokees. He was of opinion they were bad and dangerous neighbors."

36. Hugh B. McLeod to M. B. Lamar, Oct. 22, 1838, describes the Battle of Kickapootown on October 16, 1838, and sketches the Indian camp with horses tethered in the center. Lamar Papers, II, #846.

37. *Telegraph and Texas Register* (Houston), Nov. 10, 1838. Although the Indians were alarmed by Anglo-Texan invasion of their land, they reportedly did not allow Cordova to address them. Cordova remained among the prairie tribes until March 1839, trying to instigate a general war against the Texians.

38. Burton to Lamar, Aug. 25, 1838, Lamar Papers, II, #799. Burton reported 1,000 men in the field in six days. Actually none of the rebels was hanged, for fear such retribution might damage Texas's chances for annexation to the United States. The reputation of the infant republic was fragile.

39. Muster Rolls, Texas State Archives, show Warren A. Ferris appointed aide-de-camp on the staff of Gen. K. H. Douglass, Third Brigade; possibly he acted as a spy or scout.

come out and show yourself."[40] By October 1838, Texians had evidence that Mexican agents, Manuel Flores and Pedro Miracle, had visited Indians of northeast Texas to instigate war against frontier settlements.[41] Threats of a bloody massacre kept the scattered outposts in a state of alarm. With his strong show of force against Cordova, Rusk made himself an even more popular figure. There was talk of his running for president in the fall elections.[42]

When demand pressed Ferris back to surveying in late 1838, he found it hard to employ work crews. Most of the able-bodied men of East Texas were participating in the pursuit of Cordova, which took an Anglo army onto the prairies of North Texas for the first time.

Three companies of militia from Red River and Fannin Counties, under Gen. John H. Dyer rendezvoused at Fort Inglish (now Bonham, Texas) and scouted the Three Forks area in September and October of 1838. Rusk's troops left Nacogdoches on November 16 and proceeded through the Cherokee Reserve where the general satisfied himself that those Indians were not involved in the Cordova Rebellion. In early December, Rusk located Dyer's Fourth Brigade on the Elm Fork of the Trinity about twenty miles above the Three Forks (now Denton County). Five hundred well-armed, mounted Texians thus made a show of force on the prairies which heretofore had been safe refuge for the tribes. They failed to find Cordova, who reportedly withdrew westward; neither did they find hostile Indians, although they burned several deserted Indian villages.[43]

It was an unusually harsh winter with howling "northers." Warren Ferris, who was surveying on the Angelina and Sabine Rivers that winter, recalled "severe northers succeeding each other with little intermission; boys skated on the ponds near Nacogdoches."[44] On the Texas prairie

---

40. McLeod to Lamar, Oct. 22, 1838, Lamar Papers, II, #849.

41. The *Telegraph and Texas Register* (Houston), Oct. 27, 1838, carried a story from the Little Rock *Gazette* (Arkansas), exposing the Mexican plot to regain Texas. When Mexican emissary Pedro Miracle was killed on the Red River in August, his letters and journal fell into the hands of U.S. authorities at Ft. Gibson. The *Gazette* expressed some doubts as to the authenticity of this amazing journal, which detailed Miracle's instructions, his reception by the tribes, including the Cherokees, and his meeting with Cordova.

42. Rusk, on three occasions, turned down nomination for president of the Republic. This move to draft him came as early as July 20, 1838, in a letter from McLeod to Rusk: "Burton left here [Velasco] for Nacogdoches and intended to put you up in that section of the country for President" (Rusk Papers). Rusk broke with Houston over the Indian question and, as second most popular man in Texas, he was a promising candidate for the presidency. When he stood aside, Lamar's path was clear. Gambrell, *Mirabeau B. Lamar*, 189. Scholarly biographies of both Rusk and Lamar are sorely needed.

43. Scott McKinney memoirs, William C. Young Papers (Fondren Library, Southern Methodist University, Dallas), cited in DeGolyer, "Conquest of Three Forks," 34. Also see Rusk's report to Lamar, Jan. 9, 1839, Lamar Papers, II, #996.

44. Warren Ferris, Dallas *Herald*, Sept. 2, 1872.

west of the Trinity River, the Indians fell back, burning grassland as they retreated, destroying forage, and driving off the game.[45] Finally the Anglo army, short of supplies and with their horses exhausted, was forced to turn back to the East Texas settlements. Gen. Hugh McLeod called the bitter cold march across a barren prairie "unparalleled since DeSoto's." He reported the prairie land to be the "finest portion of Texas" and judged the Indians would "perceive the hopelessness of the contest," having seen that the white man could sustain such a campaign on the prairies in the winter.[46] As the militia returned to Clarksville, Nacogdoches, and San Augustine, many men were convinced that the enemy in their midst was the Cherokees and their leader, Chief Bowl.

How deeply the Cherokee were involved in the 1838 Mexican Rebellion became a matter of dispute. Chief Bowl, war chieftain of the Cherokees, protested innocence to his friend Sam Houston. Alarmed by white aggression, Bowl wrote Houston, "my people from the Bigest [sic] to the least have a little dread on their minds."[47] Houston believed the Cherokees had a right to their land. His strong condemnation of violations of Indian treaty rights alienated many of his East Texas backers who thought him more Cherokee than Anglo in his sympathies. Reassuring Chief Bowl, Houston wrote, "I have given an order . . . no families or children of Indians shall be disturbed or have troubles . . . they shall be protected and even the Mexican families, and property shall not be troubled." He urged the Cherokees to keep the peace as they had promised in the treaty; ironically, he recommended they put their trust in General Rusk as their protector. "Look to him as your great friend," Houston counseled.[48]

Warning Rusk not to invade the Cherokee Reserve and instructing Alexander Horton to survey and clarify the Cherokee boundary line with all speed, Houston left Nacogdoches for Houston City. But Houston's conciliatory Indian policy was doomed. In the fall of 1838, a new president would be elected since, under the Texas Constitution, Sam Houston could not succeed himself. The power of the protector of Indian rights was on the wane; the influence of Anglo-Texan land speculators was on the rise.

In November 1838, Houston received a report from Alexander Horton that the boundary between the Cherokees and their white neighbors had been run, despite obstacles thrown up by Isaac W. Burton and others in the Nacogdoches area. Horton, who helped negotiate the 1836 Cherokee Treaty, informed Houston that despite every "art, villainy, corruption and

---

45. *Telegraph and Texas Register* (Houston), Jan. 26, 1839.

46. Hugh McLeod to M. B. Lamar, Jan. 9, 18, 1839, Lamar Papers, II, #997, #1024.

47. Chief Bowl to George May (Indian agent), Aug. 12, 1838, Williams and Barker (eds.), *The Writings of Sam Houston*, II, 273.

48. Houston to Chief Bowl, Aug. 15, 1838, ibid., 274–275, 277.

treachery" the Anglos could invent, "We have succeeded . . . the Indians are all well satisfied, and will remain in peace if the Whites will let them alone."[49]

Assigning blame for the critical Texas/Indian predicament is not a simple task. The United States chargé d'affaires to the Republic of Texas wrote to his superiors in the State Department that the situation was "mainly attributable to the conduct of some of her [Texas] citizens, who have unwisely irritated and provoked their savage enemy by trespassing upon and surveying their lands."[50] Houston, whose hands were tied, told his friend Andrew Jackson that the bloodshed on the Texas frontier was due to the "violence of the American character." In his final address to Congress, Houston condemned a "few seditious speculators" who would "involve the country in a general Indian war." Then he left Texas for an extended visit to the United States.[51]

In point of fact, conflict was guaranteed from the moment the Texas Senate nullified the Cherokee Treaty in late 1837. That act signaled white settlers in East Texas that the reserved land was up for grabs. When the Land Office opened, settlers began to flood Cherokee lands. Early Texas historian Henderson Yoakum faulted whites for provocation, saying that the "ink was hardly dry till surveyors were in the reserve." Surveyors, eager to locate the best lands along streams, went deep into Cherokee country. Yoakum asserted: "The Indians, seeing them at work, were not slow to believe what the Mexicans had told them—that the white people would take all their hunting-grounds, and drive them off."[52]

Although Houston led Chief Bowl to believe that the treaty was still viable, running of the Cherokee Boundary was a moot issue. Houston was as unable to control the settlers and speculators as Chief Bowl was unable to control the dissidents in his tribe. Houston observed: "The Indian lands are the forbidden fruit in the midst of the garden,"[53] and Anglo settlers were not to be denied.

When Mirabeau B. Lamar became president of Texas in late 1838, he initiated an aggressive Indian policy; sanctioning Rusk and Dyer's pursuit of Cordova, authorizing Hugh McLeod to launch a March expedition

49. Alexander Horton to Sam Houston, Nov. 10, 1838, in *Telegraph and Texas Register* (Houston), Nov. 28, 1838.

50. Alcee LaBranche to John Forsyth, Nov. 10, 1838, S. Exec. Doc. 14, 32nd Cong., 2nd Sess., 9, reproduced by McLean, *Papers Concerning Robertson's Colony*, XVI, 649.

51. Sam Houston to Andrew Jackson, Aug. 11, 1838, and Houston to Texas Congress, Nov. 19, 1838. Williams and Barker (eds.), *The Writings of Sam Houston*, II, 270–272, 299–304. Marshall DeBruhl, *Sword of San Jacinto: A Life of Sam Houston* (New York: Random House, 1993), 268, suggests that Houston left Texas rather than stand by helplessly and watch his Indian brothers exterminated.

52. Yoakum, *History of Texas*, II, 248, 267.

53. Houston, speech to Congress, May 1838, Williams and Barker (eds.), *The Writings of Sam Houston*, IV, 60.

back to the Three Forks area, permitting surveyors to intrude provocatively on Indian lands, and looking for a pretext to expel the tribes from Texas.[54]

Warren Ferris shared the view of most Texians who supported Lamar's hard-line Indian policy. To them, the existence of an independent Indian nation within the Republic of Texas was preposterous. Although the civilized Cherokees were peaceful, sedentary farmers, Anglo-Texans deemed them bad neighbors. By virtue of their leadership among the tribes, the Cherokees were held responsible for the bad acts of others. Houston's "soft" Indian policy and his high-handed treatment of Congress while president contributed to increased anti-Houston feeling in the period 1838–1840. Isaac Burton, who admitted Houston was a man of uncommon natural abilities, denounced him as "dissipated, eccentric and vain."[55] Most Nacogdoches men scoffed at any guaranty of Indian lands as an unconscionable barrier to the inevitable advance of white civilization.

A cycle of violence was set in motion. The actions of white settlers, greedy speculators, and ambitious frontier surveyors like Ferris alarmed the tribes, which raided isolated frontier settlements. Anglo-Texans retaliated with military expeditions and construction of western blockhouses such as Ft. Houston (modern Palestine, Texas) on the Trinity River. Such encroachments heightened Indian fears and led to more raids. It was an old pattern of violence and reprisal.

Typical was the Killough Massacre, which occurred in October 1838. Members of the Killough, Wood, and Williams families settled on land in present Cherokee County, seven miles northwest of modern Jacksonville, in the heart of the Cherokee Reserve. Knowing their precarious situation, the farmers ventured out to clear the fields with their weapons close at hand; but, one tragic autumn day, they were caught without their rifles. In a sudden Indian attack, eighteen whites were killed or captured. Three Killough women fled on foot, one carrying a baby. They hid in the woods for days before being found by a friendly Cherokee who took them to refuge at Martin Lacy's fort.[56]

An excuse to expel the Cherokees was found on May 14, 1839, when rangers killed notorious agent/provocateur Manuel Flores on the San

---

54. Lamar learned Indian policy from Gov. G. M. Troup of Georgia, to whom he was personal secretary in 1823. Gambrell, *Mirabeau B. Lamar*, 34. In pursuing a policy of Indian removal, Lamar was following the same line being pursued in the United States by the Andrew Jackson administration.

55. Burton, "Experiences in Texas," Lamar Papers, III, #1669.

56. Ironically, people in Nacogdoches accused the Cherokees of involvement in this worst Indian atrocity in East Texas history, calling it merely "cunning" to have rescued the survivors. J. W. Wilbarger, *Indian Depredations in Texas* . . . (1889; reprint, Austin: Pemberton Press, 1967), 620–622.

Gabriel River near modern Georgetown. On Flores's body were found letters implicating the Cherokees in the Cordova Rebellion.[57]

Lamar commissioned Martin Lacy, whose home was only four miles
from Chief Bowl's camp, to deliver an ultimatum to the Cherokees. The
president of the Texas Republic accused the Indians of murder, theft, and
intrigue and ordered them to leave Texas or face extermination.[58] Young
John H. Reagan, who came to Nacogdoches in May 1839 and, like Ferris,
was befriended by Burton and Lacy, was an eyewitness at the Indian
council in June and reported the tense scene. Elderly Chief Bowl received
Lacy with courtesy and led the Texian delegation to a spring near his
home where he sat on a log and listened in silence as an interpreter read
Lamar's decree.

Although he admitted some renegades might be guilty of depredations
for which they should be punished, Bowl vehemently denied the allegations against his tribe. He told Lacy that there had been a meeting of
chiefs and head men in council. His young men were for war—so, except-
ing himself and Big Mush, were the other major leaders.[59] They believed
they could whip the whites, but Chief Bowl knew his tribe would ultimately face defeat. Reagan was impressed with the dignity and candor of
the eighty-three-year-old Bowl, who was resigned to his fate as leader of
his people. "If he fought, the whites would kill him, and if he refused to
fight, his own people would kill him. . . . [H]e had led his people a long
time. . . . [H]e felt it his duty to stand by them."[60]

Thus Bowl rejected Lamar's ultimatum and stated his determination to
defend the lands guaranteed by the 1836 treaty. When Lamar countered by
ordering the military to build a fort in Cherokee territory at Neches saline,
Bowl concentrated his people east of the Neches River near that site.[61]

---

57. The correspondence included letters to Cordova from Matamoros in July
1838 advising him to seek Indian allies by promising them land. Yoakum, *History
of Texas*, II, 257–258. Dianna Everett, *The Texas Cherokees: A People between Two
Fires, 1819–1840* (Norman: University of Oklahoma Press, 1990), 75–76, assesses
Chief Bowl's actions as consistent with traditional diplomatic maneuvering. Bowl
talked to both sides, played for time, measured his adversaries, and tried to pick
the winning side. The Cherokees had been in contact with the Mexican government
since 1833 when, of course, they held their land at the pleasure of that government. What was construed as Cherokee duplicity might as easily be seen as an
effort to secure their legitimate claims through diplomacy.

58. Lamar to Bowl, May 26, 1839, Lamar Papers, II, #1297.

59. Everett, *The Texas Cherokees*, 6, focuses on the internal politics of the
Cherokees. Chief Bowl tried to achieve consensus but factionalism split the tribe.
Texans judged him "lying or at least masking his real intentions." Ibid., 102.

60. John H. Reagan, "Expulsion of the Cherokees from East Texas," *Quarterly of
the Texas State Historical Association* , I (July, 1897), 38–46. This article is based on
Reagan's June 28, 1865, letter to his children and is, according to his biographer Ben
Procter, a more accurate recollection than that given in his *Memoirs* (1907). There
were actually two talks between Lacy and Bowl with ten days elapsing between them.

61. Neches saline was an important salt source, used by both Indians and
Anglos. The Cherokees allowed Anglo settlers to come from Lacy's Fort, forty miles

On July 1, 1839, a so-called "Peace Commission" entered the Reserve to supervise Cherokee removal. Composed of military men and hard-liners on Indian policy, the commission included David G. Burnet, T. J. Rusk, and Isaac Burton. Chief Bowl agreed to withdraw to the Cherokee settlements in western Arkansas (Indian Territory) but requested a delay to harvest the fall corn crop. For two weeks, both sides stalled for time. While the negotiations went on, Gen. Edward Burleson and Gen. Kelsey H. Douglass were readying troops. Whatever the outcome of the talks, the Cherokees were to be evicted; they were the chief impediment to Anglo-Texan expansion onto the rich prairies of north central Texas.

Troops of the Texas militia and regular army under Rusk, Johnston, Burnet, McLeod, Burleson, and Douglass camped six miles east of Bowl's position. Following an argument over command, militia leader K. H. Douglass was chosen commander-in-chief.[62] Warren Ferris was with the Nacogdoches militia under General Douglass's command. In fact, almost every able-bodied man in East Texas was present, including Nacogdoches financier Adolphus Sterne.

On July 15, Chief Bowl broke off talks and moved his encampment to the west bank of the Neches (now Henderson County).[63] The Texians pursued, first exchanging fire with the Indians that afternoon when some twenty-five men under Rusk engaged Cherokee warriors located by a spy company. The Indians advanced, fired, and then fell back into a thicket and ravine. Lines were formed and, under a blazing July sun, the battle was joined. Withering gunfire, blistering heat, and heavy smoke took their toll. When the first day's battle ended at sundown, two Texians and eighteen Indians were dead.

At mid-morning on the second day of the Battle of the Neches, Texian troops moved out in two regiments, advancing up both banks of the river. Again, a spy company located the Indians, this time in a cornfield. Troops under Burleson and Rusk arrived on the scene, charged, and exchanged a brisk fire before the Indians retreated into the thickets of the river bottom. There the main body of the Texian army engaged about 500 Cherokees formed in a line that extended a mile.[64]

---

southeast, or from Nacogdoches, some seventy-five miles distant, to boil down their salt supplies. The site is now under Lake Palestine in Smith County.

62. Jenkins and Kesselus, *Edward Burleson*, 200–202, state the militia wanted Rusk; the regulars wanted Burleson. Douglass was a compromise. Burleson was later critical of Douglass's conduct of the campaign and disagreed with his glowing report of the action.

63. The battles were fought in Neches bottomland about fifteen miles west of Tyler, Texas, at a corner of modern Smith, Van Zandt, and Henderson Counties.

64. Aspects of the Battle of the Neches were reported by General Douglass to Secretary of War A. S. Johnston on July 17, 1839, Lamar Papers, III, #1372 and #1373. Also *Telegraph and Texas Register* (Houston), July 24, 1839. Marilyn M. Sibley, "The Texas Cherokee War of 1839," *East Texas Historical Journal*, 3 (July, 1965), 18–28, is another fine summary.

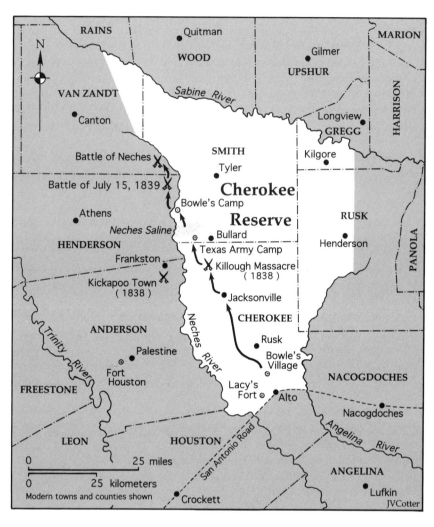

Cherokee War (1839) showing modern towns and counties and the Cherokee Reserve (shaded). Based on Jack Moore's map, *Chronicles of Smith County, Texas*, 1 (Fall, 1962). *Map by John V. Cotter.*

Chief Bowl rode back and forth behind the Indian line. Conspicuously dressed Anglo-style in a black military hat, a silk vest, a sash, and the sword given him by Sam Houston, he recklessly exposed himself to gunfire from the Texians. When the Cherokees retreated, Bowl was among the last to leave the field. He was wounded when his horse was shot from under him. Another shot caught him in the back. Then, despite John Reagan's attempted intervention to save his life, Bowl took a pistol shot in the back of the head which killed him instantly.[65] The second day's fighting, near present-day Tyler, Texas, lasted no more than two hours. Their leader dead, the Cherokees withdrew toward the Red River. Texian troops pursued, driving Indian warriors, women, and children, sick and wounded across the river into Arkansas. On July 25, the Texas army disbanded and returned home.

Following the July campaign, Ferris was with General Rusk, Robert W. Smith, and a troop of some forty men on a scouting mission in the old Cherokee Reserve. Reports circulated that hostile Indians were still in the area, perhaps returned to gather corn, so it was decided to make a forced march to the Sabine River and return via another route before the Indians could concentrate an attack. Taking every precaution against surprise, they advanced briskly through Indian country. Camped one night after seeing "mockasin" tracks all day, the recruits heard an unearthly chorus of wolves and owls. Convinced the calls were Indian signals, they panicked and fled the camp pell-mell into the darkness. Ferris recalled how they silently forced their way through heavy brush, making no great progress. At length, they found themselves dragging through a blackberry bramble. "Our pants were torn off to the knees," Ferris remembered, "our coattails . . . were left on the brambles . . . we might have been trailed by the commingled blood of ourselves and horses."[66]

When they finally regained their courage and regrouped, the troop felt rather sheepish. Warren Ferris wrote:

> We afterward ascertained that the owls and wolves that sent us out on the blackberry expedition were in reality Indians . . . that the celerity of our movements and midnight excursion saved us; that our retreat at the moment was a necessary and prudent course."[67]

On their return to Nacogdoches, Ferris and his fellow volunteers did not boast much of their achievements on this brief campaign but later convinced themselves that only forethought had saved their lives and that the Indians, probably thinking them the vanguard of a larger force, had cleared the area.

The Cherokee barrier was removed, rich lands were open to white settlement, and the surveying business again flourished. Swamped with profitable work, Ferris wrote an exultant letter to Sarah Lovejoy, proclaiming "Land is the cry!" He echoed the tenor of the times when he wrote:

> There are many who sacrifice honor and all things else to the God property. . . . Speak to one his answer is Land. Enquire kindly of his family and he answers in Leagues and Labors. The Land Mania is

---

65. Reagan, "Expulsion of the Cherokees," 46. Bowl was fatally shot at close range by Reagan's commander, Capt. Robert W. Smith. Later, many East Texans claimed to be the man who shot Chief Bowl.

66. W. A. Ferris, "Stopping Up the Trail", Dallas *Herald*, Oct. 28, 1871.

67. Ibid.

great . . . when in Turkey do as the Turkeys do, and say Land also,—
until I possess enough for future good, and for the future wealth of
myself and relations. . . . We have had some trifling difficulties with
the Indians. We have whipped off the Cherokees. I advocated the measure when it was not popular. It is good but they annoy us some still—
at times.[68]

Ferris's endorsement of the Cherokee expulsion was not shared by Sam
Houston. On his return to Texas, Houston learned the fate of his adopted
tribe and was outraged. At a public meeting in Nacogdoches, he
denounced the actions of greedy speculators and aggressive militarists
who had violated the good faith of the Cherokee Treaty. He proclaimed
Chief Bowl a better man than his "murderers." Some of his Nacogdoches
friends, like Rusk, Sterne, and Raguet, would not forgive Sam Houston of
these accusations for years. They were even more dismayed when, as a
San Augustine delegate to the Texas legislature, Houston introduced a
bill barring land speculation in the Cherokee Reserve. In a speech on
December 3, 1839, Houston decried the injustice of the campaign against
the Cherokees, denouncing the fraud and greed which motivated their
expulsion. He proposed that Cherokee land be treated as public domain,
sectioned in 640-acre tracts, and offered at public sale. Houston reasoned
such action would bring eighteen million dollars into the empty treasury
of the Republic, instead of enriching the pockets of speculators.

Enraged when Burleson and McLeod presented him Bowl's bullet-
pierced black hat as a souvenir of the Cherokee War, Houston lost all
moderation and accused the Lamar/Burnet government of being the tool
of land speculators. "The war," he said, "was produced by the encroach-
ment of the speculators—[their] locations were not made in good faith—
and if we now confirm them in their illegal locations, the bloodshed in the
Cherokee war will rest on our own shoulders." The Texas Congress,
unable to oppose a measure so obviously benefiting the majority, passed
the Cherokee Land Bill unanimously in January 1840, but Sam Houston
had made powerful enemies.[69]

Through two years of Indian campaigns and erratic surveying expeditions, Nacogdoches County Surveyor Ferris exchanged letters with Land
Commissioner Borden, explaining that illness and military duties had
delayed his preparation of the map of the county. Ferris had divided the
county into subdistricts, assigning one district to each of his deputies. He

---

68. Warren Ferris to Sarah Lovejoy, Oct. 8, 1839, FLC, Box I, Folder 4. The letter bears no postmark. It was apparently delivered by some returning traveler
from Texas to Buffalo, New York.

69. Williams and Barker (eds.), *The Writings of Sam Houston*, II, 323–347. The
anti-Houston *Telegraph and Texas Register* (Houston), Feb. 5, 1840, judged that
Houston's remarks on the Cherokee Land Bill excited the "reproach of his enemies
. . . the grief and shame of his friends." Campbell, *Sam Houston*, 89, notes that
while Houston may have received some satisfaction from this act, Congress
repealed the Cherokee Land Bill the next year.

relied on them to bring in accurate maps which, pieced together, would satisfy Borden's request for a "true" picture of boundaries and claims. Ferris complained of the impossible situation in trying to use old surveys:

> I shall forward in a day or two one [map] to be found with the dates I possess, conjecture, conflicting accounts of others. Had you required me to mark the surveys previously made you would have been pre-sented with a piece of network that would baffle description, were it possible to accomplish it.[70]

Borden, in disappointment, replied:

> It is much to be regretted that you are not in possession of the neces-sary information for representing the old surveys . . . the relative posi-tions of the different parts, the true distances from one to the other appeared to be from actual survey: consequently, it will be impossible to know from the map where the work between two rivers will meet or in what manner they will join.[71]

In late 1839, Ferris finally forwarded a map to the Land Office at the new capital in Austin.[72] Its only points of determination were streams, rivers, and Indian trails crisscrossing the vast area. The ban against sur-vey of Cherokee lands made it impossible to anchor the new surveys to older ones in Nacogdoches County.

When the Land Office called Ferris's map useless, he responded with eight reasons his deputies failed to provide accurate or complete maps of their respective districts. Obstacles he listed included: former surveyors left no copies of field notes or plats; earlier government agents had issued titles prescribing points no longer to be found; previous surveyors had been careless in establishing definite locations; names of streams (the most certain existing guides to surveyors) had been changed; and described boundaries often contained more land than called for in the title. According to Ferris, public opinion pronounced the old surveys invalid, even though they had not been officially declared void. Finally, Ferris asserted that his deputies were unwilling to run survey lines for $3 a mile (Texas money) while hostile Indians still roamed the frontier.[73]

Roving bands of Indian raiders were especially vengeful toward survey-ing parties. Although they traveled heavily armed, often with guards, sur-veyors could not work and carry rifles. Like every frontiersman, Warren

---

70. W. A. Ferris to Borden, Sept. 1, 1838 (GLO). Ferris also corresponded with Vice President David G. Burnet on the subject of surveying land for the purpose of education. See his letter of Sept. 10, 1839, in Texas State Archives (mistakenly indexed under "William A. Ferris").

71. John P. Borden to Ferris, Oct. 13, 1838 (GLO).

72. Burton was one of five commissioners appointed in January 1839 to select a new capital site. The controversial decision to move the government to an exposed position on the east bank of the Colorado River in central Texas was a blow to Houston City. Yoakum, *History of Texas*, II, 273 and Siegel, *A Political History*, 81.

73. W. A. Ferris to Borden, Sept. 9, 1839 (GLO).

Ferris had heard tales of Indians wrecking surveyors' camps, smashing their compasses, and scalping the surveyors. His own paper, the Nacogdoches *Chronicle*, carried the story of the death of surveyor Richard Sparks, surprised on the prairie, shot while attempting to survey land on the upper Trinity River.[74] In another notorious incident, the "Battle Creek Fight," which occurred on Richland Creek in present Navarro County within three days of the Killough Massacre in October 1838, a surveying party of twenty-five was attacked by 300 Kickapoos. Under cover of darkness the surveyors tried to reach a timbered thicket; only six survived. In 1839, W. P. Brashear, foolishly surveying alone and unarmed in LaVaca County near the Texas coast, was surprised by Comanches and barely escaped with his life on his horse "Git Out." Frontier surveyor John Harvey warned, "When you least expect Indians, there they are."[75] In the mid-1840s, Frederick Roemer commented: "the Texas surveyor finds his rifle just as necessary as his compass. . . . [H]ostile Indians . . . know full well that the surveyor is only the forerunner of the white intruder. . . . Therefore they pursue him with particular hatred."[76]

Such were the hazards of a frontier surveyor. Under constant pressure from clients and superiors in the Land Office, Ferris wrote to Buffalo of his mounting feelings of isolation and loneliness. He admitted that he longed to hear from his family and few loyal friends and that he was "sometimes in a sentimental mood." To sister Sarah he wrote:

> I am here among a set of worst possible ill dispositioned people who possess no feelings in common with me and I am in consequence lonesome. . . . some disagreeable reflections . . . cross my mind when I am idle . . . when reverses occur. I wish much you were here to enjoy the finest climate in the world and be near or with me.[77]

Warren Ferris wrote that money was scarce, but said "Texas is disposed to enjoy herself" even without money. Although social occasions abounded and Nacogdoches boasted "fair specimens of beauty," Ferris claimed that he shunned polite society. He found no one to be trusted. Even Senator Burton might not be useful to him or Charles much longer; Ferris predicted that Burton's reputation would not "long buffet the

---

74. Story from Nacogdoches Chronicle, carried in *Telegraph* and *Texas Register* (Houston), May 2, 1838.

75. John Henry Brown, *Indian Wars and Pioneers of Texas* (Austin: L. E. Daniel Publishers, 1896), 48–49, Wilbarger, *Indian Depredations*, 107–108, 262–264.

76. Frederick Roemer, *Texas; With Particular Reference to German Immigration and the Physical Appearance of the Country, Described Through Personal Observation*, trans. Oswald Mueller (1849; reprint, San Antonio: Standard Printing Co., 1935), 224.

77. Warren Ferris to Sarah Lovejoy, Oct. 8, 1839, Blake Collection, XLVI, 14–16.

78. Ibid. Ferris referred to Burton's certain unnamed "indiscretions" which had become public knowledge.

storm" of "vindictive malice, envy and scandal" which flourished in the young Republic.[78]

The pinch of depression in the United States was being felt even in distant Texas. Faced with a worsening economic situation and an increased sense of urgency to make himself financially secure, Ferris decided to take some risk. In a letter to Joshua Lovejoy, Ferris described the forces which drove him to take extreme measures. The issuance of cheap paper by the government caused depreciation of Texas money to but a quarter of its face value.[79] Since county surveyors were required to accept payment in the devalued currency, Ferris felt compelled to seek other income. "I immediately turned my attention," he wrote, "to a Surveying Expedition to the Three Forks of Trinity, a Section occupied by our most incorrigible foes."[80]

In August 1839, the official surveyor of Nacogdoches County was approached by Dr. William P. King, a Mississippi land speculator. Dr. King's Southern Land Company, headquartered in San Augustine,[81] hired Ferris to survey a new town at the Three Forks of the Trinity. The town "Warwick" was to be the centerpiece of a huge land promotion from which Ferris would profit enormously. Caught up in the dazzle of land speculation, Warren Angus Ferris made four desperate attempts to enter the wilderness at the headwaters of the Trinity River during the autumn of 1839.

---

79. Merchants in Texas and the United States preferred specie or hard currency and so were reluctant to accept Texas paper money, which was unsecured by gold. If accepted at all, the value of Texas money was discounted.

80. Warren Ferris to Joshua Lovejoy, May 19, 1840.

81. The Texas Constitution of 1836 expressly forbade land speculation by non-Texans. Aliens could hold no land except by title from the Republic. Therefore, King and his partners were careful to locate their headquarters in San Augustine and attract local stockholders.

★ 6 ★

AT THE THREE FORKS

Reports of a veritable garden spot on the upper Trinity River[1] in North Texas aroused the interest of speculators in distant Mississippi who, in 1838, organized the Southern Land Company and, in 1839, enlisted Nacogdoches County Surveyor Warren A. Ferris to locate land in the newly opened territory. Dr. William P. King,[2] president of the land company whose organizers first met in Vicksburg and then Holly Springs, Mississippi, came to Texas, made his headquarters at San Augustine, began to buy up land certificates, and approached Ferris as a knowledgeable and ambitious associate.

Although it was illegal under the laws of the Republic for county surveyors to locate land for private companies, Warren Ferris signed a contract with King on August 28, 1839. Ferris was to locate ninety leagues and labors (around 400,000 acres) on the Trinity River beyond the former Cherokee Reserve. On return of his field notes, Ferris would receive $900, out of which he was to pay expenses of the expedition. On the strength of his agreement with Ferris, Dr. King sold over 200 shares in the Southern Land Company on a single day, August 30. A second contract, signed September 4, 1839, stipulated that Ferris was to survey land on a bluff of the Trinity at the Three Forks. This site, to be designated the "city of Warwick," would have been the precise location that later became the city of Dallas. Ferris himself was to receive one-twelfth interest in Warwick City.[3] It was this prospect of rich reward in speculative lands that led Warren Ferris to risk his reputation and to make four desperate attempts to locate the Three Forks of the Trinity in the fall of 1839.

---

1. The potent "Myth of the Garden," so prominent in literature of the American West, persisted in early descriptions of the headwaters of the Trinity River. One of the first reports was from Lt. A. B. Van Benthuysen, returning from an 1837 ranger expedition: "The country of the Trinity is handsomely situated, well watered, plenty of timber. . . . The prairies abound in game. . . . I think that this country is the garden of America, and will in time be the most valuable part of Texas." *Telegraph and Texas Register* (Houston), Dec. 23, 1837.

2. King, a Virginian, came to Mississippi via Tennessee and was a founder both of the first bank in northern Mississippi at Holly Springs and of Holly Springs University; the former went into receivership when its state charter was denied and the latter went into the hands of the Methodist Church. DeGolyer Collection III, 15.

3. Transcripts of San Augustine Co. Probate Records, DeGolyer Collection, III, 2. Originals, misplaced or destroyed when the courthouse moved, are no longer to be found in San Augustine County records.

The area which would be Dallas County was known to early Texians as the "Three Forks," a reference to the confluence of the Elm, West, and East (Bois d'arc) Forks of Rio Trinidad.[4] It was a region of startling contrast to the Piney Woods of East Texas. Forested, sandy land gave way abruptly to a virtually treeless prairie with rolling hills carpeted in tall native grasses and broken by streams along which elm, oak, hickory, and mesquite trees grew, sometimes forming dense thickets in the bottom lands. The deep, black, waxy prairie soil, although viewed with initial suspicion by Southerners accustomed to sandy land, was the fertile stuff of a farmer's dream. From the north and west, reaching like long, skinny fingers into the Blackland Prairie, ran lines of thin sandy soil topped by blackjack and post oaks—the Eastern Cross Timbers.[5]

Although Spanish and Mexican authorities claimed the Three Forks region on vague maps, neither really controlled it. North central Texas still belonged to the Indians. It was the meeting ground of numerous tribes who camped and traded along Turtle Creek, at Cedar Springs, and along White Rock Creek. Two major Indian footpaths (or traces) crossed the Three Forks from east to west. One, the Kickapoo Trace, entered present Dallas County from the southeast, near modern Seagoville, and proceeded to a ford across the Trinity, at approximately the junction of Commerce Street and Industrial Boulevard in the present city of Dallas. From there, the Trace continued west, skirting the outcropping of Chalk Hill in modern Oak Cliff, crossing Mountain Creek to the Indian campsites on Village Creek in present Tarrant County. Another Indian trail, the Caddo Trace, crossed the northeast corner of what is now Dallas County, near present Sachse and Garland.[6] Following these Indian routes, bands of Wichitas (called variously Keechies, Ionies, Tawakoni, and Towash), as well as Kickapoos, Caddoes, and Cherokees moved through the Three Forks to camp along the tree-shaded streams. The Indian traces were also a favored route for Comanche war parties that swept in off the western plains to raid isolated settlements and confront intruding surveyors bearing that hated instrument, the compass, "the thing that steals the land."[7]

---

4. The designation "Three Forks" captured the imagination of early Texians; perhaps it reminded Ferris of the famous "Three Forks" of the Missouri River where he trapped beaver a decade before.

5. Richard Phelan, *Texas Wild: The Land, Plants, and Animals of the Lone Star State* (New York: E. P. Dutton & Co., 1976), 140–141, 148. W. B. Parker (1854) described the Blackland Prairie at the Three Forks as a sea of grass with black, sticky soil, rich in nutrients.

6. Homer DeGolyer, through his extensive research in county records, mapped the path of Indian traces through Dallas County. See maps and illustrations, DeGolyer Collection, II, 5.

7. Roemer, *Texas*, 224.

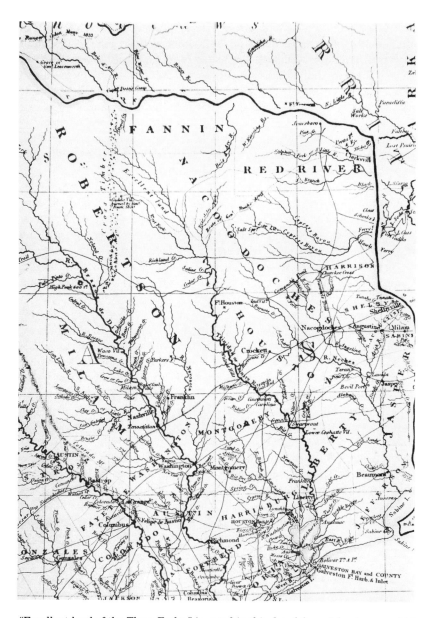

"Excellent land of the Three Forks," is noted in this detail from John Arrowsmith's *Map of Texas* (1841). The map shows East Texas towns, Indian villages, rivers, roads, Fort Houston on the Trinity, and the 1839 route of General Rusk's army. Original 23³/₄ x 19⁵/₈ inches. *Courtesy Historical Maps Collection, Dallas Public Library.*

Warren Ferris's attempts to locate King's speculative city of Warwick on a bluff at the Three Forks of the Trinity were frustrated by Indian harassment and an unexpected difficulty in pinpointing the actual confluence of three streams. Extremes in weather, either drought or flood, confused the issue. Indeed, the existence of a point at which three streams met proved to be an illusion. Only the Elm and West Forks converged near a bluff; the mouth of the East Fork was thirty miles downstream.[8]

Enthusiastic about his new assignment, Ferris invested his own meager savings in four expeditions to the Trinity in the fall of 1839.[9] In early September, with fifty-five men from Nacogdoches and again in late September with forty-four men, he tried to penetrate the Indian-controlled territory, but the sight of fresh moccasin tracks caused both expeditions to turn back. In early October, a third, better-organized attempt was made. Ferris divided his sixty men into three divisions, spent some time in the former Cherokee Reserve preparing provisions, and then made his first survey along White Rock Creek in what would be Dallas County. Again the presence of hostile Indians forced the surveyors back to the East Texas settlements.

His repeated efforts gave Ferris the reputation of an enterprising fellow, but most folks in Nacogdoches judged the survey of the Three Forks to be impractical under the circumstances. Few were willing to hazard Indian Country so soon after the Cherokee War. Finally, in November, Ferris succeeded in recruiting twenty-nine men. Well-armed and provisioned, the fourth expedition traveled slowly westward for about twelve days before they discovered signs of Indians. This time, the surveyors pursued the Indians and found them lying in ambush in a canebrake. "We charged," Ferris wrote with some pride, "and your humble servant Shot one through the heart at the distance of Eighty yards." When the rest of the Indians fled, Ferris and his men located their camp, finding five horses and provisions including meat, corn, beans, axes, ropes, and kettles. The slain Indian was armed with an amazing mix of weaponry—"an English Rifle, a Prussian Pistol, A Bowie Knife—A Butcher Knife and Bow and arrows."[10] Two days later, after seeing indications of a larger

---

8. DeGolyer explains a possible origin of the idea in that the West Fork, at times, had a double mouth on entering the Elm Fork. The two mouths, separated by a raft of silt and debris, appear on an 1880 U.S. Geological Survey map. Homer DeGolyer, "A Look at the Present Dallas Area When It Was Known As the Three Forks," unpublished article, DeGolyer Collection.

9. Ferris got $100 per league if he provided the provisions; if King paid for supplies, Ferris was to receive only $50 per surveyed league. Ferris mortgaged his East Texas land to raise money for the 1839 expeditions. During 1839, surveyors were considered part of the militia so Ferris also received a captain's pay. See transcript of Aug. 28, 1839, agreement, Ferris and King, in DeGolyer Collection, III, 2.

10. Warren Ferris to Joshua Lovejoy, May 19, 1840. Describing this same expedition in his September 2, 1871, reminiscences for the Dallas *Herald*, Ferris mistakenly put the events in 1838. As he recalled, the surveyors penetrated to the

Indian party entering the area, all but four of Ferris's men refused to stay longer in the Three Forks region and deserted him.

One of the four intrepid souls who stayed with Ferris was John H. Reagan. In his memoirs, Reagan recalled how the party traveled light, each taking only a blanket, corn flour, meat, coffee, tin cups, compass, chain, field book, and hatchet. Moving swiftly and silently by night, they reached Cedar Creek on the East Fork of the Trinity; often they were forced to hide by day in damp, cold creek beds and Reagan fell ill with chills and fever.[11] Finally, Ferris admitted that the Indians were too numerous to attempt surveys. Having satisfied himself by exploring the country, he led his men back to Nacogdoches.

Warren Ferris proclaimed his intention to resume surveying in 1840 as soon as he could raise another expedition. Not having corresponded with his Buffalo family in nearly a year, he shared the news of his fantastic financial opportunity with his half-brother Joshua Lovejoy, cautioning:

> No part of the information contained in this letter is known to our folks . . . it is absolutely necessary to keep my arrangement with the Southern Land Company a profound secret. I must only be known as County Surveyor of Nacogdoches County.[12]

As soon as the weather began to improve in the spring of 1840, Ferris was back in the field. With John Reagan as his deputy, he spent a month surveying in what is now southern Van Zandt County. Rain dogged the surveyors. They returned to Nacogdoches in May, barely having made expenses.[13]

Since Ferris had exhausted his personal finances in 1839, his 1840 surveying for the Southern Land Company was backed by the company itself. Dr. King refinanced the value of stock from $500,000 to $650,000, selling more shares and generating credit in East Texas to outfit the expeditions.[14] Stockholders cosigned a note to K. H. Douglass and

---

headwaters of the Sabine and tributaries of the Trinity, west of Jourdan's saline (now Grand Saline) before an encounter with Indians made it clearly "madness to proceed." Yet, Ferris, Reagan, and three others did proceed to explore the virgin area on foot.

11. John H. Reagan, *Memoirs: With Special Reference to Secession and the Civil War* (1906; reprint, Austin: Pemberton Press, 1968), 37–39. Reagan, who came to Ferris in Nacogdoches prior to the fourth expedition (1839), served a six-month apprenticeship before becoming Deputy Surveyor. His surveying career was frequently interrupted by bouts with a malaria-like fever.

12. Warren Ferris to Joshua Lovejoy, May 19, 1840.

13. Reagan states in his *Memoirs*, 40–41, that he and Ferris were back in the field by February 1840. It rained every day for a month, and cold winds swept the prairies of the upper Trinity. On April 15, 1840, Reagan became Ferris's deputy and also formed a surveying partnership with William Young Lacy.

14. The refinanced company was called the Wassau Exchange Company. Overextended, his credit stretched to the limit, King relied on promises of land to finance the 1840 expeditions. He also took a new partner, Judge John P. Martin of Mississippi.

Nicholas H. Darnell, merchants of Nacogdoches and San Augustine; both men agreed to be paid in land.[15] Similar agreements were reached with several individuals who signed on as assistants or guards. In addition to his post as official county surveyor and his rank as captain in the militia, Warren Ferris now carried the title "Topographical Engineer of the Southern Land Company of Texas" and owned fifty shares in the company, valued at $200 each. He was promised a fee of $5,000, "good money, U.S.," plus expenses to lead the 1840 expedition and complete the surveying in forty days.[16]

On the eve of this fifth attempt to locate the Three Forks, Ferris wrote a long, gossipy letter to his brother in Buffalo. He reported himself well and said that he had penetrated "twice to Three forks of Trinity . . . once with 4 men and once with 5—hell of a crowd—didn't do anything first trip—Indians too deep. Second trip barely paid expenses." Concerning his bargain with King, Warren Ferris urged his brother to keep "Mum—must be secret I am County Surveyor yet and in public only County Surveyor."[17]

For the first time, Ferris's optimism seemed to waver. Even the most sanguine booster knew the Texas Republic was in deep economic depression. Speculative enterprises like that of Dr. King were in trouble, gambling as they did on continued prosperity, increasing immigration, and rising land prices. Warren Ferris recognized that time was running out for the land boom in Texas. Of the economy, he wrote: "Nacogdoches on the wane. Texas bankrupt and her people rogues. . . . Times as hard as Millstones. Promissory notes not worth a damn. . . . Gold and silver fled forever and U.S. Banks all broke."[18]

Concerning Texas politics, Ferris informed Charles that Lamar's popularity declined as Sam Houston's soared upward. "He'll be next President, got no body popular enough to oppose him," Ferris judged. Everything was quiet on the Indian frontier, although the Mexicans still threatened invasion. During the peaceful interlude, Burton and other planters grew

---

15. Probate Records, San Augustine Co. (microfilm, DeGolyer Collection) include the Darnell agreement (May 31, 1840) and stockholders of the Southern Land Company: William P. King, president; Lewis V. Greer, secretary; also A. C. McEwen, A. C. Weaver, Samuel Nelson, Samuel W. Flourney, George W. Terrell, Richard Scurry, James Perkins, Napoleon B. Garner, Samuel Stivers, John A. Greer, John F. H. Claiborne, and Warren A. Ferris. McEwen was King's partner in earlier Mississippi ventures. Terrell, former attorney general of Tennessee, was a prominent lawyer in San Augustine who later became attorney general of Texas. Darnell, a young San Augustine merchant from Tennessee, migrated to Dallas and Tarrant Counties where he led a distinguished career of public service.

16. Agreement signed May 18, 1840, according to Warren Ferris's letter to Joshua Lovejoy, May 19, 1840. Adolphus Sterne states in his diary (Oct. 6, 1841) that thirty Texas dollars were worth six U.S. McDonald, *Hurrah for Texas*, 4.

17. Warren Ferris to Charles Ferris, June 2, 1840. FLC, Box I, Folder 6.

18. Ibid.

cotton and corn on what had been Cherokee land. Sensing that speculative opportunity was running out, Ferris urged Charles to take "the shute to Texas" as soon as possible, for "Texas owes us something somehow or other."[19]

One day after posting this letter, on June 3, 1840, Warren Ferris left Nacogdoches with a party of twenty-nine men. The surveyors, their guards, and assistants followed the old Cherokee Road to Neches saline, then the Kickapoo Trace through present Van Zandt, Kaufman, and Dallas Counties (roughly following present U.S. Hwy. 175) to the Three Forks region. This time Ferris was accompanied by Dr. William P. King himself, determined to survey his empire on the Trinity.

Again they divided into three surveying parties; one group under Robert A. Terrell[20] was detailed to follow the Kickapoo Trace to its crossing of the Trinity, there to locate the Three Forks and lay out the city of Warwick. An extremely dry July caused the river to run so low that Terrell was unable to determine a point where three streams met. The location of Warwick City was postponed. Ferris later described the 1840 drought conditions: "all the streams were low; the East Fork of the Trinity dry; and the clouds of dust could be seen in every direction raised by buffalo and wild horses, and water was to be found only in holes."[21]

King and Ferris established the northwest corner of the proposed King Block of surveys at White Rock Creek in present Dallas County, approximately where the creek now crosses Samuell Boulevard (or Ferguson Road). Following the direction of the streams, all lines ran northwest and southeast from that point, establishing the line for subsequent surveys. As completed, the King Block was 22 miles wide and $29^1/_2$ miles long. If outlined on a modern map, the northwest corner would be a mile and a half due east of White Rock Dam, the northeast corner about a mile north of Lake Lavon in Collin County, the southwest corner midway between Kemp and Kaufman in Kaufman County, and the southeast corner about a mile east of Van in Van Zandt County.[22]

During June and July of 1840, teams of surveyors under deputies R. A. Terrell, George W. Casey, John H. Reagan, and E. B. Harvey completed 118 marked surveys, each for a league and a labor. The King Block

19. Ibid. Lamar supported Burnet against Houston in the 1840 race for president of the Republic. As Houston's popularity rose, the influence of Burton, Burnet, and the Lamar clique declined.

20. Robert, brother of Southern Land Company stockholder George W. Terrell, later resided in Kaufman County where the county seat was named for him. R. A. Terrell was a major informant of Kate Efnor who wrote on early Texas for the Austin magazine *The American Sketchbook* during the 1870's. Efnor mistakenly credited Terrell as leader of Dr. King's expedition. Efnor, *American Sketchbook*, V, 36. DeGolyer Collection, microfilm.

21. Ferris, "Reminiscences," Dallas *Herald*, Sept. 2, 1871.

22. DeGolyer, "Conquest of Three Forks," 52–53.

totaled 543,390 acres, overlapping six counties of present-day Texas.[23] Unfortunately for King and his associates, many of the certificates issued by land boards in Shelby, Sabine, and San Augustine Counties were judged to be fraudulent, and the surveys based on them were subsequently rejected by the General Land Office in Austin.[24] Only four of the twenty-nine surveys made by Ferris in present Dallas County retain their original lines. These are all on the east side of the county and do not bear the names of the original owners. They are the T. Thomas, John Little, Daniel Tanner, and John P. Anderson Surveys.[25]

Ferris's problems coordinating the work of several deputies were revealed in his instructions to John Reagan. He ordered Reagan to cease all surveying north of the East Fork of the Trinity as E. B. Harvey had already selected and surveyed sections in that area. Reagan was to forward a plat of his work so that overlapping surveys might be avoided. "These instructions you will strictly obey," Ferris wrote, "as no end would be found to the difficulties that a contrary course would produce."[26]

Ferris returned to Nacogdoches in early August 1840, flush with the success of the summer expedition. From May to August 1840, he had completed a huge task of surveying, despite fevers that struck his men, killing one and forcing most of the others to return to the settlements. "My Expenses," he reported to Joshua Lovejoy in Kentucky, "were about one thousand dollars and for ninety of the . . . Leagues I am to receive five thousand dollars. . . . The ballance [sic] of said surveys are worth to me one hundred dollars Each—."[27]

In the first surviving description of the Dallas area in late spring and early summer, Ferris waxed eloquent on the beauty of the North Texas prairies:

> I saw in the picturesque regions there much of the wild soul-stirring scenes with which I had been so familliar [sic] in the Mountains.

23. Ferris says 118 leagues and labors. DeGolyer stated that there were 114 surveys. Efnor, *American Sketchbook*, V, 39, says 115 leagues and labors. Henson and Parmelee, *The Cartwrights*, 131, agree with the 115 league figure (509,220 acres). At any rate, the King Block, over half a million acres, was one of the largest surveys ever completed in North Texas.

24. Bogus scrip, granted by unscrupulous land boards to fictitious persons, was a serious problem in 1839, especially in the San Augustine area. Kate Efnor says that King later purchased "genuine" certificates and attempted a resurvey, but by that time it was difficult to find the original lines. Ultimately, many of his surveys were overlapped by the Peters and Mercer grants.

25. DeGolyer, "Conquest of Three Forks," 53–54.

26. Warren Ferris to John Reagan, June 10, 1840. Davis Collection.

27. Warren Ferris to Joshua Lovejoy, Aug. 20, 1840, Smith Papers; original in possession of Leland A. Smith, Mesquite, Texas. According to his memoirs, John Reagan was one of those taken ill. He spent eight weeks in bed, returning to Nacogdoches to find he had been cheated by his "supposed friend and partner," William Y. Lacy, who had stolen his field notes. The episode put Reagan in heavy debt. Reagan, *Memoirs*, 40.

Thousands of buffalo and Wild horses were everywhere to be met with. Deer and Turkeys always in view and an occasional Bear would sometimes cross our path—Wolves and Buzzards became our familliar [sic] acquaintances and in the river we found abundance of fish from minnows to 8 footers. The Prairies are boundless and present a most beautiful appearance being extremely fertile and crowned with flowers of every hue.[28]

Since Charles Ferris was still in Buffalo trying to sort out the family finances, Warren decided to invite Joshua to come to Texas; they could work a partnership, and Ferris could put his land claims in Joshua Lovejoy's name. Ferris pressed Josh to "come to Texas . . . and get a few thousand acres of Land which would be a fortune for you some ten years hence and it is now easily had."[29] Promising a welcome and a job surveying to his younger half-brother, Ferris made it clear that he was "going out for sake of profit." His personal philosophy was revealed when he told Joshua:

Money is the modern God worshipped by all the World. . . . Man is now respected, not in proportion to his learning, or his honesty no he is weighed in the ballance [sic] of dollars and cents and valued accordingly. Acquire wealth and you can accomplish anything.[30]

By inviting young Lovejoy to Texas as his partner, Ferris hoped to avoid any possible criticism of his land dealings with Dr. King; but, who was Joshua Lovejoy and what kind of partner would he make? Ferris's decision to ally himself with Josh proved to be ill-advised.

Joshua Lovejoy drew mixed reports from his family in Buffalo. He apparently left Michigan on the run from debts and sexual indiscretions. In May 1839, Charles Ferris instructed Josh to come home and work in the Buffalo post office: "Bring all your things with you and let Michigan go to hell if it pleases. . . . Don't delay then any longer but come home and leave that damned state forever—come directly."[31]

Following his older brother's advice and his own instincts for survival, Lovejoy returned to Buffalo in the fall of 1839. He worked briefly for the *Buffalonian*; but, restless for adventure, the young romantic soon headed south. He got as far as Louisville, Kentucky, before he ran out of money. In his first letter to Ferris from Kentucky, he described how he resorted to teaching in a small country school near Shelbyville. Lovejoy surprised himself, teaching subjects he had not studied since he was fourteen. He successfully bluffed his way until near the end of the term when, after expelling two boys and refusing to back down to their irate parents, he

---

28. Ferris to Lovejoy, Aug. 20, 1840. Ferris's reference to eight-foot fish in the Trinity may be an exaggeration or, perhaps, they were alligator gar.

29. Ibid.

30. Ibid.

31. Charles Ferris to Joshua Lovejoy, May 5, 1839, cited in McCausland, "Lives of the Lovejoys," 16.

lost his job. Luckily, he got another school at nearby Calloway Corners in Henry County. Lovejoy described Kentucky as "not refined" but judged it "better to be a king among hogs than a Hog among Kings." Asking Ferris of prospects in Texas, Lovejoy pronounced himself reformed of all bad habits. He was "Now a Whig and a Christian who was once a Democrat and a Dandy."[32]

Sisters Louisa and Sarah Lovejoy portrayed their brother in a favorable light. Louisa wrote to Ferris, "Brother Joshua is very handsome, very talented and one of the best fellows ever created." Sarah, who knew more of Joshua than she admitted, described the half-brother Ferris had not seen in twelve years:

> Who is he? Shall I describe him to you? Years have passed since you have seen him, the years that either model or entirely change the character of the boy. Well! With a personal appearance most remarkably prepossessing, he joins a perfection of manner rarely met—and with a temperament essentially poetick [sic], he mingles strong independent good sense, a generous heart, and a knowledge of the world singular in one so young. Are not these the elements of a great character.[33]

The family in Buffalo, Ferris in Texas, and Lovejoy in Kentucky expected Charles Ferris to depart from Buffalo any day during 1840. Joshua anticipated Charles traveling to Texas via Kentucky to bring him books and pistols, but Charles did not appear. Economic hard times, family duties, and poor health delayed his departure.[34]

Charles Ferris's situation in Buffalo was clarified in an April 1840 family letter to Texas. Charles sold his interest in the *Buffalonian* to his partner, realizing $450 which he hoped to use to travel south;[35] but he found it difficult to collect the money due him. The four-year dispute with Henry Lovejoy was settled, leaving the Ferris/Lovejoy family with three acres of prime city property which they could not sell and on which they could barely pay taxes.[36]

Charles reported that their mother, age fifty-two, looked not a bit older, Sister Sarah was "very smart," and Louisa "very pretty and . . . witty." Louisa's added note quizzed Warren, "Tell me if some bright-eyed Southern girl has not stolen your heart, or if it is as you always affirmed,

32. Joshua Lovejoy to Warren Ferris, Mar. 27, 1840. FLC, Box I, Folder 1. Josh wrote to Sarah Lovejoy in May 1840, saying that he hoped to go on to Texas for three to five years. Discouraged when his Kentucky "schollars" wrote about "Cowcumbers and Water Millions," Josh opined that their language suffered from association with Negro slaves.

33. Family letter to Warren Ferris from Buffalo, late April 1840, FLC, Box I, Folder 2.

34. Sally Lovejoy to Warren Ferris, Apr. 26, 1840, ibid.

35. McCausland, "Lives of the Lovejoys," 19.

36. Charles Ferris to Warren Ferris, family letter, late April 1840, FLC, Box I, Folder 2.

invulnerable."[37] For her part, Sarah wrote that she had seen Ferris's old acquaintance from the mountains, Sir William Drummond Stewart, and she pondered:

> Strange that men accustomed to all the luxuries and refinements of civillised [sic] life should find such charm in the boundless prairies and forests of the west, in spite of the many dangers and privations they must necessarily encounter. Yet there are many such—my brother among the number.[38]

During the fall of 1840, Sarah Lovejoy informed Joshua: "Charles is quite a literary person now. . . . He has written a prize song this summer—won the Hard Cider, Log Cabin Cup, made a speech when it was presented and had three rounds of applause."[39] It was little more than a piece of doggerel that Charles Ferris penned and Tom Nichols set to music, but the family took pleasure in the recognition won for producing the best political song to be used in William Henry Harrison's local presidential campaign. Ironically, Charles Ferris was an ardent Democrat. In his acceptance of the cup, which proved to be pewter, Ferris gave rare praise to his city:

> Buffalo, though not my birthplace, was my cradle. Hardly were the embers of its destruction cold when it became my home. . . . I watched its growth, from the weakness of infancy to its present pride and strength and beauty. . . . The Queen City of the Lakes, justly celebrated for the beauty of its position, the salubrity of its climate, the extent of its resources, the enterprise of its inhabitants, the integrity and intelligence of its citizens, and the loveliness of its ladies.[40]

Pursuit of his journalistic career led Ferris to assume editorship of *The Phalanx*, published by C. C. Bristol, the sarsaparilla manufacturer. A small paper advocating the philosophy of Charles Fourier and Albert Brisbane, it was the first daily in the United States devoted exclusively to social reform. Sarah Lovejoy wrote, "They are going to reform the world. I hope they succeed—but I have my doubts."[41] Editor and publisher were disappointed at the dearth of public interest; *The Phalanx* folded in six weeks.[42]

Sarah Lovejoy reported that Charles Ferris had also written two plays; one a farce, the other a tragedy in five acts entitled "The Ottawa Chief at

---

37. Louisa Lovejoy to Warren Ferris, dated Apr. 22, 1840, FLC, Box I, Folder 2.

38. Sarah Lovejoy to Warren Ferris, dated Apr. 26, 1840, ibid.

39. Sarah Lovejoy to Joshua Lovejoy, Sept. 17, 1840, ibid., Box I, Folder 17.

40. McCausland, "Early Buffalo Journalist," 15–16, from Charles D. Ferris's speech as reported in *Commercial Advertiser and Journal* (Buffalo), July 27, 1840.

41. McCausland, "Early Buffalo Journalist," 16–17. Charles Ferris and his half-sister Sarah Lovejoy collaborated on an article titled "Doom Averted" for Bristol's *Gazette and Herald of Health*.

42. Salisbury, "History of the Press," 206, judged the *Phalanx* was "edited by Charles D. Ferris with much ability, but the public are not philosophers, and new notions have to work their way slowly."

the Siege of Detroit." Sarah said Charles's latter work was performed once, "murdered," she claimed, when the leading actòr got drunk and forgot his lines.[43] Literary efforts brought in little cash so, although his reputation as a writer grew, Ferris was back at the post office. Sarah explained, "It is impossible for him to get enough money to go to Texas. This care is constantly wearing on his health—he has been sick all winter. Poverty is dreadful to all but rich theorists."[44]

While his brother struggled in Buffalo, Warren Ferris continued to urge Joshua Lovejoy to come to Texas. Josh was interested, but not convinced. To his sister he confided: "Warren's doing splendid—Go thou and do likewise so you will say. . . . I don't like to throw away my talents. If I fall let it be with Eyes upon me—Not in the lone forest." To "defend a city filled with Ladies—sooth them and make love—order troops—make a successful charge—return in triumph—ride thro' streets amid the thunder cheers," was more Lovejoy's style.[45] In July 1840, Lovejoy told Ferris to expect him in Texas after school ended in October: "I will try a life of adventure," Josh declared, "among the sublime western scenes a year or two, in order to gain health, energy and buoyancy. . . . I feel that Hunting and/or Surveying on the broad prairies of the West will do me good." But Warren Ferris should have been forewarned when Joshua added:

> I don't like Hard fare—I don't like fatigue—I don't like to risk my life unless there is an object of importance in the scene before me. I like the refinements of the City Life . . . —Love—Ladies. . . . I don't like to be buried in the Country.[46]

Schoolteaching or, as Ferris put it, "Teaching the young ideas to shoot" was scarcely to Lovejoy's liking. Although he had many warm friends in Kentucky, Josh was more interested in fame and fortune and judged teaching "damned thankless employment."[47] When he wrote of his ambition to join the Texas Army, Ferris cautioned:

> You speak of the Army. There was a time when I too thought that I would glory in nothing more than to land a victory but since as the Indians say I have got my belly full of military fame and Glory. I have seen hundreds bravely meet their enemies and perish and in a few short days their names were forgotten.[48]

Joshua Lovejoy came to Texas bearing an assumed name. He had tried on a number of aliases, presumably to elude Michigan problems that

43. The performance was reported in the *Commercial Advertiser and Journal* (Buffalo), Sept. 11, 1840.

44. Sarah Lovejoy's letter, May 15, 1841, FLC, Box I, Folder 1.

45. Undated note in Joshua Lovejoy's handwriting to Sarah Lovejoy with copy of Warren Ferris's letter, May 19, 1840, ibid., Box II, Folder 4.

46. Joshua Lovejoy to Warren Ferris, July 11, 1840, ibid., Box I, Folder 7.

47. Ibid.

48. Warren Ferris to Joshua Lovejoy, Aug. 20, 1840, ibid., Box I, Folder 2.

might follow him south. He wrote to Sarah Lovejoy from Michigan in 1839:

> I shall dress meanly change my name until I get money to enter Texas like a Gent. Julian FitzAlan LeRoy will answer until I get to Texas and then Clarence Linden Lovejoy or Clarence Auvergne L. will answer me thro' life. I must plot deep and consistent to sustain my name. I must not stay here long enough to be sued on my little affairs."[49]

On leaving Buffalo, Josh signed himself "John Francis" Lovejoy. In May and June 1840 from Kentucky, he was calling himself "Julian Fitzallen" Lovejoy and relating his "damned scrapes" with Kentucky girls.[50] After much experimentation, he hit on a suitable alias. When Joshua came to Texas to become the partner of his half-brother, he came under a new (and, he hoped, luckier) "Texas name," that of Clarence Avon Lovejoy.[51]

Warren Ferris's position as Nacogdoches County surveyor was up for election in September 1840. To clarify his status and open options for personal speculation in lands, Ferris did not seek reelection. The new county surveyor, A. A. Nelson, appointed Ferris his deputy, assigned to survey in the Three Forks country east of the Trinity River, including all of present Dallas and Rockwall and parts of Hunt, Kaufman, and Van Zandt Counties. At Fort Lacy west of Nacogdoches, Ferris began preparations for a fall expedition to the Three Forks. In a candid letter to Charles Ferris, he listed his assets and liabilities: "Should anything happen to me. . . . If I do not return . . . Nelson has a little book containing my accounts whilst in office." These included land scrip for fourteen sections of 640 acres each, transferred to Ferris by King and Nelson, and his one-twelfth interest in the Warwick development. Signing "Yours till death," Ferris pledged his brother, "I shall if successful this trip quit venturing and lead some less dangerous and more quiet life."[52] With John H. Reagan, several chainbearers,[53] hunters, and guards, Ferris set out the second week in October on the Cherokee Road to Neches saline, then west on the Kickapoo Trace to King's Fort.

---

49. Joshua Lovejoy to Sarah Lovejoy, Apr. 22, 1839, ibid., Box II, Folder 21.

50. Joshua Lovejoy to Charles Ferris, May 30 and June 8, 1840, ibid., Box I, Folder 7. In the latter, Josh wrote of his failure to break an engagement and win a lady: "by God to have a woman fall into my mouth like a ripe peach and then not be able to swallow her . . . "

51. Both Clarence and Avon are towns of Western New York.

52. Warren Ferris to Charles Ferris, Oct. 9, 1840, FLC, Box I, Folder 6.

53. DeGolyer listed the following as chainbearers on Ferris's expeditions into the Three Forks: D. M. and Maury Crist, R. R. West, Jordan Hamm, Robert and J. B. Nash, J. Burris, T. (or F.) Barnes, William Cooke, James Carr, John Campbell, William Aiken, a McNeill, and a Lindsay. DeGolyer Collection, III, 9. Chainmen were often seeking land themselves or were relatives of persons for whom surveys were made.

One of the chief problems for early travelers to North Central Texas was the lack of accessibility. An absence of any roads or reliable river transport seriously delayed settlement. Immigrants traveled through Louisiana via the Opelousas Road, up the Red River to Natchitoches, across the Sabine at Gaines Ferry; or they moved southwest from Fort Smith, Arkansas, along the Texas Road via Pecan Point and Jonesboro on the Red River. Either route then required an arduous overland journey along Indian traces from Nacogdoches or Clarksville. During the 1830s, Capt. Henry M. Shreve removed a "raft" of debris that blocked navigation of the upper Red River, making it navigable during high water between December and July.[54] Holland Coffee's trading post on the Red River near present-day Denison, Texas, then became the main gateway to north central Texas. Two other frontier outposts were Forts Warren and Inglish in present Fannin County, established by Abel Warren and Bailey Inglish in 1836 and 1837. An alternative to migration via the Red River was coastal steamer from New Orleans to Galveston, followed by a slow overland trip to Fort Houston on the Trinity.

In an effort to encourage immigration to North Texas, the Congress of the Republic in 1840 passed a Military Road Act, designed to open a road from the new capital Austin, north through Waco on the Brazos River, by the Three Forks of the Trinity, to Coffee's trading post on the Red River.[55] West of the road a series of forts was to be located to protect incoming settlers from Indians. To this end, Robert Sloan and an advanced party of road surveyors, followed by Col. William G. Cooke's main party, were in the Three Forks region in the fall of 1840.

Ferris's fall surveying expedition operated out of Fort King or Kingsboro, Dr. William P. King's stockade on a tributary of the East Fork of the Trinity[56] near present-day Kaufman, Texas. The fort, fifty miles upstream from Fort Houston, was the jumping-off point for surveying activities during 1840—1842. It consisted of four cabins surrounded by a wooden stockade enclosing three-quarters of an acre. From the frail fortress, a garrison of a dozen men defied the prairie Indians. It was the oldest permanent white settlement in the Three Forks region and was never abandoned during this period of frontier advancement.[57]

---

54. Edith McCall, *Conquering the Rivers: Henry Miller Shreve and the Navigation of America's Inland Waterways* (Baton Rouge: Louisiana State University Press, 1984), 196–232. Shreve and his engineers worked each spring season, from 1833 to 1839, to clear the debris which blocked the river.

55. Lamar Papers, II, #970. The idea for the proposed road was also reported in the *Telegraph and Texas Register* (Houston), Sept. 2, 1840.

56. Kings Creek is a tributary of Cedar Creek which is a tributary of the East Fork of the Trinity River.

57. Reagan, *Memoirs*, 41, described King's Fort, the only human habitation he saw between October 1840 and April 1841, as having only one house where lived four or five men. Kingsboro is sometimes spelled "Kingsborough." It once appears "Kingsport."

From King's Fort, Warren Ferris's surveying party advanced to White Rock Creek to resume where they had quit surveying the King Block in July. Over the next eighteen months, most of present Dallas County, east of the Trinity River, was surveyed. In accordance with his instructions, Ferris located league and labor "donations" for veterans of the Texas Revolution. Few of these men actually came to live on this land; some was taken up by their descendants, but much was sold, exchanging land scrip for cash from speculators or newly arrived immigrants. The first numbered survey in what would be Dallas County was a large block east of modern Ferguson Road, in the name of Adolphus Rieman.[58]

As he extended the northwest-southeast lines of the King Block, Ferris determined the direction of Dallas streets which, except in the central business district, follow the lines of his surveys. During late October, Ferris's men worked northwest up both sides of White Rock Creek to a point about a quarter of a mile south of the present intersection of Coit and Midway/Alpha Roads in North Dallas. Ferris paid his board back in Nacogdoches by surveying several plots for the Hyde family. He laid out a half-section for his employer A. A. Nelson; and, for himself, he surveyed three sections of land in the name of his half-brother, "C. A." Lovejoy. These were Lovejoy Surveys #8 and #9, now covered by White Rock Lake, and Survey #4, the present Forest Hills Addition.

As Ferris worked on upper White Rock Creek, Colonel Cooke's First Regiment of the Texas Regular Army was hacking its way through bois d'arc thickets to the southwest. The soldiers inched up the west bank of the Trinity to a point near the old Dowdy Ferry site and present Hutchins. Hunger, fatigue, and illness took their toll. Cooke was forced to leave his wagons, the sick, and forty guards under command of Lt. Col. Adam Clendenning while he, with a few men, pressed on to the Anglo settlements on the Red River. The sick party, camped on a wooded elevation of the west bank, waited nearly a month for Cooke to return with provisions. Starving, they ate their mules and horses before Clendenning decided to withdraw. They abandoned their equipment, buried their ammunition, and fell back to the Falls of the Brazos near present Marlin, Texas.[59]

Meanwhile Colonel Cooke cut his way through the dense thickets of White Rock and East Fork bottoms. Cooke, although a graduate of the Virginia Military Institute and veteran of the War of 1812, had little experience in western exploration. He hoped to reach the Red River settlements in two days; on the tenth day after leaving the sick camp, his

---

58. Or, Adolfus Reinman, a veteran of San Jacinto, whose land was settled by one of his sons.

59. A. Clendenning to Hugh McLeod, Nov. 18, 1840, Army Papers (Archives, Texas State Library, Austin; cited hereafter as TSL). Ironically, a relief party sent south by Cooke arrived on the Trinity two days after Clendenning's withdrawal.

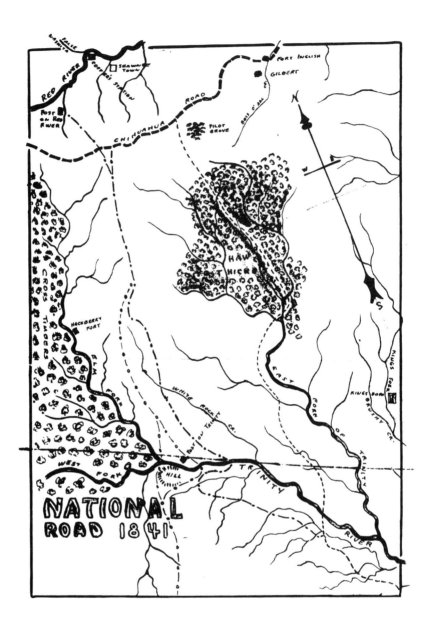

Texas Military or National Road sketch by Homer DeGolyer, showing the route of Capt. William G. Preston and the supply wagons up Preston's Trail to Coffee's Station on the Red River and Col. William G. Cooke's route through the thickets to Fort Inglish (Bonham). *Courtesy the DeGolyer Library, Southern Methodist University, Dallas.*

men struck the Chihuahua Trail which led them to Inglish's trading post.[60]

In late October or early November, Ferris's surveying party, which entered the area from the southeast, crossed the soldiers' path near present-day Mesquite, Texas; but, if Ferris knew the Texas Army was in the Three Forks region, he never mentioned it in his letters or reminiscences. Perhaps he thought their trail had been made by Indians. During November, Ferris and his men surveyed the Robert Moore plot, bounded by the modern Dallas streets of Grand, Henderson, Junius, and Monte Vista. They conducted further surveys in early December along upper White Rock Creek in the present Bachman Lake/Love Field area. Returning to Fort King in December, Ferris ran a series of surveys in Kaufman County and on the headwaters of the Sabine River in present Hunt County. Severe winter weather struck Texas that year. Ferris reported snow six inches deep on Christmas. In early January 1841, near what is now Wills Point in Van Zandt County, he and John Reagan parted company, with Ferris heading back to Nacogdoches for supplies and Reagan traveling alone to King's Fort.

In his memoirs, Reagan described his arduous forty-mile journey through Indian country during a sudden Texas "norther." It rained all afternoon, and in the timber during the night, his horse bogged so that he dismounted and led him. His rifle and one pistol were soaked. In the confusing darkness and rain, Reagan found himself traveling in circles; disoriented, he fell down to sleep. When he awoke before dawn, a fierce north wind was blowing and ice had formed on his blanket. Reagan huddled by a small campfire until daylight; then he saddled his horse and headed for Fort King. Luckily he saw no Indians.[61]

Meanwhile, Warren Ferris returned to Nacogdoches to find that he had a new partner. In late December 1840, "Clarence Avon" Lovejoy arrived in Texas. Lovejoy joined Ferris in the surveying expeditions of 1841. They completed the survey of the King Block and ran the Cherokee Line, the old northwestern boundary of the Cherokee Reserve, between Nacogdoches and Fannin Counties. The northern boundary of the former Cherokee Reserve ran west from the head of the Neches River, near the site of the Cherokee battlefield, to the northwest corner of present Hunt County.

---

60. William G. Cooke's report to Secretary of War Branch T. Archer, Nov. 14, 1840, reported in the *Texas Sentinel* (Austin), Dec. 5, 1840, and the *Telegraph and Texas Register* (Houston), Dec. 16, 1840. DeGolyer Collection., XVIII, 8. On their return trip to Austin, Cooke's party located three crossings of the Trinity in the Dallas area; one at the old Record crossing, a second at the Kickapoo crossing, and another near the old Miller Ferry. He also sited two forts; Fort Johnson on the Red River and another outpost at Cedar Springs near the Three Forks. Due to economic constraints, neither was garrisoned in 1840.

61. Reagan, *Memoirs*, 41–43.

Field notes of the expedition state the survey was made in January 1841, "commencing at the southeast corner of Fannin County. . . . Said corner being a post oak blazed on four sides about twenty miles north, of the Sabine River in open prairie, a solitary or lone tree."[62] Ferris mentioned the distances between streams and their approximate widths. He noted the crossing of the old Caddo Trace to the Cross Timbers which passed through present northeast Dallas County. This time, at a point about a mile east of White Rock Creek, Ferris indicated the route of the National Road to the Red River. After crossing White Rock Creek, Ferris outlined the borders of the Elm Fork of the Trinity extending into present Denton County. Ferris's notes, also dated January 1841, document the survey of about twenty-five sections of land in central Van Zandt County east of present Canton, Texas.

Field notes are mute on the hardships faced by the surveyors on this winter sortie into North Texas. The real character of the ordeal is better revealed in Joshua Lovejoy's letter to friend Tom Denny back in Kentucky, describing his first frontier adventure. "I have just returned from the Woods—the Wilderness," Lovejoy reported. The surveyors started their work on the headwaters of the Neches River and moved northwest to the headwaters of the Sabine. Early January cold and rain gave way to delightful March weather. All was going well until:

> We crossed Sabine and commenced running the county line of Nacogdoches and Fannin Counties—Crossed Bois D'arc [East Fork] and now found ourselves where the Indians had been . . . and now commenced our Starving . . . game all run off our Hunters could kill nothing. It rained all the while. Every creek was a mile wide.[63]

The small party of only sixteen men realized their perilous situation; they were 200 miles from the settlements, with fresh Indian signs all about. The morning of March 21 they spotted five Indians on a distant prairie hill. "Some of our men were not anxious to go on," according to Lovejoy; but his brother Warren stepped forward and the force of his example caused the rest to do the same. Amid a heavy storm of rain, hail, and wind, they reached the Elm Fork of Trinity near present Trinity Mills where they found a deserted Indian village.

The survey was successfully completed, but there was still the return trek to Nacogdoches. Again the surveyors faced a deadly combination of hostile Indians and inclement weather. By this time, the Bois D'arc Fork was two or three miles wide, so full of brush and debris that it was impossible to

---

62. Warren Ferris's field notes of the Cherokee Line, filed Sept. 14, 1841 (GLO). Also a voucher for payment to Ferris of $182, at $3 per mile surveyed. Ferris was still trying to collect payment for this survey on Aug. 15, 1843, when he wrote to Land Commissioner Thomas W. Ward from Ft. Houston pleading "a state of pecuniary embarrassment" (GLO).

63. Joshua (C. A.) Lovejoy to Tom Denny, June 1, 1841, FLC, Box II, Folder 10.

cross by raft. Four days were spent, half wading, half swimming neck deep in water, before they succeeded in getting the horses and part of the men across to dry land on the east bank. In the exertion, all the powder and firearms were soaked. At this critical juncture, the group that had crossed the river was attacked by Indians, and one man was killed before they could retreat to the main party on the west bank. Lovejoy described the pitiful situation:

> We had now been several days without Eating and had starved more or less 2 weeks, and as we had no ammunition to kill game if we could have found it. We were forced to kill a Horse—well we eat [sic] it and in 5 or 6 days reached the settlements.[64]

Proud of surviving nine months in the wilds, Joshua Lovejoy judged that surveying was pretty well "used up." He and Warren had located rich lands and planned to soon quit the surveying business. Despite the hardships, Josh reported himself fat and fit; he projected a return to Buffalo via Kentucky in the fall, after which he would take up land in his "adopted Republic" of Texas. There would be one last surveying expedition in June and July of 1841.[65]

Joshua must have written a similar letter to his sister Sarah in Buffalo, commenting on Warren Ferris's courageous leadership in the face of danger. Sarah agreed that, on rereading Warren's journal of his Rocky Mountain adventures, she too was impressed that Warren had again and again avoided certain death; "a thousand times he has been preserved . . . by the merest chance." Sarah was amazed that Joshua was an actor on the Texas scene. She wondered that one "so delicate" as Josh had not perished in the face of danger, cold, hard work, and starvation, but had survived, even thrived, all in the pursuit of wealth.[66]

Sarah Lovejoy reported that Louisa was enrolled in dancing school. The two young women had "danced thro' the cold season," attending balls and meeting friends aplenty. Although dressed plainly, according to Sarah, the Lovejoys were proclaimed "the most beautiful and sensible girls" in the place by Dr. Gibbs, cousin of Millard Fillmore.[67] Louisa's beauty was her passport, and Sarah pretended not to mind that her younger sister received the bulk of the attention.

At the request of school superintendent Oliver G. Steele, Charles Ferris produced a moral treatise entitled "The Balance Sheet." In ninety-two pages, it purported to instruct Buffalo youth in the advantages of right living and the evil consequences of crime.[68] Sarah felt that despite

---

64. Ibid.
65. Ibid.
66. Sarah Lovejoy to Joshua Lovejoy, May 16, 1841, ibid., Box I, Folder 17.
67. Ibid.
68. McCausland, "Early Buffalo Journalist," 17.

his literary successes, Charles was discouraged. Forced to supplement his income with part-time work at the Buffalo post office, his mental and physical health eroded under the strain of persistent family responsibility.

As spring came to North Texas, Indians boldly raided Anglo settlements in Fannin County. Gen. Edward H. Tarrant, who succeeded Dyer as commander of the Fourth Brigade, Texas Militia, called up volunteers to rendezvous at Coffee's Station on the Red River. The troops marched south through the Cross Timbers toward the Three Forks country, but they found only deserted Indian villages which they refrained from burning for fear of sending up an alarm. Ranging out as far west as the Brazos River and finding no hostiles, Tarrant's force turned eastward.

On May 22, 1841, the militia made a surprise attack on an Indian camp east of present Fort Worth near Village Creek (modern Arlington). Many of the warriors were out on a buffalo hunt and only about half of the 225 lodges were occupied; but the troops fell on the village with a fury, taking no prisoners. Twelve Indians were killed. The rest fled. The Texians suffered only one casualty, John B. Denton, a frontier preacher and Indian-fighter for whom Denton County was named.

Although the "battle" of Village Creek was actually indecisive, Tarrant proclaimed it a great victory, declaring he had located the "depot for the stolen horses from our frontier and the home of the horrible savages who have murdered our families."[69] Damning evidence included good guns, abundant ammunition, kettles, axes, swords and saddles, even feather beds and bedsteads. The camp apparently was occupied by remnants of several tribes: Keechies, Cherokees, Caddoes, Creeks, Seminoles, Wacos, Kickapoos, and Anadarkos. Before the Indians could regroup, Tarrant withdrew his men to the prairies east of the Trinity River. As they pulled back to the settlements, word came that support troops from Nacogdoches and Fort Houston were mustering to join the men of Red River and Fannin Counties in a final drive against the Indians of the Three Forks.

While Tarrant's men roamed the Cross Timbers in search of hostiles, Warren Ferris was able to peacefully survey the Rowlett Creek region northeast of present-day Garland, making the Howard, Alvaredo, and Crist surveys. During this respite from Indian raids, in June 1841, Ferris completed the surveys of Thomas Lagow; John, William, and Crawford Grigsby; James A. Sylvester; Miles Bennett; and Dickerson Parker. These surveys came to constitute the major portion of modern Dallas.

---

69. DeGolyer, "Conquest of Three Forks," 67–71. His account is based on the official report of William N. Porter to the Secretary of War, July 5, 1841. Army Papers (TSL). The muster roll for this expedition shows, besides John B. Denton, Holland Coffee and Jefferson "Big Foot" Wallace, as well as Capt. Mabel Gilbert and Alexander Webb, early Dallas settlers. Photocopies of muster rolls, DeGolyer Collection, XVIII, 8, from certified rolls in GLO.

The Lagow survey of a league and labor spanned White Rock Creek, encompassing much of modern Southeast Dallas, including the Texas State Fairgrounds and Tennison Park. Adjoining the Lagow survey on the northwest was the John Grigsby survey, bounded by present Grand, Lamar, Turtle Creek, and Henderson Streets, which includes part of the Dallas central business district. The Sylvester and William Grigsby surveys lay still farther northwest and contain present-day Reverchon Park, Parkland Hospital, and the Oak Lawn area. Crawford Grigsby's survey, next to the northwest, encompassed the old Cedar Springs settlement near present Loma Alto and Lemmon Avenue. Miles Bennett's survey joined the northwest line of the Crawford Grigsby survey between present Maple and Gilbert Streets. Finally, to the far northwest, Ferris laid the Parker survey which contains today's Love Field airport, Bachman Lake, and the old Letot settlement.[70]

As Texians mustered at Forts Inglish and Houston for a final drive against the Indians of the Three Forks, a "volunteer" writing in the San Augustine *Redlander* defended the expedition's motives. He disputed allegations that the military objective was "protection of the surveyors and the benefit of Dr. King's location." The writer asserted that the expedition was designed to break up the tribes, destroy their corn, and drive them out of the country; but, he admitted, the sortie also would give the militiamen "fair opportunity of examining for themselves the rich and luxuriant soil . . . making selections to suit them."[71]

Already in the field surveying, Warren Ferris, his half-brother "C. A." Lovejoy, and John Reagan were among the first volunteers to reach King's Fort. Between July 17 and 20, 1841, several hundred men answered twin calls of patriotism and greed. Early arrivals were stunned by a daring Indian raid on the fort on July 17. At five in the morning, the alarm went up. Some twenty-five brazen, well-mounted Indians raised a war whoop, swept close by at full gallop, and drove off the horses which had been tethered outside the stockade. So surprised were the Texians that few shots were fired.[72] Col. Jim Smith arrived on the 19th and organized the men from San Augustine, Nacogdoches, Houston, and Robertson Counties into

---

70. DeGolyer delineated the surveys as they relate to modern Dallas streets. "Conquest of Three Forks," 71–72. See also Sam Street's 1900 map of Dallas. Many of these surveys were for veterans of the Battle of San Jacinto who never took up their land. James A. Sylvester, an Ohio man who led the party which captured Santa Anna, traded his certificate for a mule and left Texas. Some of the claimants, like the Grigsbys, lived in the Ft. Houston area.

71. San Augustine *Red-Lander*, July 1, 1841, called for volunteers and, on August 3, 1841, defended the motives of the expedition.

72. Reported by a correspondent of the San Augustine *Red-Lander*, Aug. 3, 1841. The same story was carried by the *Texas Sentinel* (Austin), Sept. 2, 1841. McLean (ed.), *Papers Concerning Robertson's Colony*, XVIII, 329–330.

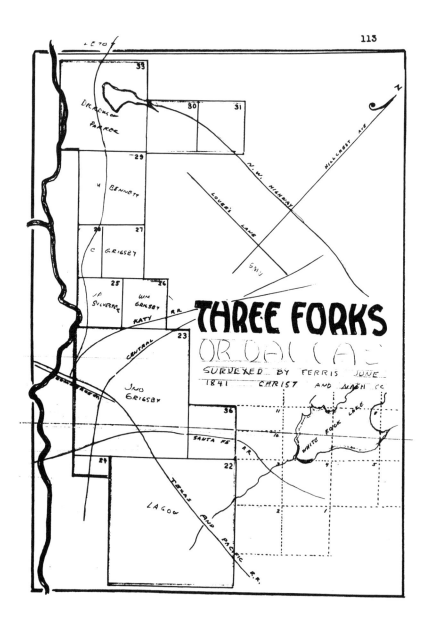

Homer DeGolyer's sketch of Warren A. Ferris's surveys (1840–1841) at the Three Forks of the Trinity, relating the surveys to modern streets, railroads, and White Rock Lake. *Courtesy the DeGolyer Library, Southern Methodist University, Dallas.*

four companies; then they followed the fresh trail of the raiders to the Kickapoo Crossing of the Trinity.

The militia swam their horses and rafted their baggage across the river to camp on the wide western prairie near a cool spring, probably Kidd Springs in present Oak Cliff. Here the Indian trail widened, evidencing the passage of large herds of buffalo and many Indians. On July 22, the Texians lounged in camp, killing a "beeve" or steer for rations and cutting "bee trees" for honey. Smith dispatched an express of three men to ride north in search of General Tarrant's Red River troops. He also sent out a spy company which was to locate the Indian camp and cornfields.

Capt. John L. Hall led the scouts, which included Ferris, Reagan, George Lacy, Samuel and Isaac Bean, John L. and Hughes Burton, a Creek Indian named Chaxty, and three others.[73] When the spy company returned to the encampment on the evening of July 24, they had located the Indian town on Village Creek, a tributary of the West Fork of the Trinity. At midnight Smith addressed the men and ordered an immediate attack on the village. The troops took up a thirty-mile march in double columns across the rolling prairies and reached Village Creek about noon, attacking the camp from two sides. They found a deserted village. The Indians had gone, abandoning their cornfields and supplies.[74]

Smith ordered the Indian village and fields torched. He learned shortly, from General Tarrant, that the Village Creek Indians had removed their families to the Brazos where some 300 warriors of numerous tribes were said to be fortifying a position. Tarrant and the Red River and Robertson County men took up the chase, but Smith withdrew his men to the east bank of the Trinity. The East Texans returned to Nacogdoches and San Augustine, while the Houston County troops went down the west side of the Trinity and crossed to Fort Houston. Thus the entire Three Forks region was scoured of hostile Indians so that all hindrance to settlement was removed.

"C. A." Lovejoy wrote Tom Denny his account of the Village Creek expedition:

> on the 10 of July I joined an Expedition against an Indian town near 300 miles North West of Nacogdoches on the West fork of the Rio Trinidad. We passed over the ground where we were in the spring surveying and after a toilsome journey in intensely hot weather we reached the town—charged in it—but found it deserted. . . . traitors undoubtedly having given them information of our intended expedition. We passed over some beautiful and fertil [sic] Prairie Country.[75]

73. Frances T. Ingmire, *Texas Frontiersmen (1839–1860), Minutemen, Militia, Home Guard and Indian Fighters* (St. Louis: Ingmire Publications, 1982). Based on muster rolls, Army Papers (TSL).

74. Brown, *Indian Wars*, 85–88, gives a detailed account of the Village Creek campaign.

75. Joshua Lovejoy to Tom Denny, Mar. 1, 1842, from Crockett, Houston Co., sixty miles west of Nacogdoches. FLC, Box II, Folder 10.

Returning militia volunteers reported that the Three Forks country was "an immense region of the most beautiful and richest soil in Texas; abounding in prairies . . . covered with all varieties of grasses, . . . thousands of buffalo and wild horses."[76] The race was on to take up the rich prairie land which would be Dallas County. Surveyors began to work up the west bank of the Trinity from Fort Houston. John Neely Bryan, a bachelor clerk from Holland Coffee's trading post on the Red River, having heard of the ford across the Trinity, rode down to look over the area. Bryan selected a site on a bluff overlooking the Kickapoo Crossing as a promising location for a trading post and town.[77] About the same time, Texas legislators negotiated a series of land grants in North Texas to the Peters Company of Louisville, Kentucky.[78]

After mustering out of the army at Kingsboro, Warren Ferris returned first to San Augustine and then to Nacogdoches where he attended a political debate between Houston and Burnet in which, he felt, "old Sam got the worst of it."[79] In mid-August, Dr. King and his new partner John P. Martin passed through Nacogdoches en route back to Mississippi in preparation for settlement of the Three Forks. Adolphus Sterne reported, "Doctor King and Judge Martin returned from Kingsborough, the latter is well pleased with the Country and is to return with his family in a short time."[80]

From Nacogdoches, Ferris headed for Crockett in Houston County where he visited his friend Isaac Burton who had recently moved there. While visiting Burton, Warren met a charming young lady from Illinois, Melinda G. Cook. In September 1841, Warren Ferris married Melinda, and six months later (April 1842) "Clarence Avon" Lovejoy married Melinda's sister Mary Cook. Apparently both young men, having staked their land claims, intended settling down to less dangerous pursuits than enduring miserable weather and dodging hostile Indians. Ferris proudly took his new bride to meet his Nacogdoches friends that fall. Sterne made

---

76. San Augustine *Red-Lander*, Aug. 3, 1841, and *Texas Sentinel* (Austin), Sept. 2, 1841, in McLean (ed.), *Papers Concerning Robertson's Colony*, XVIII, 329–330.

77. Bryan may have been in the area as early as 1840. James Beeman's memoirs (DHS) relate that Bryan told the Beeman family of his plan to establish a town at a "site he selected on Three Forks of Trinity." He showed them a penciled map when he met them at a campground in Bowie County, Texas, in 1840. Historian A. C. Greene argues that Bryan intended building a town, rather than a trading post, from the outset.

78. The original contract for the Peters Colony was granted February 4, 1841; three subsequent contracts were made in 1842 and 1843 (GLO); also Colonization Papers (TSL).

79. McDonald, *Hurrah for Texas*, 56. Houston and Burnet were engaged in a bitter, mud-slinging campaign for the presidency of the Republic. Sterne noted on Aug. 29, 1841, "W.A. Ferris returned from San Augustine."

80. Ibid., 54. Henson and Parmelee, *The Cartwrights*, 131, state that King's second wife and his children by a first marriage were living in San Augustine when King and Martin went back to Mississippi for other settlers.

a diary entry on October 2, 1841: "Mr. W. A. Ferriss got married during his transit to Houston County;" the following day he wrote, "introduced to Mrs. Ferriss, find my Friend Ferriss has a good taste, if her face is the mirror in which is reflected the Heart—she will no doubt make him a good wife—They spent the Evening at my house."[81]

In late October, Ferris and Lovejoy resumed surveying along upper White Rock Creek in the present Vickery area. It was to be their last expedition. They were out until January 1842, completing work in southeast Dallas County around the modern Kleberg and Seagoville communities. Ferris was at the height of his strong determination to gain wealth through land; his motivation was revealed in a poignant love letter written to his new bride from a cold, lonely surveyor's camp on the East Fork of the Trinity:

> My Dear Wife—How endearing the word I have just written and how different are my feelings now than they were when I was alone . . . without any one to love to console me when misfortune bore heavily upon me. . . . I find myself in possession of an Angel, a Treasure that occupies my thought, and Spurs me on to exertion because Her happiness is the grand object of my future hopes and present Labor. . . . My heart, though absent myself will be ever with you and be sure time lags heavily when I am absent from you, hence you may conclude that I will make that disagreeable interval as brief as possible. . . . Yr. loving husband, Warren.[82]

September of 1841 marked a turning point in the fortunes of Warren Ferris and in the history of the Three Forks area which would become Dallas County. En route to Mississippi, William King—speculator and town builder—died of yellow fever. Adolphus Sterne judged that King's death would set the settlement of the Three Forks back five years.[83] Gone were the dreams of Warwick and Ferris's hopes for an easy fortune.

Events were moving rapidly, with a number of interests converging on the Three Forks. While Ferris surveyed east of the Trinity, surveyor B. J. Chambers moved up the west bank from Fort Houston. In November, the

---

81. McDonald, *Hurrah for Texas*, 63.

82. Warren A. Ferris to Melinda G. Cook Ferris, Nov. 7, 1841. Smith Papers; original in possession of Leland Smith of Mesquite, Texas; copy in FLC, Box I, Folder 3. In this letter, Ferris refers to William (perhaps William S. Cook) who is with him as a chainbearer; mentions his half-brother "Clarence" who is with him and will return with him to Crockett; and inquires of the health of Melinda's sisters Mary and Susan, and that "Old Gent," Melinda's father.

83. McDonald, *Hurrah for Texas*, 64, entry of Oct. 8, 1841: after reading of King's death reported in the Vicksburg *Sentinel*, Sept. 18, 1841, Stern wrote: "news was received that Doctor King the founder of Kingsborough and Judge Martin, who lately visited this Country, died at Vicksbourgh [sic], on the River Mississippi of Yellow Fever—this is a great loss to this Part of Texas. Doctor King was an interprising [sic] man and the Country near the three forks of Trinity will be trown [sic] back at least five years unless some very strong effort is made by his Heirs or successors to carry on the work which he begun . . . "

Peters Colony was extended to include most of the area. Veterans of the summer Indian campaign came down from Fannin County to establish a stockade (Bird's Fort) on the West Fork of the Trinity near the charred Indian camp at Village Creek.[84] About that same time, John Neely Bryan and party of hunters[85] pitched their tents on the Trinity bluff above Kickapoo Crossing.

Warren A. Ferris was the first Anglo-American to extensively explore the Three Forks; he surveyed most of the land east of the Trinity—including all or part of Kaufman, Van Zandt, Hunt, Rockwall, Dallas, Collin, and Denton Counties; his surveys determined the physical layout of urban Dallas County. Yet his name would be little remembered. Due to the untimely death of William P. King, it would be John Neely Bryan who would promote and name the town "Dallas." In early 1842, Bryan visited Bird's Fort and convinced the settlers there to relocate at his superior location on the bluff at the ford across the river. It would be Bryan, rather than King and Ferris, who would fulfill the dream of town-building at the "head of navigation" on the Trinity.[86]

84. Jonathan Bird led a party that included Alexander Webb, Capt. Mabel Gilbert, and the Beeman family.

85. James B. Moore, J. H. Mais, and Joseph Hancock were with Bryan. In the Dallas *Morning News*, Jan. 21, 1899, Hancock recalled the hunters' camp. Surveyor B. J. Chambers who visited Bryan's camp described it as a country of "wild deer and wild men," Dallas *Morning News*, Oct. 12, 1888.

86. Hogan, *Texas Republic*, 87–93, comments on the mania for establishing towns between 1837–1843; each embryo town amounted to little more than a survey, a few cabins, and a claim to be head of river navigation. See also W. Eugene Hollen and Ruth L. Butler (eds.), *William Bollaert's Texas* (1844; reprint, Norman: University of Oklahoma Press, 1956), 205, describing his 1842 trip downriver on the Trinity where "on nearly all the Bluffs speculators have marked out town sites, with high-sounding names."

7

PERSONAL TRAGEDY

HAPPILY MARRIED TO MELINDA COOK, Warren Ferris spent the spring of 1842 on her family's farm near Crockett in Houston County. Despite the disappointment of his failed dream to achieve easy wealth in the speculative venture at the Three Forks, Ferris was still determined to make a success for his family. Since surveying opportunities were scarce, he tried his hand at farming and found it to his liking.

Texas experienced its most difficult year in 1842. The government was impoverished, economic growth stymied, the populace discouraged. The future of the Republic seemed doubtful. Mexico did not recognize Texas independence,[1] and now Santa Anna, returned to power in Mexico, threatened to punish Texians for the ill-fated Santa Fe expedition. Sam Houston, recently wed to Baptist Margaret Lea and drinking only cold water, was again president of the Republic.[2] His policies were as cautious as Lamar's had been reckless.

Congress moved to Houston City and later Washington-on-the-Brazos, pulling back from the exposed location in Austin, but, in what was dubbed "the Archive War," the irate citizens of Austin refused to give up the government documents. When Houston vetoed Congressional demands for a preemptory strike against Mexico, all the old charges of cowardice and incompetence were revived. Warren Ferris, echoing anti-Houston sentiment, described the dismal Texas situation to his brother Charles in Buffalo:

> Our experimental government has failed. . . . Emigration has ceased. The people are barely able to get the absolute necessaries of life . . . nine out of ten cannot pay their taxes. . . . The Post Office dept. has failed . . . *discontinued the mail.* The present threatening attitude of Mexico prevents any opulent farmers from emigrating to Texas, and the outrageous proceedings of the . . . regulators or Moderators of Shelby County has partially destroyed our character abroad.[3]

---

1. Santa Anna repudiated the Treaty of Velasco (1836), signed while he was a prisoner of war, and Mexico refused to recognize Texas's independent status until forced to do so in 1848.

2. Despite old political charges of drunkenness, cowardice, and immorality brought against him, "Old Sam" defeated Burnet three to one and was reelected president in September 1841. DeBruhl, *Sword of San Jacinto*, 280–283, recounts the bitter campaign waged largely through partisan newspapers.

3. Warren Ferris to Charles Ferris, May 10, 1842, from Crockett, Texas, FLC, Box I, Folder 6. Ferris refers to Mexican raids into South Texas in March 1842 and to vigilanteeism in East Texas (1840–1844), the Regulator/Moderator War.

Ferris notified his family of his marriage to Melinda, "a young lady of Paris, Illinois, 23 years of age, good looking and educated but poor" and of the expected birth of their first child. On his plans for the future, he wrote, "We have not been able to raise a dollar in cash since '38. . . . Surveying is *down*; land is *not worth* surveying. . . . I intend to still survey when times get better."

Like others, Ferris was forced into farming by the prolonged depression, making the best of difficult times. Describing the Cook farm where he had been working "like a Trojan" all spring, Ferris reported that he and his father-in-law had twenty-five acres under fence, owned a yoke of oxen, wagon, horse, mule, five or six cows, and hogs. Twenty acres were in corn, beans, pumpkins, and watermelons so they would not starve. Despite his recent reverses, Ferris vowed, "*I have land that I will keep till doom day* [sic] *or make something out of it.* . . . notwithstanding the hard times . . . [Texans] are unanimous in their determination to maintain their independence. . . . We will be free," he asserted, "whether we have a Govt. or not."[4] Ferris hoped for peace with Mexico, annexation to the United States, and the return of golden times in Texas.

Ferris toyed with the idea of moving to his land on White Rock Creek and surveying for the Peters Company. In May 1842, he visited the Three Forks area, "found Colonel John N. Bryan and three or four others encamped. . . . [T]here was at that time one solitary cabin constructed. Captain Gilbert made a small crop of corn in the river bottom. . . . "[5] Settlers from Bird's Fort, including Mabel Gilbert's family and the Beeman clan, had joined Bryan. The settlement consisted only of Bryan's tent and the log cabin erected by Captain Gilbert. Bryan traded furs or hides for supplies at Coffee's Station on the Red River or Fort Inglish in Fannin County; from his lean-to shelter he sold whiskey and ammunition to any welcome passersby. When a spring flood washed away the hunters' camp and corn crop, Bryan moved to higher ground on the bluff. Gilbert took his family to the west bank of the river where he located on the Military Road near Kidd Springs; the Gilberts stayed only a year before returning to Fannin County. John Beeman and his son James moved their families about four miles east of Bryan's to White Rock Creek where they built a stockade for protection against marauding Indians.[6] The land claims of both Bryan and Beeman were tenuous since they overlapped the Grigsby and Lagow surveys made by Warren Ferris in 1841, and they also fell within the newly extended Peters Colony grant.

W. S. Peters and associates of Louisville, Kentucky, had been astounded when the Fifth Texas Congress authorized an agreement with their

---

4. Ibid.

5. Ferris, "Reminiscence," Dallas *Herald*, Sept. 2, 1871.

6. An interesting description of that first year was given by William H. "Billy" Beeman to the Dallas *Mercury*, Feb. 23, 1884. DeGolyer Collection.

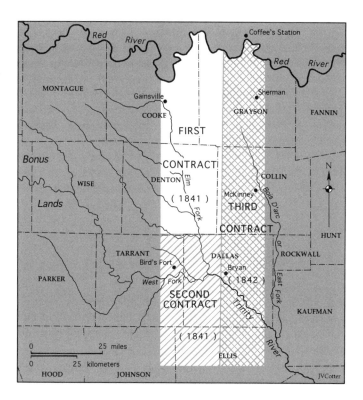

Map of the Peters Colony, showing three extensions (1841–1842) of the contract as related to modern counties. *Map by John V. Cotter.*

agent in 1841. The empresarios were ill-prepared to follow up on their contract to bring 600 families in Texas in three years. Although many Texians, including land speculators, strongly objected to a return to the empresario system, President Houston assured voters that only frontier lands would be open to contract, serving the dual purpose of opening the area and creating a buffer against Indian raids. The poll tax on expected newcomers would boost the income of the bankrupt Republic. Proponents of the empresario grant viewed the gift of land to a private company as "pump-priming," a temporary measure to encourage immigration.[7] Almost immediately it became evident that the original grant in North Texas did not contain enough unallocated land to accommodate 600 families; the Peters Company requested, and the Texas government granted, extended time and territory.[8]

---

7. Seymour V. Connor, "Land Speculation in Texas," *Southwest Review*, 39 (Spring, 1954), 140.

8. Seymour V. Connor, *The Peters Colony of Texas: A History and Biographical Sketches of the Early Settlers* (Austin: Texas State Historical Association, 1959), is the authoritative work on the subject.

In the spring of 1842, Samuel Browning, son-in-law of W. S. Peters, began surveying from the colony headquarters twelve miles north of Bryan's on the Elm Fork of the Trinity at Farmers Branch. Despite company promotions describing a paradise at the Three Forks, only one family settled at Farmers Branch in 1842. Economy measures of the Republic prevented the promised garrisoning of troops along the Military Road, mounted Indians still roamed the area, and prospective settlers doubted whether the company could deliver on its promises.

Charles Drake Ferris, marking time in Buffalo, wrote to his half-brother Joshua in May 1842, "I yet cherish the hope of paying another visit to Texas. But the time is hardly yet. The madness of this Houston mania must subside . . . then honor, talent and courage will have some hope of success."[9] In July, Charles Ferris became editor and half-owner of the *Western Literary Messenger* published by J. S. Chadbourne of Buffalo, New York.[10] This weekly journal aimed to showcase intellectual accomplishments of the American West. Editor Ferris asserted: "The West has too long acknowledged an 'intellectual inferiority' which *does not exist.* . . . American talent is no more *local* than American feeling." The following issue featured "Rocky Mountain Geysers," an excerpt from W. A. Ferris's unpublished work *Life in the Rocky Mountains.* Charles Ferris introduced the article:

> We have in our possession the manuscript journal of a gentleman who passed six years in the Rocky Mountains in the employ of the American Fur Company. It abounds with interesting and graphic sketches of personal adventure, picturesque scenery, and savage life. In future numbers of the *Messenger*, an occasional extract will be given, which cannot fail to prove acceptable to our readers.[11]

Subsequent issues contained further "teasers." Then, from January 1843 to May 1844, excerpts from Ferris's journal were serialized in each issue. The editor announced:

> We commence this week a journal of six years in the Rocky Mountains, condensed from a manuscript volume of four hundred pages, in which the author . . . kept a Diary of what he saw, heard, and experienced . . . the most full and complete account of the country, its productions, and inhabitants, that has yet appeared.[12]

---

9. Charles D. Ferris to Joshua Lovejoy, May 29, 1842. Quoted in DeGolyer, "Conquest of Three Forks," 83. The Ferris brothers clearly identified with speculative interests in Texas which opposed Sam Houston.

10. Later called the *Western Literary Review.* FLC, Box I, supp., has Charles Ferris's second contract (Oct. 20, 1842) with Harlow Case, his new partner, and sample copies of the publication.

11. *Western Literary Messenger*, July 6, 13, 1842; quoted in Paul C. Phillips's preface, Ferris, *Rocky Mountains*, 36–37.

12. Ibid. Phillips judged that Charles Ferris did a poor job of editing Warren Ferris's journal.

Sustaining interest in such a lengthy serial was difficult. The *Messenger* achieved a readership of 1,800 but was never a financial success. In July 1843, Ferris sold his interest to Jesse Clement who apparently saw less value in Warren Ferris's narrative. Final episodes were severely abridged; still, had it not been for this printing, the valuable contents of the Ferris journal would have been lost forever. A Mormon publication, *The Wasp*, of Nauvoo, Illinois, later reprinted portions of the journal which were read with interest by the Saints who were about to migrate along the Platte River route to the Great Basin area, both described so vividly by Warren A. Ferris.[13]

His journal in print, comfortably married, and expecting his first child, the only negative in Warren Ferris's life was his relationship with his half-brother Joshua. The Ferris/Lovejoy partnership soured under the emotional and physical stress of frontier surveying. Joshua Lovejoy was disappointed to find Texas not the land of riches and glory he had expected. He had been ill (probably he suffered from tuberculosis) and found the rough wilderness life far from romantic. The brothers' quarrel revolved around ownership of fourteen sections of land in present Dallas and Kaufman Counties which Warren Ferris had placed in "C. A." Lovejoy's name. Ferris felt his young half-brother had not fulfilled the terms of their partnership and should forfeit the land; Lovejoy refused. On March 24, 1842, Lovejoy and Ferris severed their partnership. Joshua ceded seven plots of land to Melinda Cook Ferris, retaining the rest.[14] Ferris was not satisfied with the settlement; he felt that Joshua had betrayed his trust. The two men exchanged harsh words and came close to violence. We know the story from Warren Ferris as he wrote it to Charles and later to his half-sister Sarah:

> Joshua F. Lovejoy alias J. Fitzallen Lovejoy, alias Clarence Avon Lovejoy is here, and ably married to my wife's sister, Mary Cook. . . . He contemplates going to New York this fall to get his property. Of him I have only to say that I was most egregiously deceived in him. After acting by him a most generous part I found myself repaid by the basest ingratitude. . . . I would also say to you to be on your guard when he comes home and give him no opportunity to swindle his Mother and Sisters.[15]

13. McCausland, "Early Buffalo Journalist," 18. Also Olin D. Wheeler's articles in *Northwest Magazine*, reported in the Buffalo *Express*, Sept. 2, 1900. FLC, Box V, Folder 6.

14. Nacogdoches County Deed Records, G, 130–131 and H, 124–125. Also Dallas County Records, A, 150–155. Original land scrip granted by Sam Houston to Thomas Toby, Texas agent in New Orleans in 1837, for his service to the Texas Revolution. The agreement between Ferris and Lovejoy, made in Crockett, was filed in Nacogdoches in April. One of the seven properties going to Melinda was C. A. Lovejoy Survey #4 (640 acres), which became the Ferris homestead; it and two other sections lay on White Rock Creek. Four sections were along the East Fork of the Trinity or its tributaries in Kaufman County

15. Warren Ferris to Charles Ferris, May 10, 1842, FLC, Box I, Folder 6. Lovejoy's sudden decision to wed Mary Cook in April 1842 was perhaps aimed at

In 1843, not having heard from the Buffalo family in over a year and believing them angry with him, Ferris wrote in more detail of the quarrel, denouncing Joshua Lovejoy as a "poor God damn pusillanimous scoundrell [sic]" and comparing him to their hated stepbrother Henry Lovejoy. Ferris explained that he had offered Joshua half of everything for use of his name. He had equipped his half-brother with a horse, bridle, saddle, pistols, and a Bowie knife for their 1841 surveying expedition, only to find Lovejoy "mulish" and "disposed to find fault constantly." According to Ferris, Joshua Lovejoy led a pack horse most of the time and only carried the compass about ten days out of the six months they were in the field. It was Lovejoy who broke the partnership and relinquished all claim to the land, cursing Ferris for "inviting him to such a God damn country" and saying "he would not suffer an hour for all the land in Texas."[16]

On return to Fort Houston, however, Joshua Lovejoy refused to sign over the fourteen sections of land and disappeared with all of Ferris's papers. "Here sir I first beheld the cloven foot," Warren confided to Charles. Forced to pursue his half-brother all the way to Louisiana where the argument continued, Ferris said Joshua Lovejoy "insisted upon performing our original Contract, which was a mean fraud to retain possession of my land untill [sic] he could sell it. . . . I asked him if he thought it just for me to give him my labor for four years for his labor for a few months. He thought it was."[17]

Lovejoy refused arbitration but, when Ferris threatened a lawsuit, Joshua offered to settle for land and enough money to leave Texas. On the heels of their agreement in March, according to Ferris, Lovejoy accused his half-brother of trying to swindle him and boasted around Houston County how he had "straitened" Ferris out when he had tried to "act the damb [sic] rascal with him." Ferris described Josh's wife Mary, sister of Melinda Cook Ferris, as "one of the most hell-fired little vixens on Gods Earth."[18] During the time they were all living together in the house of Ferris's father-in-law Lemuel A. Cook, Ferris's pregnant wife Melinda was doing all the housework. When a family quarrel arose over Mary Cook Lovejoy's refusal to share the work, Ferris almost struck her. The Lovejoys marched out and took up lodging with a neighbor, telling a pitiful tale of maltreatment at Ferris's hands.

After L. A. Cook traded his interest in the farm near Crockett to Josh and Mary in exchange for four sections of Ferris's land, Joshua reportedly

---

further disconcerting Ferris. Only a month earlier in a letter to Tom Denny, Joshua Lovejoy had expressed considerable interest in one Mary P. Thomas, "the prettiest and most intellectual looking girl that I saw in Kentucky." He hoped to visit Miss Thomas on his projected return to Buffalo. Joshua Lovejoy to Tom Denny, Mar. 1, 1842, ibid., Box II, Folder 12.

16. Warren Ferris to Charles Ferris, Jan. 24, 1843, ibid., Box I, Folder 7.
17. Ibid.
18. Ibid.

drove his father-in-law off the property.[19] During the ensuing lawsuit, Ferris and Lovejoy met in the courtroom; both men were armed with pistols and nearly drew on one another. Following the confrontation, Joshua Lovejoy placed Warren Ferris under a peace bond for a year.

Ferris reported to Charles with satisfaction that Josh was paying for his "ingratitude and rascality." He had squandered his land away and was in debt. "It is some consolation to me," Ferris concluded, "to know that the property he got of me will never do him any good."[20]

Joshua Lovejoy was also corresponding with people in Buffalo, telling his side of the brothers' quarrel to his sister, who responded sympathetically:

> The contents of those letters you may well believe were anything but pleasant to us; and only Charles, Louise, and me know what they contained. We thought it best to spare Mother the trouble as long as we could; There is enough with out that. . . . You have had more than enough of Texas—that bright beautiful sunny land, the home of free thought, and free action;—of the generous and the brave—my blood runs cold when I think of it; of what you have suffered there. . . . I want to see you very much, and talk to you of your affairs there—writing is a different thing. . . . As I cannot see you, I say act exactly as you consider right.[21]

When Sarah Lovejoy finally wrote to Warren Ferris in April 1843, she must have implied that he acted hastily toward Joshua. Young Lovejoy was, after all, only twenty-five and still immature. Perhaps he was lazy and self-impressed, where to Warren he seemed complaining and ungrateful. Ferris denied any "passionate hot-blooded unforgiving" action toward Clarence (Joshua) although clearly he felt such behavior would have been merited. "What poison may have been poured into your ears. . . . I know not for *mine enemy* lacks not the ability to colour and gild his own hate and cast odium upon my conduct," he told Sarah. Asserting his own

---

19. Apparently the Houston County land actually belonged to William S. Cook, as several of the C. A. Lovejoy surveys came into his hands. William S. Cook, possibly L. A. Cook's brother, came to Texas in July 1839 as a single man and claimed a 320-acre headright in Houston County. William Cook may have worked with W. A. Ferris as a surveyor in 1841. He witnessed the March 1842 agreement between Ferris and Lovejoy; in September and November three sections of land, two on White Rock Creek and one at Kingsboro, passed from C. A. Lovejoy to William S. Cook. Gifford White's *1840 Citizens of Texas* (Austin: Pemberton Press, 1966), 122, shows William S. Cook's headright in Houston County, filed November 7, 1839, and patented September 2, 1844.

20. Warren Ferris to Charles Ferris, Jan. 24, 1843, FLC, Box I, Folder 7. Josh sold two sections of scrip to William Y. Lacy for 175 Bushels of Corn; traded a league of land for a horse, sold the horse for another, giving a section of land to boot and fifty bushels of corn; gave away half his corn to hire teams to haul the crop, and otherwise "fooled his land away."

21. Sarah Lovejoy to Joshua Lovejoy, May 29, 1842, FLC, Box II, Folder 7. The family expected Josh home that summer and did not yet know of his marriage to Mary Cook.

blamelessness in the ugly quarrel, Ferris revealed his bitter attitude toward the half-brother he had once trusted. To him, Joshua Lovejoy was "a pitiful and contemptible coward that I shall for time present and to come forever entertain the most ardent hatred contempt and detestation."[22]

Wounded by Joshua's betrayal and Sarah's misjudgment of his character, Ferris corresponded less frequently with his family in Buffalo. He and Melinda left Crockett and moved to a farm he purchased near Fort Houston. There Ferris's first son, "Bud," was born; the child lived only a few short months. The family in Buffalo did not hear from Joshua for a year, but apparently Joshua and Mary Lovejoy stayed in Crockett where Mary gave birth to two daughters. Ferris and Lovejoy never saw each other again, but the ramifications of their quarrel echoed over the years to affect their families for generations to come. Ever after, Warren Ferris avoided placing his land in his own name, preferring to keep it in either his brother's or wife's name. From the tragic time in 1842 when Warren A. Ferris and his half-brother "C. A." Joshua Lovejoy first quarreled, paranoia and suspicion haunted the actions of the two men and their families.

Warren Ferris wrote to Charles in early 1843:

> I have purchased a farm one mile south of Fort Houston where I shall spend the present year. Melinda (my wife) and myself are well. We intend to farm it this year as there is no business a man can engage in at this time. . . . We hear little or no news. . . . Report says . . . that the U.S. intend to claim Texas, by some juggle of diplomacy. . . . I still hope for Texas though it looks like a bad chance. We are too poor to deserve to live. . . . I have never met with such times before. But we shall live, hard times cannot keep us down. . . . I shall probably move up to near Dallas at the Three Forks of Trinity next Fall.[23]

Ferris kept close tabs on the Peters Colony settlements which were scattered and exposed, with little security against the Indians. Encouraged by rumors of a truce with Mexico, settlers began to trickle into the colony. In the spring of 1843, Dr. John Cole and his sons led a wagon train to Cedar Springs just north of Bryan's village, now called

---

22. Warren Ferris to Sarah Lovejoy, Sept. 23, 1843, ibid., Box II, Folder 20.

23. Warren Ferris to Charles Ferris, Jan. 24, 1843. Ferris also commented on the "born fools," who had the "audacity and folly to invade Mexico," referring to the men of the Mier Expedition, who, in retaliation for General Woll's fall 1842 raid on San Antonio, invaded Mexico against the orders of President Houston, were captured in January 1843, and placed in Perote Castle prison in Mexico City.

24. A. C. Greene, *A Town Called Cedar Springs* (Dallas: privately published, 1984), 21–24, tells of one Joseph Dallas of Arkansas, said to be a friend of Bryan's—perhaps the person for whom the village of Dallas was named in 1843. The origin of the name has been controversial. J. M. Morphis, who visited Dallas in 1846, wrote in his 1874 *History of Texas* that the town was named for Commodore Alexander Dallas, brother of George M. Dallas. Perhaps riverboat captain Mabel Gilbert or his wife suggested the name of a naval man, suitable for a town at the

"Dallas."[24] Ferris's reference to "Dallas at the Three Forks of Trinity" in January 1843 was one of the first written usages of the name. [25]

That spring, Warren Ferris accompanied Capt. Jacob Elliot, an agent of the Peters Company, on an inspection tour of the Three Forks. Elliot, an editor of the Louisville *Journal*, had been hired to promote the colony. Traveling up the Trinity from Fort Houston, the party found the streams flooded but thought the corn crops first rate. With Capt. Mabel Gilbert, Elliott returned to the port of Galveston by canoe; Ferris accompanied them as far as Magnolia, the river landing for Fort Houston.[26]

Dreams of navigating the Trinity River came early. Both Dr. William P. King and John Neely Bryan envisioned a port town at the head of navigation, 300 miles upstream from the Gulf of Mexico. It was, after all, the heyday of the river steamboat. Red River navigation was difficult, so Peters Company agents like Jacob Elliot insisted that flat-bottomed steamers could reach the Three Forks via the Trinity. In fact, river travel was reliable only as far upstream as Magnolia Landing and then only in times of high water. Usually the water was too low or clogged with debris.

Ferris's friend John H. Reagan guided President Houston to Grapevine Springs in late summer 1843 for a peace parlay with the Waco, Tawakoni, and other tribes. Pursuing his conciliatory Indian policy, Houston offered to set up trading posts so the tribes could get supplies without raiding white settlements. Accompanied by Edward H. Tarrant, George W. Terrell, and Englishman Edward Parkinson, Houston's party stopped off at the Beeman blockhouse on White Rock Creek and rested a few days at Cedar Springs before meeting the Indians near the site of deserted Bird's Fort.

After the successful peace talks, Indian raids subsided and settlers breathed more easily. Ferris made a spring 1844 visit to the General Land Office, temporarily located at Washington-on-the-Brazos. On his return, he traveled the new National Road along the ridge between the Brazos and Trinity Rivers, noting numerous settlements along the east bank of the Trinity. To his amazement, he found three or four white families camped on one side of Chambers Creek just across from a party of some 1,500 Indians, neither group taking any notice of the other.[27]

To their dismay, Peters Company officials learned that only thirty-five of the perhaps 130 families introduced in 1842–1843 were actually living

"head of navigation." See also A. C. Greene, "Texas Sketches," Apr. 21, 1996, Dallas *Morning News*.

25. A. C. Greene reports (Apr. 21, 1996, Dallas *Morning News*) that a Fannin County deed dated August 1842 locates a lot "in the town of Dallas." The *Northern Standard* (Clarksville) referred to Dallas in March 1843, and Edward Parkinson reports on his summer 1843 visit to the "projected site of town called Dallas."

26. Ferris, "Reminiscence," Dallas *Herald*, Sept. 2, 1871.

27. Ibid.

in the colony.[28] It appeared that the company would have difficulty in meeting the terms of its contract and might have to forfeit or ask for another extension. Hostility toward empresarios was growing in the Texas legislature, and perpetually changing contracts unnerved prospective settlers. Many, fearing the company could not make good its promise of free land, decided to locate in Fannin County.[29]

In early 1844, Warren A. Ferris hobnobbed with another official of the Peters Colony when he met company agent Maj. Edward B. Ely in Dallas and traveled overland with him to Fort Houston, then by skiff to the mouth of the Trinity, across the bay by boat to Galveston, and finally by coastal steamer to New Orleans where Ely caught the steamboat for his return to Kentucky. Ely reported his opinion that steamboats could indeed navigate the Trinity to bring settlers to Dallas.[30] Peters Company promoters continued to portray rich farm lands and a flourishing city served by steamboats up from Gulf ports, but all the promotions in the world would not make the Trinity navigable to Dallas.

The year 1844 brought seasonable weather and, inspired by a truce with Mexico, peace with the Indians, and rumors of annexation to the United States, more settlers entered Texas. The *Northern Standard* in Clarksville reported: "Great numbers of immigrants are coming into the District; crossing above here, and making their way to the South Sulphur, and the Trinity."[31] Later the same paper described wagon trains piling up at the campgrounds near ferry crossings, the canvas wagontops bearing the inscription "Polk, Dallas, Oregon and Texas" in reference to the upcoming election in the United States.[32] On July 1, 1844, Peters Company agent Ralph H. Barksdale reported the introduction of 381 colonists, 197 heads of families and 184 single men, more than fulfilling the contract (which required that one-third of the settlers be located by that date).[33] Ferris described a far less populous colony: "Twelve of fifteen

---

28. *Northern Standard* (Clarksville), July 6, 1843. Charles DeMorse's newspaper was the voice of North Texas for half a century, according to Sibley, *Lone Stars and State Gazettes*, 141. After 1852, the paper was the *Standard*, dropping the "Northern."

29. Connor, *The Peters Colony*, 66–67.

30. E. B. Ely to Charles DeMorse, Feb. 25, 1844, reported in the *Northern Standard* (Clarksville), Mar. 2, 1844.

31. *Northern Standard* (Clarksville), June 26, 1844. Some of these settlers may have been heading for a new colony granted to Charles F. Mercer in January 1844. Mercer's grant lay southeast of the Peters Colony in what is now Ellis, Kaufman, and Hunt Counties.

32. *Northern Standard* (Clarksville), Nov. 6, 1844. The Democrat Party platform called for annexation of Texas and occupation of Oregon. George Mifflin Dallas was the nominee for vice president for whom (most agree) Dallas County was named.

33. "List of Emigrants That Arrived in Peters Colony Prior to July 1, 1844," Ralph H. Barksdale to Anson Jones, Dec. 7, 1844. Cited in Connor, *The Peters Colony*, 70.

families" and "some young men" employed by the Peters Company who "had settled so wide apart that in case of Indian hostilities they could not have rendered any effectual mutual protection." Still, he judged, from the year 1844, "we may date the settlement of Dallas County."[34]

When his friend and mentor Isaac W. Burton died in 1843, Ferris was named to administer his estate. Burton had moved to Crockett in 1841 and resumed his political career, representing Houston County in the Texas Congress. Ferris and Burton frequently visited Nacogdoches together and always called on Adolphus Sterne to talk politics. Burton was in Nacogdoches over Christmas 1842, so Sterne was shocked when he wrote in his diary January 19, 1843: "heard of the Death of Isaac W. Burton of Crockett, Poor Burton, he had his faults like most of us, but he was a noble generous man his bravery could not be doubted. . . . I knew him since 1832."[35] Burton was buried in the family cemetery at Crockett.

Death at an early age was common in frontier Texas. The specter struck even closer to home for Ferris in 1844. His beloved Melinda never fully recovered from the birth of their second child in May 1844. She died in October at age twenty-five, leaving Ferris, who was then thirty-three years of age, a widower with an infant son, Warren A. Ferris Jr. Devastated, Ferris left the child with neighbors and plunged into the wilderness to nurse his grief. A letter in which he shared his desolation with his brother lapsed into a sorrowful lament directed more to Melinda than to Charles:

> I have had the misfortune to lose my wife, who died on the 8th last about midnight of billious [sic] fever. Her demise has been to me a fatal blow. . . . I am now careless reckless heartless and in a word dont care a continental damn for any body or anything. . . . my Melinda fills my thoughts, at night she fills my dreams.
>
> Shade of my departed Melinda . . . how I adored thee for whom every effort in life was but to make thee happy. Now they tell me to forget thee that time will wear away my grief. Never can I forget thee nor can time repair the loss.[36]

Ferris pledged himself to carry out Melinda's deathbed wish. "I will live to rear thy infant and will endeavor to transfer some of the overflowing affection for thee to him. I will not neglect him I will compose myself and bend my future efforts to the elevation of our poor boy."[37] Apologizing for his morbid state of mind, Ferris ended on a brighter note, saying that

---

34. Ferris, "Reminisence," Dallas *Herald*, Sept. 2, 1871.

35. McDonald, *Hurrah for Texas*, 138.

36. Warren Ferris to Charles Ferris, Oct. 15, 1844, Smith Papers, original with Leland Smith of Mesquite, Texas; typescript, FLC, Box I, Folder 7. Ferris instructed that letters to him be sent in care of W. G. McDonald of Fort Houston.

37. Ibid.

eight-month-old Warren Jr. already spoke a few words, had a keen black eye, was strong and healthy.

Immediately on receiving Warren Ferris's heart-rending letter, Sarah Lovejoy responded sympathetically:

> who can console the mourner? No one save God, and he has mercifully granted that *time* should assuage *all* suffering. Deep grief, is to me too sacred to be commented upon . . . I should say in my woman's heart— let the dear friend that you have lost live in your memory . . . that *you shall meet again*. O if it were not for that thought we should go mad . . . or our poor hearts would break with the agony of the hour.[38]

Sarah urged Warren to find comfort in the child left for him to cherish and assured him that he was not forgotten by his Buffalo family who had written many letters in the previous two years which he had apparently not received. Louisa added her note expressing sorrow for his irreparable loss. The family had hoped he, Melinda, and their son would visit Buffalo the coming summer, but "Fate has willed it otherwise," she wrote, "and 'we have a sister less and heaven an angel more.'" Ferris's mother jotted a question in the margin of the letter, "Where is Joshua? We have not heard from him in two years."[39]

In December 1844, Warren Ferris corresponded with Edward Hale of New Orleans concerning Burton's estate and land which Ferris had promised to survey for Hale. Attempting to excuse his delay in carrying out business, Ferris stated that he was "deceived by Lovejoy who . . . assured me that the claims were Patented" and related how he had tried to go to the Franklin land office in October 1844 but had been "set afoot by the Indians and compelled to relinquish the journey."[40] Ferris told Hale of his misfortune in the loss of "a young beautiful amiable and accomplished wife who," he said, "left an infant son and myself to cherish her memory." He asked Hale to ascertain the cost of a "neat marble slab with suitable inscription" to place on Melinda's grave, offering to pay for the marker with "a few hundred acres of first rate land."[41]

When Ferris "took to the woods" to lose himself in grief after Melinda's death, it was probably to the thickets of White Rock Creek. Bereaved, he sought solace walking the quiet woods, away from familiar faces, his mind

---

38. Sarah Lovejoy to W. A. Ferris, Feb. 22, 1845 with notes added by her mother and sister. FLC, Box I, Folder 2.

39. Ibid. Sarah Lovejoy corresponded with Joshua but did not share the letters with her mother. In a letter dated August 16, 1845, Sarah confided to her sister Louisa that Joshua was living in Montgomery County, Texas, and had not seen Warren.

40. W. A. Ferris to Edward Hale, Dec. 22, 1844, Phillip C. Tucker Collection (CAH). Old Franklin, in Robertson County, was the land office for that district.

41. Ibid. Hale noted on the letter, "a tumbstone [sic] would cost from 15 to 30 [dollars] according to the number of letters and if he [Ferris] would send me a good title to land I would try to get one."

occupied with the bright image of his beloved wife. Ferris's long slide into despair was gradually replaced with a sense of urgency to meet, to woo, to win another wife. If he was to fulfill his deathbed promise to Melinda, he must find a woman to be a mother for his young son.

Sometime early in 1845 Ferris moved to his land on White Rock Creek, the C. A. Lovejoy Survey #4 encompassing the modern Forest Hills Addition of the City of Dallas. The 640-acre plot, bounded by today's Garland Road on the west, Lakeland Boulevard on the north, Ferguson Road on the east, and Highland Drive on the south, was mostly high ground, well timbered, and watered by White Rock Creek and its tributary Ash Creek. At the time of Melinda's illness, the C. A. Lovejoy surveys were transferred to Charles D. Ferris's name with Warren Ferris holding power of attorney to supervise the property.[42]

Ferris still received his mail at Fort Houston, in care of the McDonald family with whom he possibly left his young son. His mental distress was evidenced in a flurry of poetry writing[43] and restless travel. The poems (see Appendix A) were written mostly in 1845 and reveal his desolation and sense of loss, followed by a desperate search for meaning in his life. When he was fit for society again, Ferris resumed contact with Peters Company men. In the spring of 1845, Ferris guided agents Col. John C. McCoy and Charles S. Hensley from Fort Houston to Dallas; that summer, he traveled to Austin where, while conducting business at the Land Office, he was an observer at the Texas annexation convention.[44]

Leaving his young son with Melinda's father in Crockett, Ferris returned to Buffalo in the late summer of 1845. It was to be his last visit to see his brother, his mother, and half-sisters. He wanted to reclaim his manuscript, "Life in the Rocky Mountains," and probably felt that a change of scenery would be beneficial. En route to New York, Ferris visited Melinda's relatives, the Alexanders of Paris, Illinois.[45] He wished to tell them in person of her tragic death and investigate the possibility of

---

42. Dallas County Deed Records, A, 150–155. The deed and power of attorney were filed in Buffalo in 1847 when the land was transferred to W. A. Ferris's second wife.

43. Ferris's poems (see Appendix A)—from the melancholy "Invocation (to Melinda)"; to "Ode to Spring," a transition from sadness to belief in the continuity of life; to the poems addressed to "Laura," representing a return to society; to the verses addressed to Mary McCommas, a neighbor to whom Ferris apparently proposed marriage—track his changing moods. Originals in Ferris Memoranda Book, Davis Collection. Typescripts in Blake Collection (CAH).

44. Ferris, "Reminiscences," Dallas *Herald*, Sept. 2, 1871. The convention on July 4, 1845, with only one dissenting vote, accepted the terms of annexation offered to Texas by the United States.

45. Warren Ferris told Charles in his letter, Oct. 15, 1844, that Melinda was "the niece of Genl. Alexander of Paris, Illinois, a gent of fortune by whom she was educated as a woman should be." Milton K. Alexander, a Tennessee veteran of the War of 1812, was a founding settler of Edgar County, Illinois.

their raising Warren Jr. as Melinda had suggested in the last days of her illness. He stayed in Buffalo about a month and again stopped off in Illinois on his way back to Texas. Ferris knew he must remarry or give up his son to be reared by others. His heart on the rebound, Ferris was drawn to Melinda's cousin, Angeline Cook, who much resembled his beloved wife. On his return to Texas, they corresponded; he proposed marriage and sent an engagement ring along with a letter proclaiming his love.

> We have met, and I have found you the bright original of Melinda's picture. . . . I know that such a girl as you would make the best wife alive and believe me I would make a pilgrimage barefoot . . . to win your love. . . . let me assure you that I love you. . . . I will love you with the same undying affection I entertained for your sainted cousin. . . . If however, you do not and feel you cannot entertain kindred emotions for me then you will at once declare it for you cannot be so cruel as to permit me one hour to indulge a hopeless passion.[46]

He acknowledged that it was almost criminal to ask that Angeline leave the society of her family and friends to live among strangers, to "sink from being the pride and ornament" of her father's mansion to become "the (mere) mistress of a Texian cabin." Ferris denied that he was motivated in any way by the fact that Angeline's father was "reputed rich," saying that he had enough property to support a wife or he would not seek one. He proclaimed his utmost sincerity. "You may say that 'Men discourse like angels but live like men.' This is true in general, but not of me. I write from the heart."[47]

Angeline's response, dated October 5, 1845, came to Ferris via C. H. Hensley, the Peters Colony agent, who relayed mail from Bonham to Dallas. She wrote news of the family and friends in Illinois, saying, "You excited a great deal of curiosity in our quiet little village. Everyone wanted to know who you were and what you came for. . . . " To Ferris's offer of marriage, Angeline answered: "you have possessed my heart from the moment that I first saw you . . . you have therefore my full consent to your wishes.[48]

Angeline Cook had not discussed the engagement with her parents but felt they would approve. Her mother spoke very favorably of Ferris; her father had hand-delivered his letter unopened; and her sister Jacintha, her confidante in the romance, sent Warren her love. With such warm acceptance, lonely widower Warren Ferris was probably overjoyed. All the greater was his shock and disappointment to receive Angeline's second letter later that same month. She unequivocally broke their engagement,

---

46. Warren A. Ferris to Angeline Cook, unfinished, undated draft of a letter, probably the letter of Sept. 27, 1845, Davis Collection.

47. Ibid.

48. Angeline Cook to W. A. Ferris, Oct. 5, 1845, Davis Collection.

offering to return his ring and letters. We have only Ferris's stilted response to her rejection:

> Your letter reached me today. . . . I was very much surprised at its contents. . . . You . . . express regret that you are compelled to withdraw from the engagement. Permit me to release you fully and entirely. . . . You say that you are not at liberty to give me your reasons. . . . I am not to know whether malice has leveled her shaft at me, whether unprincipled slanderers have handled my reputation, whether I am to be made a victim of circumstances or whether you are constrained to such a course against your inclinations.[49]

Mystified, chagrined, hurt by Angeline's sudden change of heart, Ferris imagined that some defamation of his character came from a "Mr. Chessnut" who might have seen him in New Orleans in poor condition (perhaps drunk or ill with the appearance of drunkenness). Ferris explained he had become ill on the boat trip down the Mississippi; it was the effects of a diseased liver, a chronic complaint. Perhaps he was "unconsciously guilty of some error of an unpardonable nature" of which he had no knowledge. He urged Angeline Cook to reconsider. "You know that I possessed the affection of your cousin, do you think she would have placed her destiny in the hands of an undeserving person," he queried.

Ferris exaggerated the differences of their background when he concluded:

> In early youth, untutored and penniless, I left the home of my childhood and wandered forth determined to earn an honest livelihood. My impatient curiosity led me beyond the borders of civilization and I have twice from choice remained a backwoods man. I have never had any opportunity to improve my mind as I have always been remote from books and schools hence I should not be a fit companion for one who has had every opportunity to acquire all that public opinion deems accomplishments. I was aware of this and should not have approached you.[50]

Such self-depreciation, uncharacteristic of Warren Ferris, reflect his wounded pride and the low ebb of his spirits. Perhaps Angeline Cook merely realized that it was not her, but Melinda's ghost, that Ferris worshiped.

Charles Ferris, in a long letter of March 15, 1846, informed his brother in Texas that the Buffalo family had moved into a new brick home. Sister Sarah had been ill as she was so often during the long New York winter and their mother had sprained an ankle, but Charles was hopeful all would be improved with the coming of warm spring weather. He

---

49. W. A. Ferris to Angeline Cook, "My Dear Friend," undated draft of a letter. Davis Collection.

50. Ibid. This reference to liver disease is the only hint that Warren Ferris was a heavy drinker. Considering the reputation of mountainmen and frontier Texans, this would not be surprising.

expressed his satisfaction in providing the new home with amenities including a brick woodshed, cistern, attached privy, and rock-floored cellar, giving his mother and half-sisters a home suitable to a "respectable position in life."[51] But serious personal frustrations were evident when Charles Ferris summed up his own life which he viewed largely wasted.

> I have devoted my life and made a sacrifice of every opening prospect, to be near, and take care of and protect her [mother] and her daughters. . . . I have defended their rights . . . kept them at least in . . . comparative comfort . . . this is my consolation for a life in other respects wasted. . . . I gave up all my own prospects. . . . But I have no regrets to reproach myself with. . . . It is enough that I feel that I have done my duty.[52]

Saying that he still pictured himself in Texas, enjoying the sunny skies and healthful climate, taking "a kind of literary ease," caring for his herds and the education of his children, Charles urged Warren Ferris to contract land for him "in the section of the country I described to you when you were here." New York newspapers, full of accounts of emigration flowing into Texas, raised the specter of inflated land prices. Charles promised to write monthly to his brother; their mutual affection had been strengthened during the summer visit to Buffalo. Only his brother could sympathize or fully understand him, Charles felt. Of their notorious half-brother, Charles commented, "Not a word from Joshua, where is he and what about? Mother and the girls trouble themselves a good deal with anxiety about him!"[53]

The little settlements at the Three Forks—Dallas, Cedar Springs, and Hord's Ridge—were slowly developing. John Neely Bryan married Margaret Beeman, daughter of John Beeman; their first child, Holland Coffee Bryan, was born at the Beeman blockhouse in 1844 but he lived only a year. A second son, John Neely Bryan Jr., was born in 1845. Adam Haught cut the first planks to rebuild Bryan's cabin, swept away by flood, and to build a ferry for the river. Haught, who married another Beeman daughter, ran the ferry for Bryan and also operated Dallas's first saloon where the whiskey flowed more freely than the river. In early 1844, the Texas Congress authorized the building of the Central National Road, to begin near Bryan's crossing of the Trinity and proceed northeast into Red River County. Obadiah W. Knight settled at Cedar Springs, buying land

---

51. Charles Ferris to Warren Ferris, Mar. 15, 1846, Blake Collection, XLVI, 54–59.

52. Ibid.

53. Ibid. In 1844, Charles Ferris worked briefly for the Buffalo *Courier*. As an editorial writer for the Democratic newspaper, he advocated the presidential candidacy of James K. Polk. Undoubtedly Ferris was attracted by the Democratic Party platform which called for the annexation of Texas. When he was let go by the newspaper after the election, he returned to work at the Buffalo post office. McCausland, "Early Buffalo Journalist," 19.

in Miles Bennett's survey. Elder Amon McCommas and Dr. Perry Dakan purchased land along White Rock Creek to become Ferris's near neighbors.

After the Democratic presidential victory in 1844, Whig incumbent John Tyler willingly endorsed, and Congress approved, a joint resolution to annex Texas to the United States. Action at the Texas convention in July 1845 and election of Dr. Anson Jones, Sam Houston's personal choice, as president of the Republic in December assured the process. On February 19, 1846, the American flag was raised over the old wooden capitol in Austin and President Jones proclaimed, "The Republic of Texas is no more." After a decade of frustration as an independent nation, its growth retarded by financial depression, the "Texas Lone Star" attached its future to the "Stars and Stripes."

One of the first acts of the state legislature was to carve new counties out of the old ones of the Republic. At the Three Forks in 1845, Bryan and Beeman laid out a townsite wedged between the river and the Grigsby Survey. A committee to organize Dallas County was chaired by Amon McCommas. Dallas County, thirty miles by thirty miles square, was created out of old Nacogdoches and Robertson Counties in 1846,[54] and Dallas was named temporary county seat. Always the shrewd promoter, Bryan offered free ferry service to county residents if his little village were chosen the permanent seat of government.

Warren A. Ferris continued to improve his bachelor farm on White Rock Creek. His log cabin stood on the eastern edge of a large grove of trees about 200 yards east of the present junction of St. Francis Drive and Garland Road. Wild persimmon and native pecan trees flourished on his property; to these, Ferris added a hundred peach, pear, plum, and cherry trees to create a fine orchard. In April 1846, Ferris traveled to New Orleans; it rained every day of his trip.[55] He visited his small son who was still living with the Cooks at Crockett and passed twice by old Fort Houston. A new town, Palestine, was growing there. It was to be the county seat of newly created Anderson County. On one of these visits to Palestine, Warren Ferris met an attractive young lady, Miss Sarah Frances Moore. Soon their friendship developed into courtship. Ferris had found a mother for his son. It was time for new beginnings—a new state, a new county, a new marriage.

54. H. P. N. Gammel (comp.), *Laws of the Republic of Texas, 1822–1897*. . . (10 vols.; Austin: Gammel Book Co., 1898), II, 1332. An Act to create Dallas County, March 30, 1846. Beginning on the south boundary of Fannin County, three miles east of the eastern boundary of the Peters' Colony grant, thence thirty miles by thirty miles.

55. Ferris, "Reminiscences," Dallas *Herald*, Sept. 2, 1871.

Part Three

☆

Pioneer Farmer

8

EMBROILED IN CONTROVERSY

O N JANUARY 5, 1847, widower W. A. Ferris married Sarah Frances Moore of Palestine, Texas.[1] Ferris brought his bride and the three-year-old son of his first marriage to live on White Rock Creek eight miles east of Dallas. He was thirty-six years old; Frances, at eighteen, was half his age. Warren Ferris's driving ambitions and dreams of wealth cooled after the death of his first wife Melinda; now he seemed satisfied to live the quiet life of a pioneer farmer. Frances was young, strong, enthusiastic, and sensible; she would be an energetic helpmate in building the Ferris homestead in the new county of Dallas in the new state of Texas.

Frances "Fanny" Moore was born in Bedford County, Tennessee, in 1829 and came to Texas in 1840. Little is known of her parents. She emigrated to Texas, via Benton County, Alabama, with the family of her brother-in-law Marcus P. Meade, her brother A. H. Moore, her married sister Emily, and younger siblings. Frances's older sister Emily married Dr. Zachariah Ellison of Mt. Carmel, about fifteen miles east of Tyler in Smith County; another sister Martha was the wife of lawyer Cyrus H. Randolph of Crockett, a figure prominent in local politics. The Moores were a close-knit clan so Warren Ferris, far from his Buffalo family, enjoyed contact with his in-laws.[2]

To a seasoned outdoorsman like Ferris, Dallas County in the 1840s was a virtual paradise. The thickets of White Rock Creek provided some of the best hunting offered anywhere. Buffalo, wild mustangs, and maverick cattle

---

1. The marriage was performed and recorded in Smith County where the bride's sister and brother resided.

2. Nell Davis of Elgin, Texas, a descendant of Warren Ferris, has researched the Moore family line and suggests that Frances might have been the child of a second marriage of William Moore. Four of the Moore girls named sons "William." There is a six-year gap between the births of Nancy (1812) and Emily (1814) and the younger siblings born after 1820. Probably the parents never came to Texas. A William Moore is listed in the 1840 Benton County, Alabama, census, at a date when most of the adult Moore children had emigrated. Frances's oldest sister Nancy died in Alabama, but her husband Marcus Meade led the family to Texas. A brother, A. H. Moore, claimed Texas land in 1840 as a single man. There was a flock of single, but marriageable Moore girls. Martha, like Frances, was single when she came to Texas; but soon married C. H. Randolph who also migrated from Alabama. Mary Moore married Dr. John Hassell of Houston County, Texas, in 1843. Another sister, Margaret Catherine Moore, married John Grigsby II of Houston County in 1846; when Grigsby died two years later, she married John Hemby. All of the Moore girls appear to have been well educated and made good marriages.

still roamed the unfenced grasslands west of Dallas on Grapevine Prairie. An early settler recalled:

> everywhere deer, turkeys and prairie chickens were thick as ants on a hill, with bear, panthers, wolves and wildcats keeping in the daytime to the river and creek bottoms, but after dark issuing forth to ravage the plains and startle the night with uncouth shadows, and hideous screaming and howling.[3]

The wilderness that seemed so ideal to Warren Ferris must have been frightening to his young wife and infant son. Ferris was frequently away from home, leaving for long intervals as he did in the summer of 1847 to survey in Grayson County for the Peters Colony. Frances and the child endured the lonely cabin in the woods by White Rock Creek, far from her friends and family, shuddering at the cries of wild animals in the night.

While starvation was not a problem for the early citizens of Dallas, sickness was always a threat. In flood season, the streams ran full, vegetation was rank, and dense fog rested in low-lying bottom land. Malaria and typhoid were common; and, although the settlers treated the chills with calomel and quinine, many succumbed to illness. Winter brought cold winds and abrupt drops in temperature which killed the malarial fevers but introduced pneumonia and influenza. Gravestones began to sprout in the pioneer cemeteries. On August 7, 1848, Warren Ferris Jr., Melinda Ferris's surviving child, died; he was only four years old. The next week Frances Ferris gave birth to a daughter, Emily; but Emily, too, died in 1853 at age five. Children's graves marked the origin of the family cemetery which Ferris established in the eastern sector of his property near Ash Creek. Only one son, James Ferris, survived the early hard years.

Several families joined the Ferrises on the banks of White Rock Creek in the late 1840s. Ferris's neighbors, besides Perry Dakan and Amon McCommas, included James and Albert G. Collins, Benjamin Dye, Daniel Sage, Wesley and William Chenault, Stephen Heffington, and Morris Ferris, a Peters Colony settler of no relation to Warren. Downstream near the Beeman clan lived the Brutons, the Hunnicuts, the Pembertons, and the Badgleys.

These pioneer settlers of east Dallas County shared the sorrows and joys of frontier homesteading. They gathered for funerals and weddings. Most often, boys married neighbor girls. Impromptu horseraces were common entertainment in a community where several farmers, like Ferris, raised fast horses. Boots pounding on rough plank floors; they clapped to lively fiddle music and danced till late hours at winter sociables. Summer camp meetings, led by Methodist circuit riders or by local Campbellite preacher McCommas, lasted from Thursday to Sunday. Folks came from surrounding counties to the shady White Rock shores to hear three to five

---

3. Epps G. Knight memoirs, quoted in Greene, *A Town Called Cedar Springs*, 31.

sermons a day, leading up to the intense emotion of the final Sunday night service.[4] Like many self-reliant individuals, Warren Ferris was largely irreligious; but Frances and the children relished the excitement and socializing. It was welcome diversion from the struggle of daily life on the Texas frontier.

"Fanny" and "W. A." Ferris, as they came to be known to neighbors, cultivated eighty-five of their 640 acres. On the creek, near where the spillway of White Rock Lake is presently located, Ferris built a gristmill. William Laytham, an elderly English millwright, lived with the family while supervising the project. W. A. also hired a young couple, Timothy and Nancy Colwell, to help with the chores.[5] Ownership of C. A. Lovejoy Survey #4, Ferris's homestead, was transferred in October 1847 to Frances Moore Ferris. W. A. Ferris, with power of attorney, transferred the property from the name of his brother Charles D. Ferris to that of his second wife.[6] So great were his fears of Joshua Lovejoy that Warren Ferris continued the practice of putting the land in the name of someone other than himself.

Not having heard for years from Joshua Lovejoy, Ferris might have relaxed into a quiet life, but a new antagonist appeared to taunt him when Ferris was drawn into a series of political disputes that gripped the Dallas area during the late 1840s.

The Peters Company, reorganized as the Texas Emigration and Land Company of Louisville, Kentucky, found its position vastly altered when, in 1846, the state of Texas created four new counties, Collin, Dallas, Denton, and Grayson, in their former "colony." The company role changed from that of land promoter to land administrator, a role the distant stockholders and their agents played very poorly. Inhabitants of the Peters Colony were enraged when the company asserted its right to half of their land (320 acres) in payment for services purportedly rendered, that is, surveying land and acquiring patents for immigrants.[7] Colonists insisted that the company never provided these services. They demanded clear

---

4. Gerald D. Saxon (ed.), *The WPA Dallas Guide and History* (Denton: University of North Texas Press, 1992), 271–279, traces the social life of Dallas from 1842. Memoirs of George Jackson, *Sixty Years in Texas* (Quanah, Texas: Nortex Press, 1908), and John B. Billingsley (DHS) are good primary sources.

5. The *Seventh Census of the United States* (1850), Dallas County, Texas, II, 592, shows Warren A. Ferris, his wife Frances, and two children, Emily and James, Laytham, and the Colwells. Ferris's worth is listed at $2,000. Connor, *The Peters Colony*, 225, lists a Timothy Colwell claiming land as a single man in July 1848 while the 1850 census shows Colwell to be twenty-one years old, born in Indiana, emigrating through Illinois, married with one child.

6. Dallas County Deed Records, B, 19.

7. The little-known clause, allowing the company to claim settlers' half-sections, was a part of the first contract with the Republic of Texas. Under even more liberal terms of the fourth contract, the company could have claimed three-fourths of each settler's land.

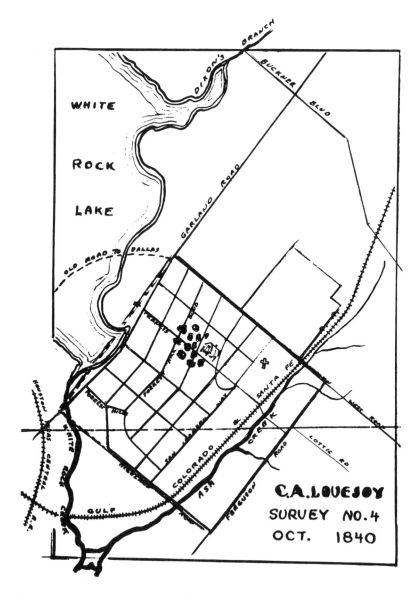

Homer DeGolyer sketch of Warren A. Ferris property (C. A. Lovejoy Survey No. 4) on White Rock Creek, relating the 1840 survey to modern streets, railroads, and White Rock Lake. *Courtesy the DeGolyer Library, Southern Methodist University, Dallas.*

title to full sections (640 acres). Individual settlers of the American West harbored a deep distrust of government land policies favoring corporate interests. Now powerful land speculators, who also opposed empresario "give-aways," encouraged the disaffected settlers in the colony; thus, a noisy coalition of anti-company factions exerted pressure on local governments and the Texas legislature.[8]

At the time of the state constitutional convention in 1845, a lawsuit was brought against the Peters Company, with a threat to nullify its contract. During the period of litigation, the Texas Land Office refused to issue patents (clear titles) to Dallas County lands. When rumors flew that the Peters contract was about to be annulled by the legislature, surveyors from Robertson and Nacogdoches Land Districts began to encroach on Peters Company lands, filing field notes on land located in the Colony. One of the chief offenders was Dallas County resident Albert G. Walker, deputy surveyor of the Nacogdoches District.[9] Walker became Warren Ferris's new nemesis.

A. G. Walker came to Texas from Kentucky in 1845, escaping a disastrous marriage which ended in divorce.[10] He began his surveying career as a deputy for David R. Mitchell, working out of Franklin, Texas, in the Robertson Land District. Then Walker was appointed deputy in the Nacogdoches District by A. A. Nelson, Warren Ferris's former employer. The new county of Dallas lay half in the Robertson, half in the Nacogdoches District, split down the middle by the Trinity River.

In Dallas, Walker gained acceptance as a congenial fiddler player at local dances.[11] Soon he came to be seen as champion of untitled settlers against the hated Peters Company. A lengthy correspondence between Walker and Nelson[12] reveals the seething controversies of the late 1840's into which Warren Ferris was drawn. In December 1846, Walker assured Nelson that the Peters Company represented no obstacle since its contract would soon be annulled. Early in 1847, Walker requested copies of Ferris's surveys of the King Block and the Grigsby grants, informing

---

8. Connor, *The Peters Colony*, 86–89. Connor later points out that most of the criticism of the Peters Company came from outside the colony, rather than from colonists themselves. Ibid., 136–138. For instance, the protest meeting held in the spring of 1849 was in Henderson County, 100 miles south of the colony. According to Connor, the dissension was orchestrated by speculators.

9. Walker was cited for his "illegal" surveying activities by H. O. Hedgcoxe, Peters Colony agent, in a May 5, 1847, letter to William G. Hale, company attorney. Connor, *The Peters Colony*, 89.

10. Walker's divorce from his wife Pauline who was still living in Henderson County, Kentucky, was recorded August 12, 1847. It was the first divorce recorded in Dallas County. Dallas County Deed Records, A, 171.

11. Saxon (ed.), *The WPA Dallas Guide and History*, 275.

12. Correspondence between A. G. Walker and A. A. Nelson in the Albert Aldrich Nelson Papers (Special Collections, Ralph Steen Library, Stephen F. Austin University, Nacogdoches, Texas). Also in Blake Collection.

Nelson that settlers wanted to locate on the even sections of land which had been reserved to the government.

Setting aside alternate sections for the government, a feature of the third Peters Company contract with the Republic of Texas, created a checkerboard pattern which was a surveyor's nightmare. Despite stepped-up efforts on the part of the Peters Company, settlement ran ahead of surveying. While old settlers waited impatiently for clear title to their land, new immigrants occupied unsurveyed tracts. The work of company "engineers" frequently failed to coordinate with earlier surveys, many made by Ferris. Misunderstanding, distrust, and resentment grew, centering on the company demand for half-sections despite its failure to deliver services. Articulate, yet often illiterate, colonists organized at the county level to make their voices heard in Austin.

Much ire was directed at the Peters Company agent on the spot, H. O. Hedgcoxe, who arrived in Texas in early 1846. Hedgcoxe's personality and actions were key factors in the heightened tension. An Englishman whose stilted accent and imperious manner irritated the rough colonists, Hedgcoxe appeared arrogant and haughty when he issued ultimatums ordering settlers off the reserved lands.[13]

As the deadline for the fourth contract approached, the state government and the Peters Company disagreed over whether the terms of the contract had been fulfilled and whether the company deserved the premium land it had been promised. In January 1848, colonists appealed to the state legislature to intervene, asking that county courts be allowed to issue land titles which the company had failed to deliver.

Another dispute arose over the precise location of Dallas County's northern boundary and the related question of which community would become its permanent county seat. State law required that the seat of government be located as near the center of the newly formed counties as possible. When A. G. Walker ran the county boundaries in 1847, he upheld the line run by Warren Ferris in 1841 as the "true line" of Old Fannin County, therefore the correct line between Dallas and Collin Counties.[14] On the other hand, John Neely Bryan and William M. Cochran promoted a line $2\frac{1}{2}$ miles south of the Ferris line which would place the village of Dallas exactly in the center of thirty-mile square Dallas County. Bryan threatened to go to Austin to appeal Walker's loca-

---

13. Connor, *The Peters Colony*, 90–91. The deadline for completion of the company's fourth contract was July 1, 1848, so Hedgcoxe, who claimed to be a civil engineer, pushed surveying efforts. The Clarksville *Northern Standard* reported on November 14, 1846, that Colonel Ball of Kentucky and a company of engineers were active in the colony.

14. Dallas County Deed Records, A, 195. Walker was employed January 13, 1847, to "run and mark" the county lines; the order was repealed then renewed in April; he submitted his survey July 13, 1847. Also Walker to Nelson, June 12, 1847, Nelson Papers.

tion of the northern county boundary. According to Walker, only about a tenth of the 3,000 people in Dallas County supported Bryan on the question of the county line. Surveyor Walker confided to Nelson, "Col. Bryan is fearful that Cedar Springs will be near enough to the center of the County for the County seat to be placed there and wishes to keep it in Dallas, in defiance of the will of the people."[15]

In July 1848, A. G. Walker learned of an attempt by a few "designing individuals" to unseat him as deputy surveyor. He ran afoul of County Probate Judge John Cole when he married Cole's daughter Louisa without her father's permission. Cole wrote to Nelson that although Walker was "said to be my sun [sic] in Law we have not had much conversation since he stoled [sic] my Daughter."[16] Judge Cole joined John N. Bryan and other critics of Walker in promoting appointment of Meredith Myers as deputy surveyor.

Warren Ferris entered the political fray when he wrote his old friend Nelson, complaining of Walker's activities in Dallas County. Involvement in a public dispute was a departure for Ferris, a man who rarely cared to draw attention to himself. He wrote as an expert surveyor, familiar with the local situation as perhaps no other man was, to align himself with those questioning surveyor Walker's qualifications. Ferris asserted:

> A majority of the citizens of this county are dissatisfied with your deputy, Mr. Walker in consequence of *his encouraging the people to locate land certificates upon government sections of land* which were by law expressly reserved to the government for the purpose of raising a fund to pay the debt of the state. Ignorant people come to the county and apply to the Surveyor to ascertain facts which he finds it to his interest to conceal in order to make a few dollars in fees. . . . Such conduct on the part of a surveyor will create great confusion and end in serious litigation to many inoffensive but ignorant people.[17]

Although he denied any motive beyond that of promoting the "prosperity of the Country" and correcting the "abuse of office holders,"[18] Warren Ferris made an implacable enemy when he criticized A. G. Walker.

Incumbent Walker and his opponent Meredith Myers both circulated petitions around July 4, 1848. Myers received over 100 signatures from citizens of Dallas County, but it was difficult to judge support since many locals signed *both* petitions. In a letter to Nelson, Myers called his opponent a "very forgetful man," reporting that Walker "forgot the time" he was to meet representatives of Collin and Denton Counties to coordinate

---

15. Walker to Nelson, July 17 and Oct. 23, 1847, ibid.

16. Cole to Nelson, Mar. 12, 1848, ibid. Greene, *A Town Called Cedar Springs*, 37, states that Walker bore a grudge against Bryan and the Dallas County commissioners. It appears the resentment was mutual.

17. W. A. Ferris to Nelson, Aug. 20, 1848, Nelson Papers.

18. Ibid.

the northern boundary of Dallas County. As a result of his negligence, there were seven miles of disputed territory, and citizens of the area were unsure in what county they lived.[19]

Dallas County Clerk William Cochran withdrew his support of Walker, telling Nelson that Walker was incompetent as a draftsman and had failed to comply with the county court's instructions in running the county lines.[20] Dr. Perry Dakan, who represented Dallas in the state legislature in 1847, wrote Nelson of three hundred aggrieved citizens "owing to A. G. Walker's mistakes" and his "reckless manner of doing his work." Dakan proposed that the county be allowed to elect its own surveyor.[21]

Despite numerous critics, surveyor Walker ingratiated himself with Nelson and managed to retain his appointment for two more years. His popularity derived from his ability to convincingly portray himself as an opponent of the Peters Company. Walker called himself the "greatest rebel against the Colony that lives in its boundaries,"[22] and complained of a conspiracy against him, "the Hedgcoxe or Colony company party was at work again in order to get a surveyor appointed for this county who was supple enough to answer their diabolical designs."[23] He was able to tar Warren A. Ferris with these accusations.

Dallas County commissioners, desperate for revenue, further aggravated the situation when, in 1848 and 1849, they levied taxes on Peters Company land in the county. The legality of such action was questionable, as neither the company nor its colonists had received clear title. When taxes went unpaid, Dallas Tax Assessor Ben Merrill offered prime land belonging to the Texas Emigration and Land Company for sale at public auction.[24] Not only company land but also over 45,000 acres of land belonging to individuals was sold that fall for delinquent taxes. It may well have been that Warren A. Ferris lost some of his land in these tax auctions.[25]

---

19. Meredith Myers to A. A. Nelson, Aug. 27, 1848, ibid.

20. William M. Cochran to Nelson, Aug. 25, 1848, ibid.

21. Perry Dakan to Nelson, Aug. 27, 1848, ibid. Walker retorted by explaining that Dr. Dakan had "got religion" at a Methodist camp meeting and allied himself with Brother Cochran (early Methodist leader), Bryan, and those critical of his northern county boundary line. Walker to Nelson, Nov. 7, 1848, ibid.

22. Walker to Nelson, Apr. 20, 1849, ibid.

23. Walker to Nelson, Aug. 16, 1849, ibid.

24. Connor, *The Peters Colony*, 122–123. The whole question of land ownership in the county remained unsettled, pending conclusion of surveying, settlement of litigation, and issuance of clear titles.

25. DeGolyer, "Conquest of Three Forks," 100, cites a letter from Hester Ferris to Warren Ferris, Feb. 4, 1850, which refers to his regrettable "loss of land." Walter McCausland states that Ferris lost much of his Texas land in 1849 and 1850. See Webb, Carroll, and Branda (eds.), *Handbook of Texas*, I, 594. Three sections on Rowlett's Creek, which Ferris surveyed in 1840 and placed in C. A. Lovejoy's name, were lost when Ferris failed to register them in Fannin County.

Capitalizing on hostility toward the Peters Company and county officials, Walker ran for the Texas Senate in the summer of 1849; his chief
opponent in the large senatorial district created for North Texas was
Warren Ferris's old friend, John H. Reagan of Anderson County.[26] Walker's
surprise victory over Reagan on August 14, 1849, was a measure of the
mounting resentment toward the Peters Company and its associates.
Walker bragged to Nelson that he had won by 199 votes, elected four to one
by the voters of the county, despite "every infamous lie . . . raised against
me by Reagan and that party." Still trying to oust Walker as surveyor, his
enemies promoted the appointment of Joel Crumpacker in 1849. Walker
told Nelson that "young Mr. Crumpacker (Reagan & Peters Company candidate)" was unfit to be a surveyor. He claimed that Crumpacker's support
of the Peters Colony contract would discredit him in Dallas County.[27]

John H. Reagan, who had soft-pedaled criticism of the Peters Company
during the campaign, later said of this disappointing election: "It was the
only time I was ever defeated in a popular election, and in this case I
deliberately accepted defeat rather than promise the people to do what I
felt sure would operate to their injury."[28] His setback sent a loud message
to Ferris and others in the county who had underestimated resentment
toward the empresarios and their "foreign" agent H. O. Hedgcoxe.

A typical irate citizen was James J. Beeman, postmaster of White Rock
Creek, who expressed his mounting frustration in a letter to District
Surveyor A. A. Nelson. Beeman arrived in the Three Forks area before
extension of the Peters Grant, but he still had not received his patent. He
complained that he had "been held in suspense for so long a time" that he
was quite "impatient of the matter."[29] No wonder the Beemans, and many
other Dallasites, favored Walker who surveyed their land and supported
their claims. Without him, they were little more than squatters. There
was tremendous antagonism toward those who, like Warren Ferris, surveyed for the Peters Company. His criticism of Walker, his past association with company agents, and his employment by them as a surveyor,
cost Ferris friends in Dallas County.

---

26. In 1846, after quitting the surveying business, Reagan took up farming and
resided at Old Buffalo on the Trinity River, the first county seat of Henderson
County. There he practiced law and was elected probate judge and a delegate to
the Texas House of Representatives. Later, he moved to Palestine in Anderson
County, where his home was near the site of old Fort Houston. Thirteen counties
comprised the North Texas senate district in 1849.

27. Walker to Nelson, Aug. 16, 1849, Nelson Papers.

28. Reagan, *Memoirs*, 58. In his history of the Peters Company, Connor doubts
that Reagan was so high-minded as the quote indicates. He just underestimated
the resentment toward the company and got on the wrong side of the controversy;
see Connor, *The Peters Colony*, 137n. Both Connor and Reagan confuse this election
with a later defeat, when Reagan lost the senatorial position to Sam Bogart of
Collin County in 1850.

29. James J. Beeman to A. A. Nelson, July 19, 1848, Nelson Papers.

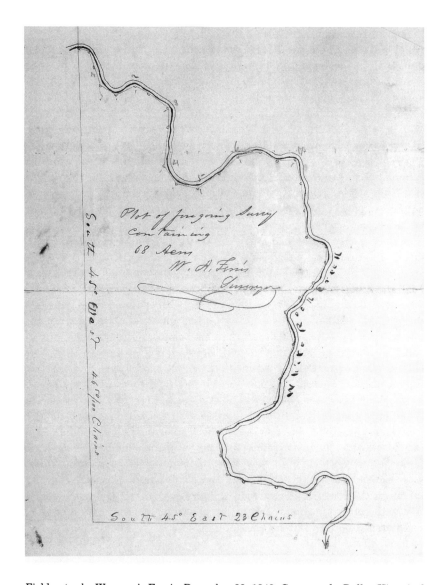

Field notes by Warren A. Ferris, December 29, 1849. *Courtesy the Dallas Historical Society.*

Nacogdoches Land District Surveyor Nelson allowed A. G. Walker to continue as deputy even while he served in the Texas Senate.[30] Walker's letters to Nelson contained frequent inquiries as to his superior's health

30. Nelson appointed A. M. Keene, Walker's friend, as assistant deputy surveyor in Walker's absence. Walker also had proposed the name of his brother-in-law John C. Cole.

and good wishes for his reelection. In 1848, Walker made two surveys in Nelson's name along the Trinity River, one in timber and one in prairie land. A master of self-promotion, Walker informed Nelson that he had named his first son "Albert" for both himself and his boss.[31] Walker denounced his political enemies in Dallas County who circulated "infamous lies" against him, including the accusation that he had surveyed land for Nelson on "shares."[32]

During his time in the Texas Senate, Walker kept Nelson informed on pending legislation which might effect his superior, such as a bill to decrease surveyors' fees.[33] Walker claimed that he was elected to "break up" the Peters Colony and that, after a hard fight, he had won the victory over "English money."[34] He took full credit when, on January 21, 1850, the Texas legislature acted to guarantee Peters Colonists full title to their land and cancel the company claim to half-sections. Gov. Peter H. Bell sent Land Commissioner Thomas W. Ward into the colony to examine proof of ownership and issue land certificates.

Mending his political fences at home, Walker began to shift position on the question of Dallas County's northern boundary. In the fall of 1849, Walker questioned Ferris's line between Old Fannin and Nacogdoches Counties and told Nelson it might have to be rerun.[35] By April 5, 1850, Walker was investing in Neely Bryan's town and supporting Dallas, over Cedar Springs, as permanent county seat. Walker urged Nelson to record Bryan's field notes and certificates, saying:

> I now feel a deep interest in the matter. I bought several lots here today and I am well satisfied the county seat will now be permanently located here . . . I gave for each lot—without improvements $62.50. So you see I now have an interest in the place [Dallas] and I therefore wish the matter settled up as soon as possible and the County seat located here, as I am convinced it will be.[36]

---

31. Walker to Nelson, Feb. 9, 1848 and July 16, 1849, Nelson Papers.

32. Walker to Nelson, July 8, 1849, ibid.

33. Walker to Nelson, Feb. 22, 1850, ibid.

34. A. G. Walker Jr. to his brother Henry W. Walker, DeGolyer Collection, III, 9. In this undated letter, the son of A. G. Walker recounts his father's lengthy political career which began with the 1849 senatorial election. Walker claims that the Peters Company offered a bribe, but his father stood firm in his determination to break up the company and give the settlers all their land.

35. Walker to Nelson, Sept. 16, 1849, Nelson Papers. This northern boundary continued to be troublesome. The county commissioners appointed Micajiah Goodwin to ascertain the "true boundary line" of Old Fannin County in mid-August 1849. Dallas County Deed Records, A, 54.

36. Walker to Nelson, Apr. 5, 1850, Nelson Papers. Although Bryan was selling lots in Dallas, he did not hold a clear title. As an "old Texan," he was not eligible for land in the Peters Colony; but he received a grant of 640 acres nonetheless, and it was finally patented in 1850.

During the spring of 1850, there was again talk of Dallas County elect-
ing its own surveyor. A. G. Walker resigned from the Senate and returned
to protect his interests when he heard that Warren Ferris planned to run
for the position. Walker accused Ferris of promising to survey for $2 a day
if elected and, in a letter to Nelson, referred to "infernal and swindling
contractors of the colony like W. A. Ferris."[37]

By introducing a bill in the Senate requiring the Land Office to issue
patents on all surveys of vacant lands, Walker had curried favor with settlers whose claims were unconfirmed. Walker assured Nelson that a

> large majority of the citizens of this county prefer me as their survey-
> or to anyone else. . . . I am satisfied you are already aware that such is
> the fact . . . that you are not inclined to listen to the misrepresentation
> of interested and designing persons to my prejudice and injury, and
> that you have no idea of displacing me and appointing any one else
> and much less Mr. Ferris who has ever been a friend to the Colony
> contractors . . . contends for their interests &&.[38]

On May 5, 1850, Walker tried to alarm Nelson by telling him that
Ferris planned to run for county surveyor if Dallas were allowed to elect
one in August. If not, Ferris threatened to run against Nelson for District
Surveyor. Then he would be

> an opponent of yours and not mine. He is out upon you. . . . He talks
> publicly of you as 'That man, Nelson',—whom, he says, he brought
> into notice and but for him you never would have been Dst. Surveyor.
> He represents you as being ungrateful. . . . There is not truth in any
> statement he makes.[39]

Next Walker charged that Ferris's surveys were full of errors and con-
tradictions, citing as examples: Ferris "calls a creek 5 varas wide in one
place and 7 in another" and "uses as landmarks trees never in existence." Walker begged Nelson to send copies of Ferris's early surveys so
that he might note other flagrant discrepancies. He demanded to know
the "infamous lies" written by his detractors, denouncing Ferris and the
Colony men who were trying to "break me down and finally to swindle
the people." He recalled that Ferris had supported Reagan over him in
1849 and asserted that it was Ferris's employment as a contractor of the
Peters Company that made it possible for him to offer to survey for $2 a
day.[40]

Warren Ferris's reputation was vindicated on May 21, 1850, when the
Commissioners Court of Dallas County ordered him to resurvey the
boundaries of the county, thereby settling the disputes which arose from

---

37. Walker to Nelson, Feb. 22, Mar. 17, 1850. Nelson Papers.
38. Walker to Nelson, Feb. 22, 1850, ibid.
39. Walker to Nelson, May 5, 1850, ibid.
40. Ibid.

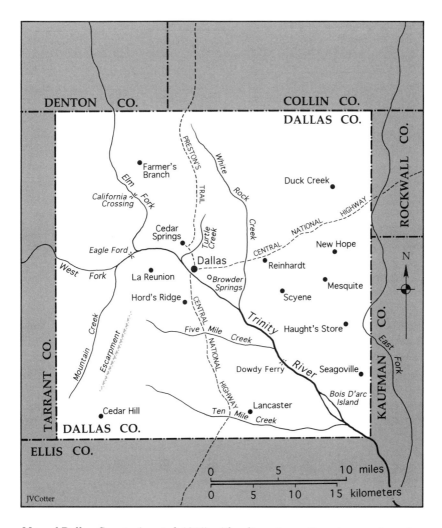

Map of Dallas County (created 1846) with adjacent counties, rivers and creeks, roads, and communities. *Map by John V. Cotter.*

A. G. Walker's faulty 1847 survey. Ferris, who had been employed in 1849 and 1850 to supervise county road building,[41] took up the surveying assignment in June. How it must have galled Walker to have his work corrected by his foremost critic and enemy in the county!

Dallas County commissioners ordered Ferris to run and plainly mark the four boundary lines of the county and to determine the exact center of the thirty-mile square. He was to begin his work on June 6 and complete the survey by June 28.[42] Due to an unusually wet summer that delayed work, the court extended his deadline to July 18. Ferris presented his field notes on July 29 and was paid $140 when the notes were filed.[43] The court then retained Ferris to transcribe field notes of land surveyed west of the Trinity in the Robertson Land District.

This 1850 survey of the county boundaries was Warren A. Ferris's last major public commission, and it was a measure of the confidence placed in him by the officials of Dallas County. The work was accomplished in record time under difficult conditions. When his field notes were filed, they not only described the physical terrain of the county borders, but also vividly recalled the hardships of surveying through high water and sticky "gumbo" mud.

The first entry in his interesting narrative report was on June 7, 1850, when Ferris and his work crew—Wormley Carter, William Babbit, James and George Sharrock, Jesse Overton, and a man named Roberts—set out from the northeast corner of the county. The previous day, Ferris had begun his survey at the point where the east line of the Peters Colony crossed the Old Fannin–Nacogdoches County line. From this point, he ran the line three miles east to the northeast corner of the county, marked by a blazed post in a highland thicket near the East Fork of the Trinity. There they waited overnight to meet surveyors from neighboring Collin and Kaufman Counties. When no one showed, Ferris and his men led their pack horses south across the heavily wooded, low-lying bottom lands of the East Fork. In three days they advanced only five miles, having to cut a passage through heavy thickets. Then the rains came.[44]

On Monday, June 10, Ferris wrote, "Rained hard during the night got up in a pretty pickle, but rolled on our course." Progress was slowed not

41. DeGolyer, "Conquest of Three Forks," 99. Ferris assisted William C. Hunnicutt in building a road from McKenzie's Ferry on the East Fork of the Trinity to Dallas (later the East Pike, U.S. Hwy. 80, Samuell Boulevard route) and worked with Edward Miles on road construction between Dallas and Dean's Crossing.

42. Dallas County Commissioners Court Minutes, Book A, 68.

43. Copy of Ferris's field notes, Dallas County Deed Records, C, 197–211. Ferris was sworn in by Acting Justice of the Peace Benjamin Frost, before whom he took his oath to "well and truely [sic] survey and mark the lines . . . without favour, prejudice or partiality."

44. DeGolyer, "Conquest of Three Forks," 102–105.

only by the weather but also by the rugged terrain. Ferris described a ridge of fine red oak timber that jutted down between Rowlett Creek and the East Fork of the Trinity but complained that the survey party was forced to cut its way through "an almost impenetrable jungle of brush, vines and briars" so tied and bound together that they could scarcely find a spot to plant their mileposts.

By the end of their first week in the field, after several days of heavy rain, the dismayed surveyors found themselves:

> still water bound, and water rapidly increasing. Camp drowned out and forced to make a midnight escape half a mile through an almost impenetrable thicket, dark as pitch, . . . the water climbing up our legs with a most alarming rapidity, this, with the strong probability of not reaching high land in the darkness caused some very disagreeable reflections, among which the strong probability of roosting in a tree until the water abated was not the most agreeable, however we were fortunate.[45]

Reaching high ground, Ferris recalled that the rain still "poured down in torrents, wet everything we had, ruined most of our provisions, and left us surrounded by seas of water." Having lost their provisions and stranded by the high water, they lived off the land, killing a deer and robbing honey from a bee tree. The flood continued for six more days so the surveyors made little progress. Circumstances dampened Ferris's enthusiasm for eastern Dallas County. He described the area around modern Sunnyvale as valueless for cultivation: "little better than an entire swamp," with "disappointing timber . . . dense wet growth of brush and vines." It took the surveyors three weeks, until the end of June, to complete the thirty-mile eastern county line.

On June 30, they marked the thirtieth mile post in the Trinity River bottom and turned the southeast corner of the county. As they continued along the southern boundary, Ferris recalled they encountered a "large slough of river out of banks, the bottoms all submerged and of course impassible, fell back to corner camped and found a bee tree. Then turned Westward ho." Ferris commented on July 1, "We were able to resume our work by doing some tall wading." The party celebrated July 4th when the fifth mile post was planted just out of the river bottoms at Ten Mile Creek or Pleasant Run (Lancaster, Texas). Ferris proclaimed with relief, "Prairie, Thank God!" On the prairie and finally out of the sticky mud, they surveyed nine miles in one day. James Sharrock and his son George became ill so the surveyors rested in camp on Sunday, July 7, waiting for replacements for the Sharrocks.

On July 9, they reached the high point of the county at Cedar Mountain (Cedar Hill) which Ferris wrote, "raises out of the plain to a probable

---

45. Ferris field notes of 1850 county boundaries survey.

height of 5 or 6 hundred feet." From this vantage point, they looked out over Mountain Creek Valley and the West Fork bottoms to the Cross Timbers eight miles to the west. Ferris remarked, "The inhabitants on this side of the river possess a treasure of no little value in the Cedar Mountain which affords cedar timber in great abundance."[46]

Turning the southwest corner, they moved along Mountain Creek, across indifferent sandy soil, through fair timber, to Grapevine Spring Prairie. In the vicinity of modern Grand Prairie, along the western county line, Ferris commented, "The prairie is generally first rate in quality notwithstanding some hogwallows are intersperced [sic] on it."[47]

At the northwest corner on July 14, Ferris and his party paused two days, waiting in vain, for surveyors from Denton and Collin Counties. "We turned on our course Eastward," Ferris wrote. Surveying the controversial northern county line, Ferris attempted to correct errors made by Peters Colony surveyors Phelps and Orr.[48] Unfortunately, Warren Ferris's procedures and the language of his report on this northern line did not fully clarify the controversy.[49] On July 19, the surveyors reached their point of commencement where the Peters Colony line crossed the northern county boundary. On July 21 and 22, Ferris backtracked to the fifteenth mile post, then ran a line south fifteen miles to the center of the county where he marked "Post Center" on a lone blackjack oak tree, thereby completing his assignment for the Commissioners Court.

Ferris's field notes illustrate the markings used to blaze trees. They also list a variety of timber found in the county: red and blackjack oak, hackberry, mulberry, ash, locust (mesquite), haw, and cottonwood in the bottoms. The notes mention various existing roads that penetrated the county in 1850: in the eastern sector, Dean's Crossing Road, the National Road going toward Greenville and Paris, Bennetts' and Coats' "rail" or plankroads, the Kickapoo Trace, Edwards Crossing Road, Lanier Crossing, and the mail road from Dallas to Buffalo, Texas; in the west,

---

46. Ibid. The quality of this mature cedar timber can still be seen in the preserved buildings of the Penn family farm in Cedar Hill State Park.

47. Ibid. The indentations in the soil, called by the pioneers "hogwallows" or "buffalo wallers" because of the animals' propensity to roll in them, were actually created by cracks formed in the hard, dry prairie soil during periods of drought, later to fill with water during periods of rain.

48. Josiah S. Phelps and a Mr. Orr surveyed for the Peters Company in 1846, extending the line between the Fannin and Nacogdoches Land Districts which became the boundary separating Dallas County from Denton, Collin, and Fannin Counties. According to George Jackson, Phelps was killed by Indians while surveying on the West Fork of the Trinity in April 1849. Jackson, *Sixty Years in Texas*, 166–167,

49. Robert H. West, former Dallas County Surveyor, stated in an interview with the author, Feb. 27, 1991, that he felt Ferris must have been ill, hurried, certainly not reporting in his usual manner as he worked the northern boundary line of Dallas County. The precise location of the line is a matter of dispute even in the 1990s. See Dallas *Morning News*, Jan. 27, 1993.

the road to Ft. Worth; and, to the north, the road to Coffee Bend (Preston Road) and the Bonham Road.

At times the surveyors passed and even stayed overnight at scattered farmhouses, and Ferris cites their owners: in the south, Miller's and Widow Kirtland's; in the west, Silas Parks's farm, John F. Porter's, Billingsley's, Hughey Robinson's, Riley Watson's, Holland's, Robinson's, Bradshaw's, Goodwin's, and Jackson Hitt's; on the northern line, John Holland's, Mount's, McCullough's, and John Vance's; en route to the center of the county, Overton's, Walker's, and Smith's places. Various creeks and streams which composed the tributaries of the Trinity River are listed: Rowlett Creek, Red Oak Creek, Ten Mile Creek, Prairie Branch and Mountain Creek, Bear Creek, Denton Fork, Spring Branch, and White Rock. Thus Warren Ferris, in his detailed field notes, gives the reader a thorough picture of the physical borders of Dallas County in 1850.

Ferris and his assistants completed their survey and returned home in time to participate in the hotly contested August 5 election for permanent county seat. Bryan's town of Dallas received 191 votes, edging out Judge William Hord's settlement west of the river, which received 178 votes. Cedar Springs came in third with 101 votes; many disgruntled residents of that community decided to boycott the run-off on August 31. Voters who lived west of the Trinity River were unable to reach the polls in Dallas because of a broken cable on Bryan's ferry. Adam Haught, ferryman, saloon owner, and Bryan kinsman-by-marriage, distributed free whiskey to the stranded voters on the west bank who were finally allowed to vote if they still cared to do so. Despite cries of "foul," Dallas became the county seat, tallying 244 votes compared to 216 for Hord's Ridge.[50]

After 1846, when Joshua Lovejoy was reportedly living in Henderson County, Warren Ferris lost touch with his alienated half-brother; but Sarah Lovejoy reestablished contact with Josh in 1848. After three years of silence from her long-lost brother, Sarah wrote with relief to "C. A. J. F." Lovejoy in Petersburg, Texas:

> You may well believe that your letter was gladly welcomed . . . although it contained no joyful tidings except that you were alive and not deeply distressed. Amid our own many trials we have thought how often of you, with many forebodings and many hopes. . . . We wrote until we gave up in despair of ever hearing from you and my last letter was sent by Warren, who promised that you should get it, but we concluded that he had failed.[51]

The correspondence found Lovejoy still down on his luck. He asked Sarah and his mother for money, but the Buffalo family had none to

50. Greene, *A Town Called Cedar Springs*, 37–38.

51. Sarah Lovejoy to Joshua Lovejoy, July 31, 1848, FLC, Box II, Folder 7. Although Joshua wrote in 1846 of joining the army fighting in Mexico, apparently he did not do so.

spare. In fact, they were selling off lots, parceled from their three acres, to pay taxes. Their rent house brought in some money. In the other house, the family of nine resided: Sally Ferris Lovejoy, age seventy-one; her two unwed daughters, Sarah and Louisa; Charles Ferris, his wife Hester, and their four children, Charles (Charly), Edward (Ned), Ellen May (Nelly), and George W., the youngest. Charles Ferris worked tirelessly at the Buffalo Post Office to meet the bills and keep a roof over the family. Responding to Joshua Lovejoy's inquiry, Sarah assured him that his inheritance, the lots on Carroll and Exchange Streets, were preserved. She reported that their cousin, Nelson Wing of Michigan, demanded settlement of the $800 debt owed him by Lovejoy, but that the Buffalo family had truthfully told Wing they had no idea of Joshua's whereabouts. Sarah, whose health was always delicate, had been gravely ill—at the "brink of the grave" she said—but she was slowly recovering. Although neither she nor Louisa were married, the comely Louisa had many offers. Both young women were married within the next three years, long before they heard from Joshua Lovejoy again in 1853.

In 1842, a dashing Swedish sailor came to the Niagara frontier. Laurentius G. Sellstedt, age twenty-three, spent some time sailing the Great Lakes before he settled in Buffalo in 1845. "Lars" Sellstedt took up the study of art; with remarkable native talent, he painted Lake Erie and the port towns he loved. Frequently he produced portraits which he traded to local families for his room and board.[52] Sellstedt resided with the Lovejoys and painted Sally Lovejoy's family in a charming domestic scene.[53] The artist was captivated by Louisa Lovejoy; he married the twenty-seven-year-old beauty and swept her away to New York City.

Louisa had little more than a year of happiness in her marriage to Sellstedt; however brief, it was a time of fulfillment for them both. In 1851, Louisa's sudden death threw the fledgling artist into deep bereavement which he later described in his autobiography. The touching tribute

---

52. Henry W. Sprague, "Lars Gustav Sellstedt," *Buffalo Historical Society Bulletin*, XVII (Apr., 1912), 39–74, presented to BHS on April 30, 1912.

53. The unfinished genre painting is a kitchen scene, now darkened with age, with mother Sally Lovejoy making bread in a bucket. Her daughter-in-law Hester Ferris sits near a window, holding her baby Sarah Louise. Either Sarah or Louisa Lovejoy is faintly discernible, shown knitting or sewing. About the room are the other children of Hester and Charles Ferris. George's head is barely distinguishable by the door and beside him is his sister Nelly. The two oldest Ferris brothers, Charles and Ned, sit in the foreground. The painting was in the possession of Winifred Ferris of Los Gatos, California in 1941; there is a photograph copy in the Ferriss/Lovejoy Collection. It is described in McCausland, "The Life and Work of Lars Gustaf Sellstedt," 1943, FLC, Box VI, Folder 1. There are also portraits of Sally and Louisa Lovejoy by Sellstedt, and two poems written by Sellstat to Louisa, "To My Absent Louisa" and "The Dark-eyed Sailor."

54. Lars G. Sellstedt, *From Forecastle to Academy: Sailor and Artist* (Buffalo: Matthews-Northrup Works, 1904), 281.

to his departed wife asserted: "God never sent a more beautiful soul to dwell in mortal body than that of Louisa Lovejoy, and our love was pure, perfect, and sweetly mutual."[54]

Sarah Lovejoy wrote to her brother Joshua to tell him of Louisa's marriage and subsequent tragic death. Sellstedt she described as a professional artist, "gentlemanly in manners, of cultivated intellect," with "strong religious principles and a kind heart." Sarah told of how the newlyweds left in February 1850 for New York City, bound ultimately for St. Thomas in the Virgin Islands where Sellstedt hoped to perfect his art. Disappointed by his lack of artistic success in New York City, Lars brought Louisa home to Buffalo in late 1850. There she was struck with dreaded cholera and severe dysentery, dying on the fourth night of her illness. "Remember Louisa as you do in her early girlhood," Sarah urged Joshua. "You can have no idea how brilliantly beautiful she was at the time of her death, in person, mind, and manners."[55]

Prior to Louisa's marriage to Sellstedt, in October 1849, Charles Ferris left Buffalo, supposedly bound for Texas. Depressed by the unwelcome news that his wife Hester was pregnant with their fifth child, worn by the family's years of financial struggle, disappointed in his own personal ambitions, Ferris was in a gloomy state of mind. A long period passed with no word from him. Hester Ferris posted a frantic letter to Texas:

> Brother Warren, we are all in a state of great trouble and anxiety on account of not hearing from you or Charles. . . . He left home on the first of October intending to go south in fact direct to your place, we have not heard from him but once since he left, that was about three weeks after he left home. . . . I hope you will answer this as soon as possible, for I am [so] anxious to hear something of Charles that almost any news would be preferrable [sic] to such dreadful suspense. . . . He has had plenty of time to get to your house before this.[56]

Hester urged Warren Ferris to write, good news or ill, in care of "a friend of ours—Hiram Damon, Buffalo." She shared news of Louisa's marriage to Sellstedt, their trip to New York City, and plan to visit the West Indies. Of her sons, Hester wrote, "The boys wish they could see their uncle Warren, and often talk of going to live on a prairie beside him. They are two great boys headstrong enough to be sure and need their fathers presence to curb them." Of Joshua Lovejoy, Hester reported that the family had heard nothing in over a year, perhaps he had joined goldseekers flocking to California.[57]

Warren Ferris probably responded immediately to Hester's urgent letter, but his next surviving letter dated June 11, 1851, was addressed to

---

55. Sarah Lovejoy Damon to Joshua Lovejoy, May 21, 1853, as cited in DeGolyer, "Conquest of Three Forks," 107.

56. Hester Ferris to Warren Ferris, Feb. 4, 1850, as cited in DeGolyer, "Conquest of Three Forks," 100–101.

57. Ibid.

sister Sarah. Ferris wrote that he had heard nothing from Charles and that he also was concerned over this brother's apparent disappearance. Neither had he heard anything of Joshua. "[A]lthough he did beat me in a most ungenerous not to say unbrotherly manner," he stated, "yet I should be well pleased to hear where he is and what he is doing." Ferris fretted that Louisa had married some foreign "profligate who will abandon her." With Charles absent, Warren Ferris was uneasy about his mother's welfare; he urged Sarah, "come here and spend your days in this sunny land . . . you would be happier and it would enable me to do something for Ma that distance and my heretofore errant life has hitherto prevented."[58]

Describing his life in Dallas with Frances and the children, Emily, James, and six-months-old William, Ferris continued:

> We have here a home that I think would please you. Our buildings are situated in the East edge of a large grove that amply shades our large yard, we have an orchard of two or more hundred trees among which are a hundred Peach. They now [are] loaded with fruit our Apples and Pears and Plums have not borne. We have six head of Horses, 25 or 30 cattle, 60 or 80 head of hogs—85 acres in cultivation—have just harvested a fine crop of Wheat—say 4 or 500 bushels—will have as many oats and 5 or 600 bushels of corn besides cotton to the Value of 100 or 200 dollars. . . . Mother and children all in fine health—in addition to this we have Two dogs, 3 cats, and 200 chickens—besides bees enough to supply us with an abundance of honey the year round. So you see I have become a thorough farmer.[59]

Warren Ferris addressed this letter, so solicitous of his Buffalo family, to his half-sister Sarah Lovejoy, not knowing of her marriage in February 1851 to Hiram Damon. Sarah, at last, escaped spinsterhood to which she long had felt doomed. Sarah and Hiram Damon had four children and apparently enjoyed relatively prosperous circumstances during the years of their marriage, as Sarah was able to send her brother Joshua money from time to time. It was to Joshua Lovejoy in May 1853 that Sarah revealed more about the mysterious disappearance of Charles Ferris.

According to Sarah, Charles had been in poor health when he left Buffalo in October 1849, thinking that a few months spent in Canada might restore him. He wrote once, requesting money and clothing and saying he would remain in Canada a bit longer before heading for Texas. The family heard no more until June 1851 when they received shocking news that Charles Ferris was presumably lost at sea aboard the ship *Unicorn* in terrific winter storms along the Atlantic coast during December 1850. Five months elapsed without the vessel reaching port; and, as the owners of the ship in Sydney, Cape Breton, received no word of her, they considered the vessel lost with all her passengers. Sarah

---

58. Warren Ferris to Sarah Lovejoy, June 11, 1851, FLC, Box II, Folder 20.
59. Ibid.

Lovejoy Damon yet hoped the family might have news of Charles's survival. She testified to his "worth as a son and brother," saying had it not been for his exertions the family would not "have retained one foot of the land we now have."[60]

No record was ever found of the fate of a ship called the *Unicorn*. Lloyd's list showed a brig of that name abandoned off the coast of Portugal in November 1850 while en route from Philadelphia to Londonderry, but the crew was saved. In November 1851, a vessel of that name was abandoned while on a voyage from Liverpool to Saint John, New Brunswick, but again the crew and passengers were saved. Another *Unicorn*, used to deliver mail from Cunard steamers calling at Halifax, was sold to the Portuguese in 1846. Perhaps the ship with which Charles Ferris perished was a small coasting vessel whose loss excited little notice.[61]

Thus Charles Drake Ferris, whose brief life as a Texas pioneer was interrupted by a New York fraud trial, whose ambitions were thwarted by economic collapse, and whose budding journalistic career was weighed down by family responsibilities, dropped from sight, his fate never truly known by his friends and relatives.

---

60. Sarah Damon to Joshua Lovejoy, May 21, 1853, cited in DeGolyer, "Conquest of Three Forks," 108–109.

61. McCausland, "Early Buffalo Journalist," 21. In the 1940s, McCausland researched the fate of the ship *Unicorn* but found no insurance or shipping records which verified its 1850 loss at sea. FLC, Box V, Folder 8.

9

AT HOME ON WHITE ROCK CREEK

IN DALLAS, WARREN A. FERRIS attempted to extricate himself from the controversy that still swirled around the Peters Company. Hoping to distance himself from past associations with land promoters, Ferris only longed to resume a quiet life on his White Rock Creek farm. However, the dispute was not to die easily.

When the fourth contract expired in 1848, the Peters Company was eager to close out its troublesome Texas venture. Haunted by fears of endless litigation, the directors hoped to settle the problems and collect their premium land.[1] Agent H. O. Hedgcoxe completed surveying and, in January 1849, submitted a map of the Colony to the Land Office in Austin, where state officials were unfriendly to Peters Company claims. On Gov. Peter H. Bell's orders, Land Commissioner Thomas W. "Peg Leg" Ward[2] traveled through the colony listening to settlers' grievances. While the lawsuit against the company, charging failure to comply with terms of the fourth contract, was still pending, no clear titles could be issued. To further complicate the matter, the Peters Company filed a countersuit, arguing that government actions made it impossible for the company to fulfill its contract.[3]

The man who would resolve this impasse was James W. Throckmorton. Throckmorton, whose family came to Collin County in 1842 as Peters Colonists, was a state legislator in 1851 when the dispute between the settlers and the company came before the session.[4] At issue was the question of how to secure titles for the settlers and still live up to the state's obligations to the Peters Company. Throckmorton judged that the company

---

1. Upon successful completion of the contract, the company was to receive 600,000 acres of premium West Texas land in payment for its promotion of colonization. Connor, *The Peters Colony*, 135.

2. This was the same Thomas W. Ward who, on Sam Houston's orders in 1842, tried to remove the archives from Austin in the struggle that became known as "The Archive War." Ward, longtime commissioner of the General Land Office, lost a leg in the Texas Revolution and an arm later in celebrating her independence.

3. The countersuit was filed by Willis Stewart, a forceful lobbyist for the company who was sent to Texas in late 1849 to try to settle problems with the colonists. Connor, *The Peters Colony*, 126–128.

4. Claude Elliott, *Leathercoat: The Life History of a Texas Patriot* (San Antonio: Standard Printing Co., 1938), 21. Throckmorton, age twenty-six when elected to the Texas House, served on a joint committee to work out an agreement between the Peters Company and its dissatisfied colonists.

had fulfilled the terms of the contract: between 1841 and 1848 it had introduced over 2,000 families to north central Texas.[5] Throckmorton's compromise solution, passed by a relieved legislature on February 10, 1852, called for dropping the lawsuits, allowing settlers to locate claims until August 4, 1852, and compensating the company (for relinquishing its claim to half-sections) with an additional amount of land. The legislature never dealt with the legality of the half-section claim and was remarkably generous, granting the company over a million acres of land (estimated value $300,000) in West Texas.[6] Congratulating themselves on successful completion of their work, the legislators adjourned to their home districts only to find their constituents infuriated by the compromise.

Henry O. Hedgcoxe, reinstated as Peters Company agent, operated from an office north of Dallas. Under terms of the compromise, he was empowered to receive claims and issue certificates. To the settlers, this high-handed Englishman represented years of unjust treatment. They dubbed him "Lord Hedgcoxe Duke Grand Mogul etc. of the Three Forks of the Trinity."[7] To obtain their land titles, settlers were forced to deal with this obnoxious fellow whose arrogant pronouncements enraged them. True to form, Hedgcoxe promptly inflamed the citizens by issuing a circular declaring the claims of 400 settlers invalid. The stage was set for what came to be known as the "Hedgcoxe War."

Violent reaction to the compromise agreement flared throughout North Texas. At indignation meetings, speakers emotionally attacked company "pirates" and "extortionists." An Austin newspaper outlined Peters Company abuses, including disregard for its charter, harassment of settlers with unreasonable demands, overcharging for surveys and invalid certificates, selling land already in possession of another, and retaining the best land for itself.[8] Encouraged by disgruntled land speculators who found themselves excluded from a million choice West Texas acres,[9] settlers demanded a special legislative session to correct the Throckmorton Compromise which they viewed to be little more than fraud and robbery.

John H. Reagan, Ferris's former deputy surveyor and now a district judge, spoke to a rally of irate colonists in Dallas on May 15, 1852, coming

---

5. Connor judges this an exaggerated figure since it was based on company records. Ward's enumeration fell far short of this figure.

6. Premium land lay in what became Baylor, Archer, Clay, Throckmorton, Young, Jack, Shackleford, Stephens, and Palo Pinto Counties, straddling the headwaters of the Brazos River.

7. John J. Good to John H. Reagan, Aug. 17, 1852, Connor, *The Peters Colony*, 140.

8. The *State Gazette* (Austin), May 22, 1852, cited in Elliott, *Leathercoat*, 23.

9. Connor, *The Peters Colony*, 138, points out that the first of these mass meetings was held in Limestone County, outside the Peters Colony, and was organized by noncolonists.

out strong against the Peters Company. Reagan learned a hard political lesson in 1849 when his pro-company stance cost him election to the Texas Senate; apparently he decided this time to join the popular hue and cry. Although he cautioned against violence, Judge Reagan now urged "united resistance" against the "petty tyrant" (Hedgcoxe) of "foreign nabobs" (Texas Emigration and Land Company). The Dallas meeting offered resolutions against the compromise law and Hedgcoxe's reappointment. Those in attendance vowed to aid and assist any oppressed colonist, "peacably if we can—forcibly if we must."[10] This ominous threat became the theme of protest meetings in North Texas during the summer of 1852.

At a second, larger rally in Dallas, on July 10, Reagan spoke again. Those present appointed a committee of "investigators" who on July 12 forcibly entered Hedgcoxe's office to examine company records.[11] A crowd, disappointed when the committee failed to make its report on July 13, censured Sen. Samuel A. Bogart, Reagan's political rival who supported the legislative compromise.[12] The committee report concerning the accuracy of company records was promised for the evening of July 15.

The hot and angry crowd shifted restlessly while they listened to Reagan harangue for hours on the night of July 15. The report of "investigators" of Peters Company records reinforced fears that the company intended to defraud the colonists of their just land claims. Reagan purportedly tried to dissuade the people from "a resort to violence"; but, by the end of the talk, the temper of his audience was at a fever pitch.

Later that night in Dallas, armed citizens milled the streets, drank whiskey, mustered their courage, and elected John J. Good, who had military experience in Mississippi, as their "commander." At first light, they marched north on Hedgcoxe's office, reaching their destination early in the afternoon of July 16. Hedgcoxe was warned in time to grab some of his valuable records and hide in a cornfield.[13] McKinney resident T. B. Wilson, recalled the day's events, "They, after tanking up on E. Whitley's corn juice, proceeded thro' the streets . . . to the office of the company. It was motley crew."[14]

---

10. *Northern Standard* (Clarksville), July 31, 1852. Such bombast capitalized on the fact that the Peters Company originally had British investors.

11. Connor, *The Peters Colony*, 142. The second meeting was reported in the *Northern Standard* (Clarksville), Aug. 7, 1852. Committee members included: A. Bledsoe, Samuel B. Pryor, Alex Harwood, James H. Smith, J. M. Crockett, and B. Warren Stone. Connor identifies Stone and John J. Good as land speculators and leading agitators in the episode.

12. Samuel A. Bogart of Collin County filled A. G. Walker's senate seat when Walker resigned in 1850; he then defeated Reagan in a special election for the District 3 position. Representing Collin, Cooke, Dallas, Denton, Fannin, and Grayson Counties, Bogart supported Throckmorton's Compromise.

13. Elliott, *Leathercoat*, 25.

14. Ibid. T. B. Wilson recollections, McKinney *Daily Courier-Gazette*, Dec. 26, 1906. This description conflicted with that of B. W. Stone who wrote to the

The mob seized company files and maps and ordered Hedgcoxe out of the colony. He departed the next day; en route to Louisville, he stopped by Austin to lodge a protest with Governor Bell:

> The men were armed with rifles, double-barreled shotguns, bowie Knives and revolvers to attack an old man broken in health. A band of armed men . . . more than one hundred . . . violently entered my office, seized and carried away maps, books and papers . . . with threats and force entered my private residence.[15]

Captain Good and his "army" returned to Dallas, placed the company papers in the courthouse for safekeeping, and joined a raucous victory celebration. According to Good, Dallasites gave the returning vigilantes a "brilliant reception" with feasting and reveling that lasted well into the day. An effigy of Senator Bogart was promenaded around the square on a rail, then swung from a blackjack oak and burned. William Myres, a reputed spy of the Peters Company, was seized by the mob and given a rough "rail ride" before his release. All company agents received one month's notice to get out of North Texas.[16]

With paranoia running so high, Warren Ferris wisely kept a low profile. He was a known associate of Peters Company men. Ferris did not participate in the attack on Hedgcoxe's office, but he did attend the protest meetings in Dallas. When Reagan was later charged with inciting the mob action of July 16, Ferris was one of those who signed a statement swearing that his friend's words did not inflame the crowd:

> we were present and heard Judge Reagan address the citizens of this county on several occasions during the excitement which resulted in taking the papers etc. from the possession of Henry O. Hedgcoxe. . . . [The] object of Judge Reagan's speeches on every occasion . . . was to allay the existing excitement.[17]

The colony was in an uproar. What would follow the night of lawlessness? Would claims placed with Hedgcoxe still be valid? What had happened to confiscated company records? Now that Hedgcoxe had fled the colony, who would accept claims? A series of meetings throughout the colony demonstrated the disarray. On July 20, in McKinney, moderates condemned the Dallas mob, but on July 29 Denton colonists supported

---

Northern Standard (Clarksville) on July 20 and was reported Aug. 31, 1852. Stone called the forty men who marched from Dallas some of the "best in the colony."

15. H. O. Hedgcoxe to Gov. Bell, Sept. 3, 1852, cited in Elliott, *Leathercoat*, 25.

16. John J. Good to John C. Easton, July 17, 1852, reported in *Northern Standard* (Clarksville), Aug. 7, 1852.

17. *Northern Standard* (Clarksville), Sept. 10, 1853. Ferris was one of a number of Dallas County leaders who signed the statement. Other signers were Sam Pryor, Wes Chenault, Wormley Carter, Hiram Bennett, W. C. Haught, and A. Bledsoe. Reagan took a full-page paid advertisement in several papers to establish that he had been invited to Dallas to secure colonists' rights and had no connections with land speculators.

armed action against Hedgcoxe and called for the resignations of Bogart and Throckmorton. Further resistance, "peacably if we can—forcibly if we must," was endorsed.

At the urging of Peters Colonists,[18] Governor Bell called a special session of the legislature, which worked out a plan for colonists to file claims based on the residue of Hedgcoxe's papers and the official map filed in the General Land Office.[19] As resentment and anger gradually subsided, Warren Ferris must have heaved a sigh of relief. The episode marked the end of his public life. From this point forward, Ferris was a very private man, concentrating on his farm, his family, and his books. His friend John H. Reagan gained popularity from his role in the affair, and Throckmorton's constituents soon forgave him and returned him to the legislature. Both Reagan and Throckmorton went on to play leading roles in Texas politics.[20]

During the mid-1850s, Warren Ferris continued his correspondence with the Buffalo family. Not knowing if his mother was still alive, Ferris wrote Sarah of his hope to someday see the family again. "If mother is yet alive, tell her that I never forget her . . . tell her that nothing would give me more pleasure than to have her with me and to show her my wife and children"[21]

That the family kept up hope of word from Charles Ferris is evident in Warren Ferris's letter:

> In your last you stated that Charles had entered on board a vessel bound for Canada and, not having been heard from, the vessel was supposed to have foundered at sea. Now vessels sometimes are driven far from their course and wrecked upon desert islands where mariners might support their existence for months or even years before an opportunity offered to find a conveyance home. I had still hoped that you might hear from him living. If, however, such is not the case, it would be vain to indulge any further hope.[22]

---

18. Connor, *The Peters Colony*, 144. Demands issued by delegates from six counties attending a convention held in McKinney, July 29–31, 1852. Connor, who analyzed delegates to this convention, found the majority to be non-colonists. He judged the Hedgcoxe War "no spontaneous movement of the colonists. It was originated by, developed by, and led by outside land speculators."

19. The special session opened in January 1853 and by February had worked out legislation favorable to the colonists. Peters Company papers seized by the Dallas mob never reached the Land Office. The loss of the stolen papers, which probably were destroyed by fire, further complicated issuance of patents. See Connor, *The Peters Colony*, 149, and Elliott, *Leathercoat*, 30.

20. Throckmorton served as post–Civil War governor of Texas and U.S. congressman. He died in 1894 and was buried near McKinney. John Reagan was postmaster general of the Confederacy and U.S. senator from Texas. He died in 1905 and was buried at Palestine.

21. Warren A. Ferris to Sarah Lovejoy, August 1855, cited in DeGolyer, "Conquest of Three Forks," 109.

22. Ibid.

Five years after Charles Ferris's mysterious disappearance, his brother advised the Buffalo family to go about the business of living. Louisa Lovejoy Sellstedt's demise at so young an age and Charles Ferris's apparent death struck a double blow to the family. Sarah and Hiram Damon were living in Cazenovia, New York, where Damon clerked in a general merchandise store. Elderly Sally Lovejoy still resided in the brick house on Seneca Street in Buffalo with her daughter-in-law Hester and five grandchildren. Sarah Damon described to Ferris his nieces and nephews: the oldest, Charly, was seventeen, "talented, full of good impulses, but sometimes too easily led by others"; Ned, age fourteen, was "bright but idle unless he has strong inducements"; Ellen May or "Nellie," age ten, "a genius, born to be an authoress"; George W., a boy of seven, "in him . . . lie the strongest materials—for good or evil, as directed"; the youngest, age three and a half, "the little witch" Sarah Louise.[23]

In his letter to Sarah Lovejoy Damon written August 24, 1855, Warren Ferris painted the picture of a contented farmer, withdrawn from public life but well aware of the rapid development of his community. "I am quietly settled on White Rock Creek in this county on a place where I have buried two of my children and where I shall in all probability close my career," he wrote. Now W. A. and Fanny Ferris had five living children, ranging from six years of age to eight months: James (b. 1849), William (b. 1850), Charles (b. 1852), Mary Catherine (b. 1853), and Henry (b. 1855).

Ferris told the Buffalo family of his life on the Texas frontier where, like most pioneers, he exhibited personal resourcefulness. "I have," he stated proudly, "framed and built a house myself . . . my own plough, and other tools . . . by industry and economy we manage to keep above water." The bears, wolves, and wildcats which once annoyed the Ferris farmstead were fast disappearing, but game was still plentiful. Supplementing their diet with deer, turkey, squirrel, and fish from White Rock Creek, the Ferrises lived very well.

Ferris reported that Dallas County also prospered. By the mid-1850s, steam-powered threshing machines were busy cutting wheat which, after processing at local flour mills, brought a good price in East Texas. According to Ferris, Dallas area cotton was also good, but not as profitable as wheat because of transportation problems. Sugar, cloth, and manufactured items were costly since goods headed for Dallas were hauled by wagon over 200 miles from either Houston or Shreveport. Rich prairie soil and a long growing season helped the Ferris family enjoy relative prosperity; but, like most farmers, they always owed a debt to the local merchant.

The future looked bright to Ferris: "a general spirit of improvement . . . will soon place us in an enviable position." He predicted with pride, "the

---

23. Sarah Lovejoy to Joshua Lovejoy, May 21, 1853, FLC, Box II, Folder 1.

Portrait of Sarah "Sally" Gray Ferris Lovejoy, mother of Warren A. Ferris, painted by Lars G. Sellstedt, noted Buffalo artist, in 1850 when Mrs. Lovejoy was sixty-five years of age. Oil on canvas. Original painting held by the heirs of Winifred J. Ferris. *Photograph courtesy the Photographic Archives, Harold B. Lee Library, Brigham Young University, Provo, Utah.*

country is rappidly [sic] improving and we shall soon have in point of climate and rich agricultural lands a country unsurpassed."[24]

"The Town of Dallas is becoming quite a little place," Ferris bragged,
"we can get nearly everything we wish except rare books."[25] Dallas was
not only the county seat but also the hub of overland stage routes that
reached out in every direction. The town boasted its own newspaper, a
new courthouse, one fine hotel, a carriage factory, a brewery, saw mills,
flour mills, and cotton gins that drew customers from a wide area. New
men were coming in and old settlers moving farther west. In 1854, Neely
Bryan sold his interest in the town to Alexander Cockrell, a Peters
Colonist from Kentucky. Bryan took off for Indian Territory, while
Cockrell began to develop the townsite. He replaced Bryan's ferry with a
wooden toll bridge and laid a plank road across the Trinity River bottom,
giving immigrant wagons better access to the western plains. After
Cockrell was killed in 1858, his enterprising wife Sarah Horton Cockrell
became the leading business figure of the town. Ferris's former business
associate from Nacogdoches, Nicholas Darnell, managed Sarah Cockrell's
new hotel, the St. Nicholas. William Caruth and his brother Walter established a general store, near the courthouse at Main and Record Streets,
and almost immediately began buying up land. These events and all the
"doings" of Dallas were recorded by publisher James W. Latimer in his
Democratic newspaper, the *Herald*.[26]

Dallas evidenced a concentration of money and talent unusual to the
Texas frontier. The Peters Colonists, largely non-slaveholding emigrants
from the Upper South, possessed capital assets that were readily available for commercial investment. In the mid-1850s, the short-lived "La
Reunion," a French socialist colony established west of Dallas, provided
an influx of educated professionals and gifted artisans.[27] Taken together,
Dallas businessmen displayed a canny talent for seeing larger trends,
seizing opportunities, and advancing their community. These, combined
with the ambitions of progressive farmers like W. A. Ferris, propelled the
development of Dallas County.

During the late 1850s, Warren Ferris gained experience as a farmer. He
read agricultural and scientific journals and experimented with planting a

---

24. Warren A. Ferris to Sarah Lovejoy Damon, Aug. 24, 1855, ibid., Box II,
Folder 20.

25. Ibid.

26. Saxon (ed.), *The WPA Dallas Guide and History*, 47, 50–51, 258. Latimer
brought his press down from Paris, Texas, in 1849. First calling the Dallas paper
the *Cedar Snag*, Latimer soon changed the name to a more dignified *Herald* and
began expounding anti-abolitionist views.

27. It was perhaps of interest to Warren Ferris that social reformer Albert
Brisbane visited Dallas in 1852 to establish La Reunion. Ferris's brother Charles
promoted the Fourierist philosophy of this same Brisbane in his Buffalo publication, the *Phalanx*.

variety of crops. The Blackland Prairie was a natural haymeadow with gently swaying native grasses that reached head high in spring. Settlers first grazed their cattle on the vast, rolling meadows; later they acquired heavy steel plows to break the deep sod and began to plant crops.[28] Prairie soil was well suited to wheat, but farmers also wanted to grow corn for feed. Ferris learned by experience to distance his corn rows and plow deep, thus capturing spring rains and producing a decent yield, even in years of summer drought.[29]

Vagaries of weather were the bane of Dallas farmers, and the year 1858 stood out in the memory of all. A series of natural disasters plagued the area. Spring floods collapsed Cockrell's first bridge across the river, then the summer brought a prolonged dry spell. Grass withered, livestock died of thirst, even Ferris's gristmill on White Rock Creek shut down for lack of water. With winter came heavy snowfalls, sleet, and rain which damaged the winter wheat crop. Texas weather was always unpredictable. As if these calamities were not enough, farmers were again pestered by wheatbirds (horned larks) which destroyed the spring crop just as it was coming to harvest.[30]

Ferris was one of the first Dallas County farmers to experiment with growing cotton.[31] Every southern farmer longed to harvest this money crop, but many thought prairie land unsuitable. Ferris and others proved Blackland Prairie cotton equal to that of the lower Brazos and Trinity River bottom lands. Its stalks were small, but prairie cotton was just as productive. Although Ferris admitted that "No crop is more tender or requires more careful management," he advised its large-scale cultivation, for aesthetic as well as economic reasons. He judged, "there are few plants that can vie with cotton in beauty, aside from its great commercial importance and utility."[32]

The chief obstacle to a cotton culture was lack of reliable transportation to get the Dallas County product to market. Dreams of navigating the Trinity were still alive. In 1852, Adam Haught, James Beeman, Ferris's neighbor Amon McCommas, and others attempted floating cotton downriver to mar-

---

28. Phelan, *Texas Wild*, 144.

29. In "Maize or Corn," Dallas *Herald*, July 1, 1871, W. A. Ferris shared the results of his agricultural experience. He advised farmers to select choice seed, plant corn rows four to six feet apart, plow early and deeply, and thin the stalks, promising "if the hints here offered are followed out, I will warrant the crop produced to be a fair one either with or without summer rains."

30. Saxon (ed.), *The WPA Dallas Guide and History*, 51–52, 47.

31. William M. Cochran planted the first cotton in 1846. The first cotton gin in the county (1849) was located near Cochran's at Farmer's Branch. "Blackland Base for a City," *Southwest Business Magazine*, 19 (Oct., 1940).

32. W. A. Ferris, "Cotton," Dallas *Herald*, July 15, 1871. Describing a July cotton field, Ferris wrote "the deep green foliage contrasting with the red or yellow blossoms, and snowy whiteness of the opening cotton . . . presents a scene of surpassing beauty."

ket in Galveston. Crewmen poled a handbuilt flatboat, the *Dallas*, as far as Porter's Bluff, seventy miles downstream; it took the boatmen four months to negotiate even this short distance.[33] Either low water or logjams made steamboat navigation of the Upper Trinity impossible.

By the 1850s, the riverboat town of Jefferson in East Texas was the main outlet for export of inland cotton. Farmers hauled their produce overland by wagon; at the busy Jefferson dock, it was loaded on steamboats and floated down Cypress Bayou to the Red River and New Orleans. Freighting costs from Shreveport, Jefferson, and Houston kept the price of manufactured goods high. Two transportation issues dominated thoughts of Dallas businessmen in the late 1850s: the need for a permanent iron bridge across the Trinity and the desire to attract proposed railroad routes, one north/south from Houston to Denison and the other east/west from Shreveport to El Paso.

In the census of 1860, W. A. Ferris identified himself a "farmer" rather than a surveyor. He owned over a thousand acres in Dallas and Denton Counties, valued at close to $10,000; he had ten horses, fifty cattle, and a hundred sheep, worth nearly $1,000.[34] Ferris attributed this abundance to his own industry and perseverance, saying he did not admire men (perhaps here he was thinking of Joshua Lovejoy) who depended on their luck for existence. In Dallas, he commented, there were professional men who, despite their abilities, were too poor to marry. Counseling his nephews, Charly and Ned, Ferris urged an education that stressed industry rather than idleness so that when they "launch out into active life toil will be easy and success certain."[35]

Warren Ferris's fortunate situation was in sharp contrast to the pinched existence of his alienated half-brother. Having heard nothing from C. A. (Joshua) Lovejoy after 1846, Ferris presumed him to be in the California gold fields, but Sarah Lovejoy Damon corresponded with Joshua frequently in the 1850s. Sarah tried to locate her brother in early 1853 and finally got a letter through to him and his wife Mary. It was the first news Lovejoy had of Charles's disappearance, Louisa's death, and Sarah's marriage. He was in LaVaca County in South Texas, out of money as usual, and still trying to find a profitable "situation." Sarah, always the loyal sister, sent money, and her letters tracked him as he moved restlessly from one Texas county to the next, herding cattle, haul-

---

33. Jackie McElhaney, "Navigating the Trinity," *Legacies*, 3 (Spring, 1991), 4–13, offers an excellent summary of persistant efforts to utilize the river. Barrot Sanders, "Dallas to Galveston on the Mean Trinity," Dallas *Morning News*, Jan. 19, 1986, cites A. C. Haught's logbook, which described the disappointing venture. Heavy rains soaked much of the cotton and the massive flatboat sank in the river at Porter's Bluff. Some bales were salvaged and sold at depressed prices in Galveston.

34. Agricultural Census of 1860, Dallas County (Dallas Public Library).

35. Warren Ferris to Sarah Damon, Aug. 24, 1855, FLC, Box II, Folder 20.

ing freight, farming, and teaching school. Joshua Lovejoy had not lost his flare for the melodramatic, as revealed in a 1854 letter which told a tale of danger and disappointment:

> I sat down in sickness—in poverty . . . and mourned the loss—apart from society of the world for two years till my head commenced turning gray—until the support of a wife and children demanded exertions. . . . I have been since then in 'perilous times'—I have sat in the Wilderness a hundred miles from succor—My horse saddled at my feet—my gun cocked in my lap, my revolver cocked in my belt—Thus have I sat all night my back against a tree. . . . there I sat for hours— every nerve strained . . . but the attack was not made. . . . The nerves relaxed—and the memory of home—came stealing over the heard [sic] and in the wilderness—there—where every rustle of a leaf might be the step of an Indian or Mexican—I wept—till life seemed valueless— but tears softened . . . life was not mine but belonged to helpless wife and children—widowed mother and sisters. . . . Life is valueless I have no hopes or pleasures to live for—save to struggle on—for the support of those dearer far dearer than life—.[36]

Concerning the fate of Charles Ferris, Lovejoy refused to believe him dead. He was convinced that Ferris disappeared to escape family responsibilities and start a new life. Lovejoy claimed to have met a cousin who told him that "an old Texian" had recognized "CDF" in Louisville. Warning his sister not to get up false hopes, Joshua promised to investigate.[37]

In 1854, Lovejoy invested in cattle, oxen, and two wagons to haul freight for the state government in Austin. By the following year, he was writing that he was ill, having trouble collecting debts due him, and needing money. Sarah Damon sent $200 to the post office in Brenham, Texas, where he received his mail. When next she heard from him, he had taken up farming again; this time trying to raise cotton in the fertile Brazos Valley of Washington County. On payment of a debt owed him, Lovejoy rented a farm; invested all his money in farm implements, seed, and livestock; and determined to "make cotton . . . the only thing that brings money in the South." Gambling to make a killing on his corn, cotton, and hogs, Lovejoy dreamed of wealth which would allow him to visit Central America, Cuba, or Brazil, but he lost everything when his crop was wiped out by a severe Texas drought.[38]

---

36. Joshua Lovejoy to Sarah Damon, May 10, 1854, ibid.

37. Ibid.

38. Joshua [Lovejoy] to Sarah [Damon], July 30, 1856, ibid., Box III, Folder 1. Lovejoy wrote that he "rented a farm for 140$ bought 79$ corn—60$ for meat—80$ farming implements tools Harness etc—35$ for two cows—16$ for Hogs—took mules etc for my debt . . . thought the next year I would fatten my hogs with my own corn—and have but little expense—I worked like wild—hired some—planted from 3 to 5 hund [sic] bush corn—and from 5 to 8 hundred Dollars worth cotton when shipped to Galveston or Orleans—Well a *little dry time* commenced in May and still continues."

Sarah urged Joshua to bring his wife and children home to live in the nearby family rent house on Carroll Street. She even offered to send him "railroad money" for travel expenses.[39] Writing her brother of family news, she informed Joshua that Louisa's estate was being divided; her husband Lars Sellstedt had left Buffalo and the family heard from him only by letter. Sarah Damon told her brother of the death of her first child, a baby son, and of her own poor health which led the doctor to send her to Saratoga Springs for a rest cure. On any question of Charles Ferris's survival, she insisted, "can't be true about Charles—we know he was in the ship *Unicorn* in the awful Christmas storm of 1850 . . . [which] left no doubt of his fate."[40] Sarah sent an additional $300 to her brother in care of the post office at La Grange, Texas. Markedly subdued, Lovejoy told his sister, "I am living such a retired country life that I can neither instruct nor amuse you." Although he frequently spoke of returning to Buffalo to claim his inheritance, Lovejoy wrote from Washington County in 1856 that with "cholery" in Houston and yellow fever in Galveston—there was "too much sickness on the waters, too much risk to come home."[41]

Drought ruined the majority of Joshua Lovejoy's crops and his chance of getting to Buffalo in 1856. The once dashing adventurer now made a pitiful plea for money:

> If mother could see me toiling between the plough handles my face sun burnt . . . seamed by sickness and sorrow—and suffering—My hands in the same fix she certainly would not hesitate long which way money ought to go.[42]

In the spring of 1857, Joshua Lovejoy was in Brenham where he received Sarah Damon's draft for $400. Farming near Vine Grove in Washington County, Lovejoy experienced little success. Another long, hot, dry summer with no rain from mid-May to the end of September caused "short" crops of cotton and sugarcane. Money was scarce, but Lovejoy still hoped to visit Buffalo in the fall.[43]

Sarah Damon wrote that she had heard from Warren Ferris in Dallas and that he had asked about Joshua. Lovejoy instructed his sister, "You will not give my address to W. A. Ferris—I have abundant reasons for being at war with the *name*." He claimed Ferris "once attacked and shot at me missing the right side of my head 2 inches."[44] Although Warren Ferris made several inquiries, Sarah Damon followed her brother's admonition and never shared with Ferris the meanderings of "C. A." Lovejoy.

39. Sarah Damon to Joshua Lovejoy, May 21, 1853, ibid., Box II, Folder 1.

40. Sarah Damon to Joshua Lovejoy, Apr. 4 and July 18, 1854 ibid., Box II, Folder 1.

41. Joshua Lovejoy to Sarah Damon, July 1, 1856, ibid., Box II, Folder 20.

42. Joshua Lovejoy to Sarah Damon, July 30, 1856, ibid., Box III, Folder 1.

43. Joshua Lovejoy to Sarah Damon, Mar. 1, 1857, ibid., Box II, Folder 20.

44. Ibid.

Probably Warren Ferris was concerned about Lovejoy's whereabouts more out of dread than affection. He lived in constant apprehension that his half-brother might suddenly reappear and challenge his ownership of the White Rock Creek land.

During the late 1850s, Sarah Damon and Joshua Lovejoy continued the family practice of exchanging newspapers.[45] Sarah sent Josh an Episcopal family newspaper, commenting that it did not "meddle in slavery" so would not be obnoxious to postal authorities busily censoring abolitionist literature coming into the South.[46] For his part, Lovejoy wrote of the "pinching times" in South Texas due to overdependence on cotton. He said that Northern people were unpopular in that area and asserted "We are very anxious to be out of slaveholding country."[47]

In February 1859, "C. A." Joshua Lovejoy wrote from Industry, Texas, in Austin County where he was teaching school. It was here that he received Hester Ferris's letter bearing word of the death of his beloved sister Sarah. Sarah Lovejoy Damon, whose spirit was always stronger than her body, died of a heart attack in October 1858. Joshua Lovejoy was stunned by the sad news. He offered his condolences to Sarah's husband Hiram Damon and assured Hester that he would come to Buffalo as soon as possible to console his mother.[48] Charles Ferris's disappearance and the deaths of both Louisa and Sarah laid the Buffalo family low.

Joshua Lovejoy visited Buffalo in August 1859. He was interested in the settlement of his sisters' estates, even trying to secure guardianship of Sarah Damon's two children.[49] During his visit home, Josh reached an understanding with his aging mother Sally Lovejoy; upon permanently returning to Buffalo, he would inherit her house.[50] Thus on the eve of the Civil War, Joshua Lovejoy left Texas and took his family to live with his

---

45. McCausland, "Some Early Texas Newspapers," *SHQ*, 49 (Jan., 1946), 384–389, discusses the papers mailed from Texas to the New York Lovejoys, including two 1839 issues of the Houston *Morning Star*.

46. Sarah Damon to Joshua Lovejoy, Apr. 30, 1858. FLC, Box II, Folder 1.

47. Joshua Lovejoy to Sarah Damon, Mar. 24, 1858, ibid., Box III, Folder 1.

48. Hester Ferris to Joshua Lovejoy, Jan. 24, 1859, and Joshua Lovejoy to Hester Ferris, Feb. 28, 1859, ibid., Box I, Folder 9.

49. Sarah and Hiram Damon had two surviving children, Walter who was six, and an infant daughter, Louisa, one of twins born in 1857. In November 1859, suits were filed in the Superior Court of Erie County, New York, by Joshua Lovejoy against members of his family, seeking guardianship of Sarah's children and control of Louisa's estate. Ibid., Box II, Folder 9, and Box III, Folder 18.

50. Joshua Lovejoy to his mother and Hester Ferris, Oct. 20, 1859, ibid., Box I, Folder 13. Josh wrote of his safe return to Texas despite a siege of yellow fever raging in the Houston-Galveston area. Sarah "Sally" Lovejoy's will, written in 1854, left the house on Seneca Street to her son Joshua and left money ($500) to Hester and her children. If Charles Ferris did not return, the rent house and two lots were to go to Hester. Sellstedt was left $400 in "affectionate memory." The rest of the property and money was to be equally divided with fourths to go to Warren, Joshua, Sarah Damon, and Charles's family. By 1859, Charles, Sarah, and

mother in the house at 247 Seneca Street in Buffalo, New York. Where did that leave Hester Ferris who had so loyally cared for her mother-in-law for ten years since the disappearance of Charles Ferris?

Sellstedt were out of the picture. A copy of Sarah Lovejoy's 1854 handwritten will is located in the Davis Collection.

THE BROTHERS' WAR

THE CENSUS OF 1860 reported Warren A. Ferris a farmer, age fifty, with wife Frances and nine children; Robert (1856), Louisa Jane (1858), and Edward (1860) had been added to the Ferris family. Another daughter, born in April 1864, was named Sarah Ellen. Tragedy struck too often, however. Two Ferris boys died during the 1860s. William (Willie) Ferris was sixteen when he died on July 12, 1866.[1] Almost exactly a year later, five-year-old Price Ferris skipped down to the horselot to feed salt to his favorite colt. The mare kicked him in the stomach. Mary Catherine and her mother carried the youngster into the house, and Jim Ferris rode for the doctor in Dallas; but Price died the next day, July 6, 1867.[2] The last child of Warren and Frances Ferris was born in 1869. She was Frances Laura.

Ferris, so far from his own family in Buffalo, maintained a warm relationship with his wife's relatives. One of Frances's brothers, Willie Moore, was blinded by an arrow in a freak accident and lived for a time with the Ferrises. The Ferris children frequently exchanged visits with their cousins, children of Emily and Zachariah Ellison, who lived east of Tyler in Smith County.

In the late 1850s, Dr. Ellison sought advice from Ferris on setting up a water-powered grist mill on his large plantation in the Old Flora Community.[3] When Ellison retired from medical practice and moved to Tyler to school his children, he expected that profits from the mill, along with proceeds from corn and cotton grown on his plantation under the supervision of his son-in-law Thomas Veasey, would support the family. Mary Catherine Ferris, oldest daughter of W. A. and Fanny, was living with the Ellisons during this volatile pre–Civil War period and is thought to have related the story of an abortive slave revolt on the Ellison plantation.

According to Mary Catherine, a loyal, elderly slave revealed the slaves' plan to "kill all the white folks." The informer told Veasey that the revolt was timed for a night when local young white men gathered for a monthly

---

1. W. A. Ferris's memoranda book, Davis Collection

2. Mary Catherine Ferris Cannon memoirs, ibid.

3. Z. Ellison to W. A. Ferris, Apr. 5, 1857, ibid. Dr. Ellison shared Ferris's interest in breeding and racing horses. This letter refers to his stable and his decision not to bring a horse to Dallas but to "keep him, where he is known. . . . He will do a good business at home this year, having proved himself, and without competition." The Dallas *Herald*, May 9, 1860, gave Ferris's livestock mark and brand.

hunt. While the whites were chasing their hound dogs, the slaves planned to meet at the Presbyterian churchhouse. A lighted candle, passed three times at the window, would signal the "all clear" and the revolt would ensue.

Veasey and the young white hunters gathered as usual and pretended to start off on their hunt, but they went only a short distance, then cut back and entered the church where they gave the signal to draw in the rebels.

As Mary Catherine recalled the near revolt:

> the first to come in was some of Uncle Dr.'s women and men. Several bunches came in but some got scared and run [sic], but they got some and found out who the rest were. Some were hung, some were whipped, the rest were badly scared.[4]

This Smith County incident illustrates the fear which gripped white Southerners and the violent reprisals that followed any rumor of abolitionist activity or perceived slave rebellion in the years before the Civil War. In Dallas County during the hot summer of 1860, such tension unleashed a lynch mob. On July 8, 1860, Dallas's entire three-block business district burned to the ground, leaving only the new brick courthouse damaged but standing. There were six other unexplained fires in north central Texas towns that same day. Editor Charles Pryor of the Dallas *Herald*, who lost his press in the fire, called it arson and blamed local slaves.[5] Rumors flew of an abolitionist plot to incite a slave rebellion; Yankee Methodist preachers were prime suspects. The ministers were run out of town, slaves were threatened, beaten, and finally a Dallas "vigilance committee" hanged three blacks at the foot of Main Street near the river.[6] Anti-abolition feeling ran so high that a man might be whipped for

---

4. From *Chronicles of Smith County, Texas*, VII (Spring, 1968), 42–44. Copied from the original by W. R. Conger, Dallas historian. The story purportedly came from Mary Catherine "Kate" Ferris. Born in 1853, she would have been under ten years of age prior to the Civil War. Support for the story is evidence that Dr. Ellison was sued for holding "Indians" (free blacks who had married into the Creek Nation) as slaves. According to a letter to the author from Nell Davis, Dec. 9, 1989, this situation precipitated the uprising, but the men remained in bondage until after the Civil War. Thomas Veasey, husband of Rebecca Ellison, was killed in the war.

5. Handbill printed in McKinney the week following the fire, reprinted in the Dallas *Morning News*, Dec. 20, 1890.

6. Donald Reynolds, *Editors Make War* (Nashville: Vanderbilt University Press, 1966), 97–110. Calmer heads concluded that the Dallas fire was an accident, originating in the second floor of Peak Bros. Drugstore when a new type of matches ignited in spontaneous combustion. It was 110 degrees, dry, and windy on that July day. Others feel arson was instigated by secessionists; certainly the fires created public hysteria and strengthened the hand of those who favored secession. All of the fires occurred in areas of North Texas where Union sentiment was strong. See also Richard B. McCaslin, *Tainted Breeze: The Great Hanging at Gainesville, Texas, 1862* (Baton Rouge: Louisiana State University Press, 1994), 23–24, for a summary of the 1860 "Texas Troubles" and their impact on public opinion.

saying a good word about Abraham Lincoln.[7] John Brown's raid on Harper's Ferry fueled rumors of abolitionist plots to set fires and incite slave revolts in North Texas. Lincoln's election in the fall of 1860 was the last straw; Dallas County voted three to one for secession.[8]

Warren Ferris wrote to his Buffalo relatives in October 1860 and again in March 1861 describing Texas enthusiasm for secession. Hester Ferris responded in disbelief, "as to your predictions, we can not shut our eyes to the fulfillment of them; but we hardly think there will be any war."

Hester wrote that Hiram Damon and his two children had been living with Ferris's mother; but, when Damon remarried and moved out, Hester returned to Seneca Street to care for her feeble mother-in-law Sally Lovejoy. Hester's two oldest sons, Charly and Ned, still were interested in taking up their father's Texas land[9] and becoming sheep ranchers, but neither had the funds to make a move. In his note added to the March letter, Charly Ferris, age twenty-four, informed his uncle that he had been working in the theater but was sick of dramatics and had decided to enter the oil business, which he expected to be a "big thing." Ned Ferris, who was studying law, wrote that Buffalo was "played out" and proclaimed his intention to "leave this miserable hole and make tracks for Texas." Ned hoped Texas secession would not damage his plans for the future and asserted, "I think you of the confederate states are a little the best off. Up here people are out of work, money scarce and the devil to pay generally; some of the effects of black republicanism."[10]

Ellen May Ferris was, it was reported by her mother, a serious scholar who soon would graduate from Buffalo Central High School and planned

---

7. William E. Hughes, *Journal of a Grandfather* (St. Louis: Nixon-Jones Printing Co., 1912), 45–54, tells of his questioning by a Dallas "Citizens Court" in the fall of 1860 simply because he was heard discussing the Lincoln-Douglas debates, which he had witnessed. A young man from central Illinois, down with a flock of sheep which he and his cousins were grazing on Mountain Creek, Hughes was hauled into a Dallas hotel room to be examined as a "suspicious character" sent to stir up local Negroes. His claim to be a Southerner by birth won his release with a warning and a round of drinks for all.

8. Over Governor Houston's objections, the Texas legislature called a secession convention in Dec. 1860. The "Secesh Men" carried the vote 152 to six. Their action was followed by a popular vote in the counties in February 1861; Dallas voted for secession, 741 to 237. Pro-Union sentiment was probably stronger than the votes indicated as many Unionists boycotted the election, regarding it to be illegal.

9. In 1860, the State of Texas awarded the heirs of Charles D. Ferris 960 acres in West Texas. This land in present Donley Co. near Clarendon was granted for Ferris's military service in the Texas Revolution. Special Act Bounty Warrant #13/34, Feb. 11, 1860, in Thomas L. Miller, *Bounty and Donation Land Grants, 1835–1888* (Austin: University of Texas Press, 1967), 262. Walter McCausland mistakenly placed the land in Denton County. Webb, Carroll, and Branda (eds.), *Handbook of Texas*, I, 593. At the time of the letter a claims court, created after fire destroyed military records in 1855, was considering Charles Ferris's application; it was not clear how Texas secession would effect the outcome of that case.

10. Hester Ferris to Warren Ferris, Mar. 31, 1861, FLC, Box II, Folder 1.

to be a teacher. George, the youngest son, wanted to be a sailor. No mention was made of the youngest child Sarah Louise. Hester Ferris concluded her letter with some exasperation: "I shall most likely move again as Joshua and his family arrived here a week ago today with the intention, I expect, of living with his mother."[11] It was the last letter exchanged between Warren Ferris and his Buffalo family before the war cut off Texas correspondence with the North. By the following month, shots had been fired on Fort Sumter in South Carolina—and the war was on.

Warren A. Ferris left no doubt as to his loyalties; he was a life-long Jeffersonian Democrat, strong on states' rights. Ferris later wrote that the South fought with "high personal honor," saying that Southerners seceded even though they knew they were fated to lose to the Union's superior resources and numbers. In an intriguing turn of phrase, he asserted that Southerners "preferred death to slavery."[12] Due to his age and old injuries, Ferris did not serve actively in the Confederate Army, but he did enlist in the Home Guard, specifically the White Rock Mounted Rifles organized by his neighbor John H. Daniels.[13] Home defense was important since, with the federal troops withdrawn, the Texas frontier was again exposed to Indian attack. On one occasion, early in the war, Captain Daniels's men were called to duty. They left Dallas on May 8, 1861, expecting to see action at Fort Washita in Indian Territory; but the White Rock Riflemen returned home four days later, having found no Union troops on the Red River.[14]

Dallas experienced no fighting during the Civil War, so Ferris was never again called to duty. Indeed, North Texas became a refuge for those trying to escape the ravages of war. Many Southerners sent their slaves for safekeeping and themselves sought a haven "safe from the gunboats" in the Texas interior. Dallas's population grew and its economy prospered, especially in the last years of the war. At the heart of a vast wheat-producing area, Dallas was headquarters for the Central Confederate Quartermaster and Commissary. Where Fair Park is now located, horses, mules, and grain were collected for shipment to the Confederate Army in Arkansas. The worst local hardship of the war years was inflated prices due to the shortage of sugar, coffee, seeds, paper, medicine, and other manufactured or imported items. Families like the Ferrises had to invent substitutes and fall back on making their own clothes and shoes.[15]

---

11. Ibid.

12. Warren A. Ferris, Dallas *Herald*, Sept. 6, 1871.

13. The militia company was organized by Daniels, a veteran of the Mexican War, on Feb. 6, 1861 and Warren Ferris enlisted on Feb. 9. Military records, Texas State Library, cited in DeGolyer Collection, III, 10.

14. Dallas *Herald*, May 8 and May 15, 1861, FLC, Box I, Folder 4. McCaslin, *Tainted Breeze*, 42. The Dallas troops were part of a larger force that marched from North Texas to seize Ft. Washita but found it abandoned.

15. Saxon (ed.), *The WPA Dallas Guide and History*, 56–57.

Joshua Lovejoy returned to Buffalo in early 1861 expecting to be welcomed, but, according to his daughters Alice and Florence, he got a cold reception from his mother and Charles's wife Hester Ferris. Hester, who had been caring for her mother-in-law for nearly a decade, was suddenly ousted from the home on Seneca Street to make room for the prodigal son from Texas. According to his mother's 1854 will, Lovejoy was to receive her house in return for managing her affairs. But, to his chagrin, Josh discovered that Sally Lovejoy had rewritten her will in 1860, instructing that her estate be divided four ways: between Warren, Josh, Sarah Damon's children, and Hester.[16] Sarah Gray Ferris Lovejoy died in 1864, but that did not end the family quarrel over her property. The bitter dispute led to a messy court case when Joshua Lovejoy challenged the second will on the grounds that Hester Ferris had unduly influenced his mother. In 1869, the court upheld the 1860 will, but it was not probated until 1876.[17]

Alice Lovejoy, who was sixteen at the time, recalled the origins of the family quarrel:

> I understood when my father came home from Buffalo in 1859 to Texas that his mother had agreed to give him her homestead furniture family portraits and all . . . at her death, Father expected to go back to Buffalo in 1860 but the Southern troubles prevented . . . until 1861 in the Spring, it was our intention to stop in Southern Ill. that is Mother and us children but Father having received some hints that his mother had been doing some thing different to her agreement with him . . . we all hurried on to Buffalo . . . we all knew that a lawsuit with Grand mother was certain and Father was getting ready as fast as circumstances would permit.[18]

Alice's older sister Florence described the scene in Buffalo:

> When we arrived in Buffalo in the Spring of 1861 We were received by our Grandmother and Mrs. Ferris's family in the coldest and most disagreeable manner. Mrs. Lovejoy seemed to be intensely bound to Mrs. Ferris [Hester] and family—they did not want us to sleep in the house—they did not want us to bring our trunks from the Depot to the house—We were insulted every day—my Father was treated like an alien rather than like a son.[19]

As Alice Lovejoy remembered, her father tried time and again to get his mother to make a financial settlement on his portion of the Buffalo land

16. Interestingly, a handwritten copy of Sally Lovejoy's 1860 will is in Box 3, Folder 7, William Caruth Family Papers, 1841–1958 (DHS). Perhaps Warren Ferris gave his original copy of his mother's will to Caruth as collateral on debts.

17. Probate of the estate of Sarah Lovejoy, Feb. 10, 1876, by Warren T. Ferris, son of Zebulon Ferris. Davis Collection.

18. Alice Lovejoy's testimony given in the spring of 1864 as evidence in the court case. FLC, Box II, Folder 1.

19. Deposition of Florence Lovejoy who was seventeen in 1861, twenty at the time of her writing in 1864. Ibid., Box II, Folder 1.

which she had already sold; Sally "would get mad and would not hear to settling but after the Ferris family moved out she would talk a little more calmly about settling." Florence Lovejoy stated that her grandmother became more unreasonable after each visit from Hester and her children:

> they used to go to Grandmother's bed room and have a whispered con-
> versation and always nearly—when they went away Gmother was dis-
> satisfied and our family and father in particular was insulted scolded
> and abused. . . . Father had no influence with her (Grandm) at all—
> She gave Mrs. F everything in the shape of clothing and house linen. .
> . . Paid her taxes, insurance. . . . father was always treated as though
> he was no relation.[20]

Joshua Lovejoy had the gall to contact his Michigan cousin, Nelson Wing, to whom he was already in debt. Apparently he asked for another loan, using the Buffalo property due him as collateral. Refusing at first to make the loan, Wing advised, "Don't quarrel with your mother. Talk kind-ly to her. Write what she says."[21] Thus in the days of her last illness, Sally Lovejoy's heirs squabbled over her property. In the court case that followed her death, Lovejoy's teenage daughters were dragged in as wit-nesses. Alice testified that Florence observed a settlement between her father and grandmother in which lawyer McMahon was also present; the terms of this agreement called for Joshua to control his mother's affairs, in return for which he agreed to pay her bills and provide a home for the rest of her days.[22]

On his return to New York after twenty-two years in Texas, Lovejoy tried to reestablish contact with his old Michigan friends, some of whom had advanced their careers through association with former President Millard Fillmore. Hoping to get a government position, he corresponded with Gardner R. Lillibridge, Charles D. Millerd, B. G. Noble, George Warner, and R. E. Morse. Their responses, although not producing a "sit-uation" for Josh, are instructive. Lillibridge, who had invented a barley substitute for coffee, reflected on the "unnatural war" and "troubled times." He expressed surprise that the South had mounted "so formidable an army," and observed, "They [Southerners] may take Washington if we don't give McClellan more troops."[23] B. G. Noble, who worked in the cus-

---

20. Ibid.

21. Nelson H. Wing to Joshua Lovejoy, July 13, 1861. The following year, Aug. 8, 1862, Wing agreed to a loan for $1,000. This agreement was witnessed by Millard P. Fillmore. FLC, Box II, Folder 1.

22. Apparently this agreement held between 1861–1864 as records show Joshua Lovejoy paid bills, authorized repairs on 247 Seneca, leased property at 236 Carroll, and mortgaged property to N. H. Wing for a $1,000 loan. Ibid., Box II, Folder 1. The Buffalo City Directory (BHS) shows Lovejoy as a boarder in the home of Sarah (Sally) Lovejoy on Seneca, until after her death in 1864 when he appears in the Directory as owner of the property.

23. G. R. Lillibridge to Joshua Lovejoy, Apr. 19, 1862, FLC, Box II, Folder 1.

toms house, returned Lovejoy's inquiry, marveling that his friend was forty-six years old, still boyish, and without a job.[24]

New York grocer Charley Millerd's response to his long-lost but well-remembered friend is revealing. "Where is Lovejoy? Nobody could tell—someone said you were in Texas. I really thought you were dead. Asked N. H. Wing—no clue. I gather from your letter you are unmarried. I'm a little surprised knowing your social temperament."[25] George Warner of Dexter, Michigan, said he judged by Lovejoy's letter the "unpleasant state" of his family relations; Warner advised Josh to get his dealings in black and white, noting, "I see by it [letter] that your life has been to some extent a 'checkered one' in regard to business matters."

R. E. Morse, Josh's most successful contact, wrote from Curacao, West Indies, where he was U.S. Consul General. Morse recalled "his spring-time" when he and Lovejoy had been friends. Mostly Morse commented on the "War in the U. States all absorbing subject with you as here it effects seriously trade and commerce of the world." Morse judged the "failure to crush the rebellion due to Democratic politicians who prolong the war."[26]

Believing that his half-brother Charles D. Ferris was still alive and had deserted his family to start a new life, Joshua Lovejoy placed "Missing Persons" advertisements in several eastern newspapers.

> WANTED—information on whereabouts of Chas. D. Ferris who left Buffalo fall of 1850. Last heard of in St. Peters or Sidney 1851—supposed to have been married about that time at or near Chambers Bay under the name of Henry A. Johnson.[27]

Although he did not serve in the active army, Joshua Lovejoy capitalized on wartime opportunities. On July 6, 1864, Lovejoy was appointed recruiting officer for Lockport, Niagara County, and given thirty days to enlist men for the 118th Regiment, New York State Volunteers, at a draft rate of $100 per man.[28] Later that year, Lovejoy and a partner in Cairo, Illinois, worked out a scheme to substitute refugee blacks for white draftees. His letter to J. L. Price on November 6, 1864, revealed his fear that an inquiry might raise ugly questions about activities in which he was involved. Lovejoy pressed Price, "did Mr. Carpenter talk or act or show or say we were partners together? did he pay for men? how many? how much? Did he leave Cairo with men? How many in

---

24. B. G. Noble to Joshua Lovejoy, May 4, 1862, ibid., Box II, Folder 1.

25. C. D. Millerd to Joshua Lovejoy, Aug. 11, 1862, ibid.

26. R. E. Morse to Joshua Lovejoy, Sept. 11, 1862 and May 1, 1863, ibid.

27. The advertisement, placed by attorneys of J. F. Lovejoy, Aug. 1, 1865, in New York, Texas, Louisiana, Montreal, and California newspapers, drew no response, so far as is known. Lovejoy thought Ferris a bigamist as well as a fellow who would desert his family. Ibid., Box I, Folder 8.

28. Special orders, Adjutant General's Office, Albany, New York, July 6, 20, Aug. 27, 1864, ibid., Box II, Folder 2.

Cincinnati?"[29] On December 27, 1864, Josh received a letter from LeRoy H. Briggs of Cairo on the subject of refugee "darkies" coming up the river—with a view to getting them in the Union Army as substitutes for whites. "Get nigs in service here [Cairo] and credit them to localities in the north." Briggs felt there was a great deal of money in recruiting colored regiments and thought there would be no problem in securing the cooperation of officers "which can be done in most cases for a small amount—credit 'niggers' any place you wish."[30]

Some of the Northern branch of the Ferris family took a more direct role in the Civil War. Young Charly Ferris, eldest son of Charles and Hester, served two years in the Union Army. In the 21st Regiment of New York State Volunteers, Charly, who was more suited to theatrical than military life, contributed a "Civil War Song" dedicated to the gallant boys of Buffalo. A cousin, Capt. Warren T. Ferris, son of Zebulon Ferris, saw action at Port Hudson with the 116th Regiment of New York Volunteers. George W. Ferris, Hester's youngest son, was a merchant sailor in 1864–1865, writing home to his mother from exotic Pacific ports.

The eldest sons of Charles Drake Ferris, Ned and Charly, were impetuous young men who, lacking paternal guidance in their formative years, were a trial to their mother. Both men died in their thirties and neither married. Ned Ferris, the fledgling lawyer, died in 1869; his older brother Charly died the following year. Warren Ferris's two nephews who so longed to "make tracks for Texas," never lived to fulfill their father's dream of a fresh start in the Southwest. When daughter Ellen died in 1874, it was a crushing blow to Hester Ferris. Nelly was a promising poetess, much cherished by her family. Of the children of Charles Drake Ferris, only George carried on the Ferris name in Buffalo. His son Lawrence and daughters Winifred and Amy preserved letters, portraits, and childhood memories derived from long talks with their grandmother.

Hester Ferris lived into her eighties. Her husband gone, three of her adult children dead in a five-year period, she became an embittered old woman. Except to say "adventuring was in his blood and he couldn't help it," no one in the family ever faulted Charles Ferris for his disappearance. Sympathy clearly rested with Hester. It could not have been easy for her to board with her mother-in-law and raise the children alone while Charles was off adventuring. There was always a reluctance to discuss her husband's fate; on the face of it, the explanation "lost at sea" was accepted. The children were told that their grandfather had been a man of literary talent and sober character. Beyond that, the family raised a

---

29. Joshua Lovejoy to J. L. Price, Nov. 6, 1864, ibid.

30. LeRoy H. Briggs to Joshua Lovejoy, Dec. 27, 1864, ibid.

wall of silence on the subject of Charles Drake Ferris.[31] Joshua Lovejoy was remembered as the "black sheep" of the family—"sort of irresponsible, a 'ne'er do well'—always roving . . . brilliant but shiftless . . . something of a Casanova."[32] Perhaps, it was said, he was a man born at the wrong time and place. Their opinion of Joshua Lovejoy was quite generous, considering that he had tried to cheat the Ferris children of their inheritance.

The aftermath of the Civil War was harder than the war itself for many Southerners. Dallas County, like much of Texas, experienced a serious breakdown in law and order in May and June 1865. With the collapse of the rebel government, local law enforcement authorities found it impossible to prevent looting. Roving bands of military deserters, civilian refugees, and Indian raiders threatened North Texas so that when federal troops entered Texas in the summer of 1865, they were given a friendly reception. As they marched northwest to Austin and Dallas, the restoration of order was welcomed.[33] A Dallas *Herald* article of December 9, 1865, reported the first party of federal cavalry passing through the city en route to Sherman in North Texas. Colonel Brown's Indiana troops were "well disciplined," according to the paper; the editor noted that "foolish" blacks, gathered to welcome their liberators, were disappointed when the Union Army failed to confiscate and distribute rebel property among them.[34]

In 1860, two-thirds of Texas voters supported secession; the other one-third, "Unionists," either fled the state, converted to the rebel cause, or kept quiet during the war years. As the federal army of occupation moved in, old Texans with Union sentiments clamored for protection. The initial reaction of conservative Southerners was to accept defeat gracefully as long so it did not mean any drastic change in lifestyle. Moderates like John H. Reagan, who served as postmaster general of the Confederacy, and James W. Throckmorton, who opposed secession but served as an officer of the Confederate Army, were willing to acknowledge slave emancipation.

---

31. Letters of descendants of George Ferris to Walter McCausland; Winifred Ferris and her sister Amy, Apr. 9, 15, 30, May 15, 1944. They, and their brother Lawrence, knew their grandmother Hester Ferris in her old age. Ibid., Box VI, Folder 9.

32. Winifred Ferris to Walter McCausland from Los Gatos, California, July 5, 1941, ibid.

33. Randolph B. Campbell, *A Southern Community in Crisis: Harrison County, 1850–1880* (Austin: Texas State Historical Association, 1983), 218–219, describes the chaotic situation in much of Texas during April and May, 1865.

34. Dallas *Herald*, Dec. 9, 1865, and Jan. 6, 1866, reported passage of Union troops and supply wagons through Dallas. On Feb. 3, 1866, the *Herald* noted that the Indiana troops mustered out and would be replaced by 6th regulars. McCaslin, *Tainted Breeze*, 164–165, states the Gen. George A. Custer sent Lt. Col. Thomas M. Browne and 200 men to Sherman in late 1865 to protect North Texas Unionists who had been harassed throughout the war.

Throckmorton, elected governor of Texas in 1866, had little patience with opportunists who flocked to Austin, their pockets bulging with the names of "loyal" men to be appointed to office. No Texan, he said, could respect those who "skulked from danger and drew no sword in defense of either belligerent and who now flock around the slain carcass like filthy beasts and vultures."[35]

During the early phase of Reconstruction, John J. Good, Dallas County's leading secessionist and rebel officer, was elected judge of the district court—a local indication of lack of Southern remorse about the war.[36] When Texas, like other rebel states, passed Black Codes strictly regulating African American behavior and sent "secesh" men back to Washington, outraged Radical Republicans gained control of Reconstruction. In July 1867, Throckmorton was ousted, and military rule was established over Texas. A squad of the 17th U.S. Infantry occupied Dallas. The Freedmen's Bureau became active, opening schools for blacks, protecting their rights, and registering them as voters.[37] Only those whites willing to take the "ironclad oath," that they had not voluntarily aided the Confederacy, were eligible to serve as jurors or hold office after the summer of 1867; however, these restrictions were not always strictly enforced.[38] In Dallas, local Unionists of ability, acceptable to ex-Confederates, came forward to assume leadership and the response was one of grudging compliance to Radical Republican rule.[39]

---

35. Elliott, *Leathercoat*, 103. Barry A. Crouch, "'Unmanacling' Texas Reconstruction: A Twenty-Year Perspective," *SHQ*, 93 (Jan., 1990), 283–284, urges a new evaluation of Throckmorton as Elliott's biography is over fifty years old and fails to take into account recent research. Crouch offers a useful update on Reconstruction historiography, against which one may measure the local experience of Dallas County and Warren A. Ferris.

36. Randolph B. Campbell, "A Moderate Response: The District Judges of Dallas County during Reconstruction, 1865–1876," *Legacies*, V (Fall, 1993), 5–7. As judge of the 5th Judicial District, Good was accused of discrimination against Unionists and Freedmen.

37. Thomas H. Smith, "Conflict and Corruption: The Dallas Establishment vs. The Freedmans's Agent", *Legacies*, II (Fall, 1989), 24–30, utilizes records of the Freedmans Bureau to document the struggle in Dallas of agent William H. Horton to protect the rights of Negroes in courts dominated by ex-Confederate officers like John J. Good.

38. Campbell, *A Southern Community in Crisis*, 276–280. Some civilian officials who could not take the Test Oath continued to serve so long as there were no complaints against them and no Unionist sought their office.

39. Campbell, "A Moderate Response," 4, attributes Dallas acceptance of Negro enfranchisement to the white majority's realization that they would shortly regain control and to their desire for stability, economic progress, and renewed prosperity (that is, coming of the railroad), which were promised by Republicans. Apparently economic goals were more potent than political grudges. Campbell's pioneering studies of Texas counties indicate that a pre–Civil War power elite retained control after Reconstruction. Crouch, "'Unmanacling' Texas Reconstruction," 297.

Old Lemuel Cook, father of Warren Ferris's first wife Melinda and of
Joshua Lovejoy's wife Mary, described the postwar situation in Texas
when he wrote to the Lovejoys from Woodville in 1868:

> Dear children I address you a few lines to let you know I am still a Live
> and in reasonable health considering my age [80] and my family is well
> They consist of my [third] Wife Caroline Laura and my Wife's youngest
> daughter Sophia. . . . times is quite dull since the War has ended mony
> [sic] is scarce tho provision is plenty fine crops this year. . . . I lost a
> good deal in the Confederate war I had two mailroutes. . . . I carried
> them two years for $3400 [Confederate] I lost it all I was Sheriff two
> years The state owed $600, the convention two years ago repudiated
> all debts made in time of the war. . . . I had a mail route in the United
> States last year from Livingston by Woodville to Nacogdoches at
> $2000 but they have not paid me punctual. . . . I want you to write. . . .
> If you are in high fluent circumstance I would be glad you would send
> a Twenty dollar Greenback.[40]

Prior to the Civil War, Cook took up land in Cherokee County where at
age sixty-three he remarried[41] and became a Baptist minister; after the
war, he moved to the Big Thicket area of Southeast Texas to be near his
daughter Elizabeth. Of keen interest to Joshua Lovejoy was the news that
Cook's daughter Caroline (Carrie) had wed a Union soldier, Edward
Henry, who was stationed with the "occupying" army in Dallas.[42] Carrie,
proud of her Boston Irish Catholic husband, bragged to her uncle that she
"always intended to marry a Yankee—you see my principles."[43] In a second letter to New York, L. A. Cook stated that he was trying to get an
appointment to a government job, open to a "loyal" man such as himself.
He commented that people in Texas were reconciled to the election of
Gen. U. S. Grant as president and wished him well.

Joshua Lovejoy lost no time in writing to Edward Henry and his com-
manding officer Capt. Henry Norton, concerning the whereabouts of
Warren Ferris. Captain Norton answered, "A gentleman by the name of
Warren A. Ferris lives on 'White rock' creek, about six miles from Dallas,
said to be about fifty years old and surveyor by profession."[44] Young
Edward Henry responded to Lovejoy's letter:

40. L. A. Cook from Woodville (Tyler Co., Texas) to Mary and Joshua Lovejoy in
Buffalo, N.Y., Aug. 25, 1868. FLC, Box II, Folder 2.

41. Cherokee Co. Marriage Records, Book A, p. 191, show Cook's marriage on
June 22, 1852, as the first marriage to be recorded in the county.

42. Edward Henry was a member of the infamous 17th Infantry which had
gained a reputation for rowdiness in Galveston and Brenham. See William L.
Richter, *The Army in Texas during Reconstruction* (College Station: Texas A&M
University Press, 1987), 29, 54–65.

43. L. A. Cook to Joshua and Mary Lovejoy, Aug. 30, 1868, FLC, Box II, Folder 2.

44. Capt. Henry Norton, 17th U.S. Infantry, Dallas, Texas to Joshua Lovejoy,
Sept. 14, 1868, ibid. Captain Norton was popular with Dallasites, and the departure of his troops was lamented in the Dallas *Herald*, May 29, 1869. Richter, *The*

> I have just received a note from Capt. Norton from you enquiring [sic] for Warren A. Ferris of this County. As my wife Caroline J. Cook happens to be a sister-in-law of his she asked me to go out and see him to tell him her family were all well etcet—I have been there three times to see him since we were stationed in this town he is not dead but alive and working in his cotton patch the last time I saw him.[45]

Caroline Cook Henry wrote a long newsy letter to her uncle Joshua and his wife Mary in October 1868. She candidly described her new husband and life in Reconstruction Texas:

> You wished to know something about my husband. He enlisted in the service in Boston—His co[mpany] being stationed in Woodville some length of time, is how I formed his acquaintance—A short time after we were married the Company was ordered to Dallas. . . . Mr. Henry having only one year to serve, from the time he left here, he and myself thought it best for me to still remain in Woodville. . . . I will describe him to you, has blue eyes, dark red hair, and fair complexion is about 5 ft and half in height, and very heavy built, and is inclined to be rather good looking according to my judgment of beauty—. . . . Yes my husband and myself are both union, my husband is a strong Democrat, though I am inclined to agree, to some extent with the opposite party—My Father, is not against me, neither is my brother-in-law, Mr. Sheppard, he has always been a strong advocate for the Union. . . . During the war, I met with a great deal of opposition, in regard to my "Yankee" principles, on the part of my Father's family but they have all converted into Yankeeism—I think my step-sister, and also our half-sister, will take a Yankee provided they can get one—There are a great many Union men in this county—though most every one was opposed to me marrying a Yankee.[46]

Carrie Henry answered her uncle's inquiry about the amount of land her father owned near Woodville and encouraged Lovejoy to seek his wife Mary's share, as Cook's third wife coveted it for her children. Carrie reported that in Texas, compared to Buffalo, things were cheap, although money was scarce. The principal crops of Southeast Texas were corn, potatoes, and sugarcane, large planters having abandoned cotton for cane. She assured Lovejoy that the "slaves can be hired and made to work very well." Finally, Carrie informed her uncle, "Warren Ferris is not dead—he is still living near Dallas."[47]

So, as early as the fall of 1868, Joshua learned that Warren Ferris was alive and living on the White Rock Creek survey which bore his alias, "C. A." Lovejoy.

Army in Texas, 180, admits that the Dallas experience does not support his thesis that the Army was intrusive and much resented by white Southerners.

45. Edward A. Henry, G Company, 17th U.S. Infantry, Dallas Co., Texas, to Joshua Lovejoy, Sept. 17, 1868, ibid.

46. Caroline Cook Henry to Joshua and Mary Lovejoy, Oct. 22, 1868, ibid.

47. Ibid.

Lovejoy determined to somehow wrest the land from Ferris by using Edward Henry as his agent in Dallas. He wrote Dallas attorney James K. P. Record, giving Henry power of attorney in the estate of the "late" C. A. Lovejoy. Young Henry was eager to be of service to his in-laws but was perceptive enough to see that the discrepancy between the names, Joshua F. and Clarence A. Lovejoy, weakened Josh's claim to the Dallas land. Saying his company was about to be transferred, Henry sent regrets that he would not be able to "carry out this matter." W. A. Ferris had gone to Jefferson with a load of cotton so it would not be possible to see him before the transfer of duty. Henry requested particulars and necessary papers concerning the land; although he had not "swallowed Blackstone," he was puzzled as to how J. F. Lovejoy could empower him to act in the estate of C. A. Lovejoy.[48]

The next letter from Edward Henry came from Sulphur Springs, Texas, where the federal troops had been transferred to deal with a daring outlaw, Cullen M. Baker, the so-called "Swamp Fox of the Sulphur."[49] Brazen anti-Union activity led to martial law in Hopkins County in 1867–1868. With tacit approval from community leaders, masked nightriders ruled the backcountry, intimidating free Negroes and government agents. To deal with the problem, 400 Union troops were stationed in northeast Texas, which Edward Henry called the "seat of rebellion." Twelve blacks and three soldiers were killed in two weeks, and, according to Henry, "we can't go alone a mile out of town without being shot at." Henry proclaimed, "my politics are republican—I believe in abolition—not nigger equality."[50] Finally, before returning to guard duty, Henry advised Lovejoy, "If you own any land in Dallas county I'd advise you to say your name is Clarence A. Lovejoy and not J. F. or else you can't give the power of attorney to anyone."[51]

When next he wrote to Joshua Lovejoy, Edward Henry was in Richmond, Virginia, waiting to muster out of the army and join his wife Carrie and their new baby daughter in Boston. Henry expressed sympathy for some unclear marital calamity which had struck Lovejoy:

---

48. Edward Henry to Joshua Lovejoy from Dallas County, Oct. 25, 1868, ibid.

49. Cullen M. Baker gained a reputation as a daring Robin Hood, continuing the fight against Yankee invaders in the name of the Southern "Lost Cause." He captured a Union supply train singlehandedly; then appeared in disguise at troop headquarters to ridicule Yankee authority. When pursued, he would disappear in the thickets of the Sulphur River bottoms. Actually, Baker was little more than a bully and murderer. When he was killed in 1869, it was by a posse which included his father-in-law. Webb, Carroll, and Branda (eds.), *Handbook of Texas*, I, 98. Also, Richter, *The Army in Texas*, 146–147.

50. This is an interesting expression of opinion from a Union soldier from Boston. While they accepted Negro emancipation, even many Yankees balked at blacks as jurors or voters.

51. Edward Henry to Joshua Lovejoy from Sulphur Springs, Hopkins Co., Texas, Nov. 3, 1868, FLC, Box II, Folder 2.

> I am sorry to hear of your sad reverse of fortune to think of your home being broken up I expect it is a sad picture to illustrate. husband and Wife to be parted Oh "God" it is a sad thing to think of the crosses and trials we must bear in this world. Death must be a welcome to some persons.[52]

Henry recommended that Lovejoy sell his Dallas land which would probably bring him a good sum of money, and commented,

> As to Warren A. Ferris he seems to covet that land as a miser would if he cultivated it it might be some good to him but it is no good to him now he thinks that you will give him right and title to all of your estate now you sell all your land in texas.[53]

Writing from Boston on July 15, 1869, Henry queried, "I forgot to ask you how you settled that place of yours on White Rock Creek near Dallas, Tx." He thanked Lovejoy for putting his trust in him, but "There was one part of the Power of Attorney wrong—that was signing yourself in the name of J. F., when it is recorded with initials C. A. Lovejoy." Henry told Joshua Lovejoy that he and Carrie were returning to Texas and offered to take care of the land matter if Josh liked.[54]

Out of touch with his Buffalo family during the war years, Warren Ferris did not learn of his mother's death until 1865. Not without reason, he lived in dread that Joshua Lovejoy would reappear and attempt to seize his land with the support of the Union Army of occupation.[55] After visits from Joshua's emissary, Edward Henry, Ferris warned his teenage sons never to allow a stranger into the house. On one occasion a young hired man was caught by the Ferris boys, searching their father's trunk, going through his papers.

Rena D'Arcy, granddaughther of Warren Ferris, recalled hearing of the episode from her father Charley:

> When my father was a boy of 12–14 . . . [he] came home from hunting to find a young man that had been working for grandfather 2–3 mons. All the family was gone. Grandf. was out on a sarveying [sic] trip. This boy was in Grandf.'s room going thro' the contents of this little old Black trunk daddy pointed his gun at him and ask[ed] him what him what he was doing he (the boy) said hunting mony [sic] then the older boy Uncle Jim come [sic] in he did not believe he was hunting mony so

---

52. Edward Henry to Joshua Lovejoy, Spring, 1869, ibid. This reference to an apparent "separation" of Joshua from his wife Mary is intriguing. Whether their marital problems were personal or financial is unclear.

53. Ibid.

54. Edward Henry to Joshua Lovejoy, July 15, 1869, ibid.

55. Crouch, "'Unmanacling' Texas Reconstruction," 298–299, calls for more research on the economic impact of Reconstruction. Ferris's attitude toward Radical rule was perhaps influenced by threat of economic loss. Fears of higher taxes, inability to market his farm produce, and especially of Lovejoy using the Union Army to wrest his land from him were important psychological factors in his thinking.

uncle Jim said I will shoot you if you dont tell the truth The boy then
said he had been sent by Jousha [sic] Lovejoy to steal a paper from my
Grandfather they taken [sic] him to Dallas an told him to get out.

when Grandfather come [sic] home they told him G. said Jousha
would give anything for that paper as long as I have that he will not
dare come back here to make truble [sic] for me and don't never let
anyone see the inside of that trunk and Uncle Jim told his children
the same and they won't hardly let the family see the papers and that
is that.[56]

Through the difficult years of the Civil War and Reconstruction, Ferris
continued to work his farm on White Rock Creek. A little community
called Rinehardt grew up along the route of the old National Road,
between Dallas and Duck Creek (Garland). Here gathered Ferris's neighbors—the Chenaults, the Sages, the Daniels, the Herndons, the Collinses,
the Dyes—for camp meetings, horse races, and for funerals. The number
of graves in the family cemetery grew as Ferris allowed neighbors' loved
ones to be buried there.[57] Old dreams of easy wealth faded; now things
improved slowly and with great effort. Ferris built up his library, taught
a little surveying, and watched his family and community grow.

Like others, Warren Ferris experienced hard times after the war. It
was a "cornbread" economy. Money was scarce and hard to earn. Some
men pastured cattle, put herds together, and drove them up the Shawnee
Trail to northern markets. Others went west to the Texas plains to shoot
buffalo and haul in the hides. Everyone expected cotton to be the big cash
crop when the war ended. When hostilities drew to a close, cotton was
selling for $1.80 a pound; but the price of cotton fell dramatically while
the price of manufactured goods and groceries like sugar, coffee, and
liquor consistently rose. Cotton brought thirty cents per pound in 1866,
seventeen cents in 1870, and thirteen cents in 1875.[58]

Farmers resorted to barter, begged for credit, and struggled to scrape
together cash to pay taxes and hold onto their farms. Unimproved land in
Dallas County was practically worthless. Most of Warren Ferris's land lay
fallow while his debts piled up at the Caruth Bros. store. In 1866, Ferris
sold fifteen acres to his neighbor Marion Herndon for $100; in 1869, he
sold more land to Thompson W. Daniels. Both of these parcels of land
from the C. A. Lovejoy surveys ended up in the hands of the Caruths.[59]

---

56. Rena D'Arcy to Walter McCausland, June 12, 1951, FLC, Box IX, Folder 4.
This episode probably occurred in 1865 or 1866.

57. One of the first outside the Ferris family to be buried in the cemetery was
Elizabeth Chenault, first wife of Wesley M. Chenault; she died in the typhoid epidemic of 1858. Wes Chenault then married Lucy Sage.

58. Karen G. Britton, *Bale O' Cotton: The Mechanical Art of Cotton Ginning*
(College Station: Texas A&M University Press, 1992), 49.

59. Caruths' store on the courthouse square closed during the Civil War, but
reopened in 1868. Dallas *Herald*, May 4, 1867. When customers could not meet

Some local farmers still dreamed of floating their cotton to market down a navigable Trinity River. In 1868, Dallas celebrated the arrival of Job Boat #1 up from Galveston along the snag-clogged Trinity after a journey of one year, four days. Enthusiasts in Dallas built their own steamboat, the *Sally Haynes*, and petitioned Austin to clear obstructions on the river. But the days of river navigation were numbered; it was the railroad that offered salvation for a stagnant postwar economy.

The years after the Civil War were desperate, often lawless years. Ex-rebels, drifters, and outlaws wandered down from Missouri and Kansas to North Texas. Men from Quantrill's Raiders, still nursing old grievances and holding old loyalties, looked for a fresh start in Texas. Many of the Missourians had relatives in the Dallas area. Cole Younger, Myra Belle Starr, and the James brothers hovered around the Scyene community east of Dallas, trading for fast race horses, often stolen.

According to a family story, young Charley Ferris witnessed a tense moment in 1864 when William Quantrill and his men, including Frank and Jesse James, came to town. Although they were on the run from their own Confederate commander, these renegades were "not bad men" according to Dallasites who furnished them horses and welcomed them to dances held in their honor. Only Thomas Crutchfield, a Republican, refused the Missourians service at Crutchfield House, the hotel on the town square. When Quantrill pulled out his pistol and shot the dinner bell, Crutchfield agreed to serve the men but not their leader.[60]

Myra Belle Shirley (better known as Belle Starr) also arrived in Dallas County in the 1860s. She was followed to Texas by her beau Cole Younger and others of the Younger clan. During the next decade, Belle, with her plumed hat and six-shooters, was frequently seen in Dallas gambling casinos or racing her fast horse down the dusty streets. By 1870, Dallas, still a primitive frontier village on the banks of the Trinity, was trying to outgrow its rough reputation. Population was approaching 3,000. Gambling, dancing, and whoring were common; there were sixteen gambling houses, eight licensed saloons, six pool halls, and one shooting gallery. On unpaved Main and Elm Streets after a spring rain, horses and wagons labored through mud five feet deep. Many of the buildings were built up on stilts and there were board sidewalks. Cattle herds often stampeded through the streets, and cowboys worked off exuberance by

---

their bills, William and Walter Caruth would take land or livestock as payment. In the 1860s the brothers married the Worthington sisters, Mattie and Anna, whose father owned a great deal of property in the east part of the county. When William died in 1885, the Caruths had the largest landed estate in Dallas County. The Caruth Papers include account books for 1871–1872, showing Ferris family debts which were paid off in land after Warren Ferris's death.

60. Lucy Pounds Smith to Walter McCausland, Oct. 11, 1959, recalling a family story from Bob Ferris. FLC, Box VI, Folder 9.

shooting up the New Idea saloon.[61] But there were also five churches—
Methodist, Presbyterian, Christian, Episcopalian, and Baptist.
W. A. Ferris's near neighbors, respected citizens like the McCommases,
the Collinses, and the Herndons, watched their sons and grandchildren fall
in with outlaw bands. They knew men like the Youngers back in Missouri,
and lines between the "lawful" and the "lawless" were fuzzy in those troubled postwar years. Rosanna McCommas, granddaughter of Elder
McCommas, ran off with Jim Reed, first husband of Belle Starr. Mike and
Dave McCommas followed young ruffian Joel Collins who led his own outlaw band. Later Joel and his brothers Henry and Billy Collins along with
Albert Herndon were involved with the Sam Bass gang.[62] Ferris's oldest
sons, Jim and Charley, were at an age to get into a heap of trouble—just at
the time when they lost the softening influence of their mother.

Frances Moore Ferris died at 3 A.M. on April 23, 1869. She never
regained her strength following the March 7 birth of her daughter
Frances Laura, the thirteenth child in twenty years of marriage. Fanny
Ferris was forty years old, worn out from childbirth and the hardships of
frontier living. Like so many pioneer women, she had been a full and
equal partner with her husband in managing family affairs. Warren A.
Ferris, age fifty-eight, was left a widower for the second time, with nine
living children ranging in age from one month (Frances Laura) to nineteen years (James). Her unusual will, which Ferris filed with the Dallas
County Probate Court in May 1869,[63] took full advantage of Texas law
regarding the property rights of women.[64] Texas women could protect
their property, especially if they had the foresight to draw up such a will.
Ferris was the executor of Fanny's estate, amounting to all of their property, which had always been in her name. It was Fanny's overriding wish
to hold her large family together after her death; therefore, she stipulated
that her acreage on White Rock Creek, the Ferris farm out of C. A.
Lovejoy Survey #4, not be divided until April 1874. She requested:

---

61. Memoirs of John C. Gallaher, in W. S. Adair's column, "Knew Dallas When
Frontier Village," Dallas *Morning News,* July 27, 1924.

62. Dallas District Court, Criminal Docket, 1873–1876, (DPL). Numerous
charges were lodged against Albert Herndon, Mike McCommas, Myra Reed (Belle
Starr), and her brother Sug Shirley, including arson, carrying arms, and theft of
livestock. See also Tom Peeler, "Crooked Cowpokes: True Grit on Dallas Outlaws,"
D Magazine X, (Dec., 1983), 198–205.

63. Dallas Co. Records Probate Book, Part One, #182, filed May 15, 1869, with
Judge A. Bledsoe's County Court, witnessed by neighbors Sarah, Harriet, and
Mary Sage, who testified as to Frances Ferris's sound mind when she dictated her
will on April 13, 1869.

64. Mexican/Spanish protection of married women's property, which was adopted by the Republic, and later the state of Texas, was in stark contrast to U.S. law,
derived from British Common Law, giving women no rights to property they
brought to marriage. Community property provisions of Texas law gave women
claim to one-half of property accumulated after marriage.

> That the said estate shall be managed by my husband for the support
> of our children. . . . It is my desire that my children shall remain
> together for the period of five years and that they shall cultivate as
> much of the farm as they can . . . that the rest of the farm be rented
> out that the rents shall be applied to keeping the farm in order and . . .
> be applied to raising and instructing the children.[65]

Frances Ferris stipulated that the rents and income be used exclusively
to benefit those children who "remain together" upon the farm. After five
years she requested that Dallas County appoint a commission to divide
her estate equally among "such of my children as may be living at that
time." In case of Warren Ferris's death before 1874, she asked that
Thomas J. Nash of Duck Creek be executor of the estate. Finally, Fanny
made special bequests to insure that all her children would be "well
mounted." The older boys, Jim and Charley, already had their own horses. Mary Catherine was to receive the horse called "Frenchman," Henry
was to have the colt from the Chenault mare, Robert the colt from the
Jackson mare, and the remaining children, Louisa, Edward, Ella, and
Fannie were to receive colts from mares to be bred over the next five
years.[66] Thus Frances Ferris guaranteed her minor children the protection of home, education, and transportation until the youngest, Fannie,
was at least five years old.

Frances Ferris's will included a survey, made by her husband, of their
470-acre farm. Composed of most of C. A. Lovejoy Survey #4 and a bit of
Lovejoy #8, bounded by White Rock and Ash Creeks on the west and east,
marked by certain "witness trees" and four hard rocks planted at the corners, the Ferris land was delineated from that of their neighbors, Wes
Chenault, John H. Daniels, James Jackson, and Marion Herndon. It was
all that was left of the thousands of acres Ferris had once claimed.[67]

In July 1869, Ferris suffered the bite of a wild raccoon that came into
the house through a window on a sultry summer night. Thinking it was a
house cat trapped in the cabin, W. A. first shooed the animal, then
attacked it with a hoe and tried to stomp it. Fifteen-year-old Mary
Catherine recalled the pandemonium. Her father had just returned from
a horseback trip to East Texas, bringing home one of the Ellison cousins
for a visit. It was a beautiful bright moonlit night; the family slept with
all the doors and unscreened windows wide open to catch the breeze.
Ferris himself put a bed down in front of the door as he wanted all the air
he could get. Mary Catherine, assuming her deceased mother's role,

---

65.. Last will and testament of Frances M. Ferris, Dallas Co. Records Probate
Book, Part One, #182.

66. Ibid.

67. Davis Collection and the Caruth Papers include several deeds of sale and
surveys of land originally held by W. A. Ferris. An excellent handdrawn map in the
Caruth Papers shows Ferris land out of Lovejoy Surveys #4 and #9 which came
into the hands of the Caruth family.

rocked the baby to sleep and had just retired when she heard something climb in the window and jump to the floor. Her cousin called, "Uncle Ferris, there is a dog under my bed; come drive it out." Ferris entered the room, stomped his foot, and ordered "Begone!" Then the coon gave a terrible scream and Ferris exclaimed, "The cat bit me!"

The next few moments were bedlam. The frightened animal ran into the front room, attacking and gnawing the rocking chair. Brother Ed, who was sleeping with his father in front of the door, escaped the house while Ferris slammed the bedroom doors, jumped out the window, got a hoe, and ran to the front door. When the cry "Mad Cat!" went up, brother Charley, who was sleeping upstairs, grabbed the beam of a spinning wheel, and ran downstairs to protect his sisters. Still half asleep, young Henry Ferris grabbed the pet cat in both hands and, holding her out in front of him, ran to the window and threw her out.

Mary Catherine admitted that she was deathly afraid of anything mad. When she heard "Mad Cat!" she jumped out her window, ran across the yard, and climbed up on the outhouse, refusing to come down when her father called for her to bring a light. She would not come down until after the thing was dead and they had discovered that it was a raccoon. Ferris and his sons stunned the animal as it came out the front door, and the dogs killed it.[68]

Although the tumult took a comic turn, the consequences of a bite from a rabid animal could be fatal. Through the following hot day, Ferris's leg festered to an indigo blue. He hesitated to split the wound and spread the poison so he cauterized the bite with a hot iron and sent one of the boys on horseback for a doctor. When Dr. Stevenson only sent word that he knew no further treatment, the children began to beg their father to ride for help to a man who owned a "mad stone." Ferris finally agreed, not because he had any faith in the cure, but to placate the children. He rode about ten miles, through brush and undergrowth, arriving in the early afternoon at the place of the man who had the stone. The stone was immediately applied, as Mary Catherine recalled:

> It clinched to the place and remained until twelve o'clock at night. As I said my father had not believed in the mad stone; so as an experiment, he would apply the stone to the scratches he had received while riding through the brush, and it would not stick at all. But after being rinsed and put back to the bite, it would clinch again until the poison was all absorbed and then it wouldn't stick at all.[69]

The stone's efficacy was proof enough for Ferris. Mary Catherine stated that her father "came home a firm believer in the mad stone and wrote

---

68. Mary Catherine Ferris Dozier Greenwood or "Aunt Kate" as given in an interview to Homer DeGolyer in 1939. DeGolyer, "Conquest of Three Forks", 115–116.

69. Ibid.

three columns describing it and its effects for the Dallas *Herald*."[70] W. A. Ferris's article was sent to New York and England for publication, according to his daughter. Of course, the true worth of the mad stone was not proved for nine days, and during that time, still uncertain of the outcome, W. A. instructed, "Children, in case I do go mad, run quick and get a neighbor . . . to shoot me."[71]

In his article for the *Herald* describing his experience, Ferris revealed that John Favens, who lived on the West Fork of the Trinity River, was the owner of the mad stone. Purported to be one of three such stones in Dallas County, the Faven stone was about one inch square, irregular in shape—looking something like coral or a hornet's nest. A bundle of membrane-like tubes comprised the stone, which Faven soaked in hot water then placed on Ferris's wound where it stuck so tightly it did not fall off even when he walked about. Ferris was fascinated by the experience and wished he had a microscope to examine the stone more closely. One should not scoff at such things, W. A. asserted; the stone sucked the deadly "virus" from his leg and saved his life. Indeed, Ferris had to kill one of his dogs which became rabid after being bit by the same raccoon.[72]

Having survived the bite of a hydrophobic cat, Ferris resumed his enjoyment of the outdoor life. At every opportunity he could be found roaming the thickets of White Rock Creek where he loved to hunt. Despite a slight limp, he walked the trails with a quick, vigorous stride. Young boys, who encountered the short, stocky fellow with the Van Dyke beard and piercing blue eyes, were fascinated by the old man who was always willing to thrill them with his stories of frontier adventure, told in incisive, cultured diction.[73]

Warren A. Ferris made his last survey, for R. C. Buckner,[74] in 1871, but he continued to share his knowledge by giving instruction to several young men in the county who wished to become surveyors.[75] One of his students was John R. West whose sons and grandsons followed the

---

70. Ibid.

71. Ibid.

72. W. A. Ferris, Dallas *Herald*, July 8, 1871. Mody C. Boatright, Wilson M. Hudson, Allen Maxwell (eds.), *Madstones and Twisters* (Dallas: Southern Methodist University Press, 1958), 5, a Texas Folklore Society publication, states that such "stones" were actually calcinated bone that came from the stomach of ruminants like cows or deer.

73. Although there is no known photograph of W. A. Ferris, a physical description was given by his youngest surviving daughter Sarah Ellen in a letter to Walter McCausland, May 17, 1951. FLC, Box IX, Folder 4.

74. R. C. Buckner was the founder of Texas Baptists' Buckner Orphans Home in Dallas.

75. One of the last public acts of W. A. Ferris was recommendation of surveyor B. L. Frost, perhaps one of his young students. In the Dallas *Herald*, July 27, 1872, Ferris stated: "I was present when the observations were made . . . and find them correct. I would . . . recommend Mr. Frost . . . who richly deserves employment . . . as a surveyor."

surveying profession for generations in Dallas County. An admiring neighbor judged Ferris the "best mathematician in the state" and said that there were more books in his library than that man had ever seen in one Texas house. Ferris spent many winter days poring over his cherished volumes of Shakespeare and other classics which he kept in a large walnut double-bookcase.[76]

Beginning in the summer of 1871, Ferris contributed frequent articles to the Dallas *Herald*. A series of over twenty articles published in 1871 and 1872 reveal his wide interests, values and prejudices, and reflections over a remarkably eventful life. This outflowing of opinion came in the last twenty months of his life, as if to share his experience was an urgent necessity. Early articles took the form of letters to the editor, usually signed "W. A. F." They were sparked by some point of disagreement or reaction to opinions expressed by others in the *Herald*.[77]

When Horace Greeley spoke as an expert on agricultural progress at the opening of the State Fair in Houston, Ferris's spirited retort was carried on the front page of the Dallas paper: "It seems to me like sending coals to Newcastle to send to New York, for a Republican chief, who has been all his life devoted to politics, to inform the people of Texas on the subject of farming." Ferris judged that Greeley offered not "one practical . . . idea that is new" and showed "an extreme ignorance of the experimental knowledge acquired by the people of Texas during the past 30 years." Surmising that political motives brought Greeley to Texas, Ferris concluded with a challenge:

> I will undertake to find 50 farmers in Dallas County, who can condense on one-fourth a sheet of paper more genuine, practical knowledge derived from observation and experience of the greatest value to emigrants than contained in this vaunted lecture.[78]

Responding to Greeley's advice on overcoming Texas's perennial water shortage, Ferris contributed an article on "Irrigation" in which he advocated the building of stock ponds or "tanks" to catch the winter and spring rains. He gave specific directions, based on his own experience, as to how such tanks should be built. In addition, he pointed out: "In large towns like Dallas, situated on the banks of rivers, one steam engine with a sufficiency of hose would water five hundred gardens twice a week at no great expense." Ferris assured his readers "that no man has at heart a stronger desire to see our country prosperous" than he.[79]

---

76. DeGolyer, "Conquest of Three Forks," 117.

77. Ferris also contributed articles to the *Herald* during the 1860s. An example is his scathing attack on Bonneville, Dec. 1, 1866, written in reaction to Caleb Forshey's article of Sept. 20. The fragment of another early writing recounting the death of fur trapper William H. Vanderburgh is found in the Davis Collection.

78. W. A. Ferris, Dallas *Herald*, July 15, 1871.

79. W. A. Ferris, ibid., Aug. 5, 1871.

In the midst of a Texas dry spell, with no rain between April and August and the cotton yield down two-thirds, the *Herald* carried an interesting exchange of opinion between Warren Ferris and John Henry Brown. John H. Brown, a "johnny-come-lately" to Dallas, was a noted Texas historian who quickly established himself as an expert on local history. In a somewhat condescending manner, Brown disagreed with Ferris's prediction of frequent dry weather. Recounting his own experience in South Texas, Brown asserted that drought in the Dallas area would be rare. Warren Ferris fired back his "Reminiscences," a useful account of Dallas weather between 1837 and 1846, which was also something of a personal diary.[80]

Brown and Ferris shared a low opinion of Gov. E. J. Davis and his Radical Republicans, and both men attacked the "carpetbag" excesses in the pages of the *Herald*. Deploring "reckless mismanagement" and overtaxing by Republicans, Ferris especially criticized Radical influence on education of youth:

> As long as "They" continue in power . . . those God-forsaken creatures who call George Washington [a slaveholder] a scoundrel . . . [they] will teach our youth to despise their fathers as traitors . . . confiscate the little a disastrous war has left us. . . . [we must] establish our own schools . . . with schoolmasters whose sympathies are with us.[81]

A hint of populism appears in Ferris's judgments on the relationship between the growing city and its surrounding countryside. Saying the town and country should "march hand in hand together," Ferris urged city folk to sympathize with the vagaries of nature under which the farmer labored and not overtax their rural neighbors. Having lost much of his own land to taxes, W. A. Ferris knew all too well the injustice. Ferris demonstrated his wide reading and knowledge of engineering when, in a series of articles, he reacted to the building of a new brick courthouse in Dallas and the construction of the first iron bridge across the Trinity. Dallasites took great pride in these two postwar projects, but to Ferris they were prime examples of useless spending. He felt less ambitious structures would be more suited to the hard economic times. Denouncing the "reckless spirit of spending for internal improvements that will ruin the people," Ferris concluded:

---

80. Ibid., articles of July 29, Aug. 5, 26, Sept.2, 1871. This exchange led one commentator to dub Ferris Dallas's first "weatherman."

81. W. A. Ferris, ibid., Sept. 16, 1871. Like many Southerners, Ferris exaggerated the length of Radical rule, speaking of twelve years of misrule. He was particularly concerned about Republican control of public schools, opposing the comprehensive education law passed in 1871 by the state legislature; see Crouch, "'Unmanacling' Texas Reconstruction," 286–287. In a murky but fascinating allegory entitled "A Vision," Dallas *Herald*, Jan. 6, 1872, Ferris dreams of the restoration of Democratic rule to the beleaguered South. In every way, Ferris reflects the early "Dunning school" view of Reconstruction challenged by modern historians.

We, in the country, are willing to be taxed for reasonable and judicious improvements in the city of Dallas. . . . We shall be proud of the growing city in our midst . . . but we do oppose the indiscriminate application of public funds to improvements of doubtful . . . utility. . . . Let us be careful to build no real capitols for imaginary States.[82]

On the other hand, Ferris agreed on the importance of the coming railroad. Mary Catherine claimed that her father "sold thousands of acres of land for fifty cents an acre to bring the Railroad to Dallas."[83] Probably Ferris contributed to a fund of $5,000 raised by Dallas County to lure the railroad. Not only Dallas merchants but also conservative farmers understood the necessity of being adjacent to the proposed rail route.

In all his writings, Warren Ferris displayed the modesty and wit which had always been his style. He revealed himself as a man of strong opinion and poetic imagination. One article, "Book of Nature," was as close to a religious statement as Ferris ever made. He asked: "Should we not study the great volume of nature—should we not draw wisdom from the past to guide us in the future? Should we not carefully read and correctly interpret these lessons, written by the Supreme Architect of the universe?"[84] Like so many of the Romantic period, Ferris found morality and inspiration in nature. He loved to contemplate the majesty of God's creation and found spiritual strength therein rather than in organized religion.

More and more, Ferris's thoughts returned to the majestic vistas of the Rockies whose romance and beauty he recalled in poetry and prose. Warren Ferris must have felt a large measure of satisfaction when his descriptions of Yellowstone's wonders were vindicated in the amazing photographs of William Henry Jackson. Fantastic geysers, shimmering pools, roaring waterfalls, quiet meadows, crystal lakes, and towering mountains were no tall tales or whimsy invented by trappers like Ferris. Congress was so moved by Jackson's photos that on March 1, 1872, they preserved two million acres as the nation's first national park.[85]

The last ten of Ferris's newspaper articles, appearing in three months between November 1872 and January 1873, concerned his Rocky Mountain adventures. Although his memory was sometimes at odds with earlier versions he had written, his reminiscences were unfailingly colorful. It must have surprised his friends and neighbors to read of Ferris's exciting past. Those who thought "W. A." just an ordinary Dallas farmer

---

82. W. A. Ferris, Dallas *Herald*, Sept. 9, 16, Dec. 30, 1871.

83. Lucy Pounds Smith to Walter McCausland, Oct. 11, 1959. Mary Catherine Ferris told this story to her grandson Felix Dozier. FLC, Box VI, Folder 9.

84. Ferris, Dallas *Herald*, Sept. 2, 1871. According to Nell Been Davis, this statement of belief reflects the teachings of the Second Degree, the "Fellowcraft" degree, of the Masonic Lodge and might indicate that Ferris advanced to that degree which is well-suited to one of his scientific bent.

85. Robert V. Hine, *The American West: An Interpretive History* (Boston: Little, Brown and Co., 1973), 180–181.

were amazed to realize that he was an "old Mountain Man" who had experienced countless adventures. While Ferris spent long hours at his desk or roaming the White Rock thickets, the farm went slide and the debts to Caruth Bros. store mounted.

Warren Ferris lived to see his two oldest sons marry and to enjoy a grandson, William Monroe Ferris, son of Jim and Martha (Stanford) Ferris.[86] Ferris also experienced the landmark year of 1872 when the railroad came to Dallas. Perhaps he was in the crowd at the East Dallas depot on July 16 when 7,000 people welcomed the Houston and Texas Central Railroad. If so, he may have been amused to hear the speeches of John Henry Brown and John Neely Bryan. In his own mind, Warren Ferris could recall Dallas County as a sea of waving grasslands, a flurry of vivid spring wildflowers, a tangle of bottomland thickets, teeming with wildlife, made hazardous by roaming Indians. So much had happened. So much had changed.

On February 8, 1873, Warren Angus Ferris died at age sixty-two. A new editor of the Dallas *Herald*, not knowing him, carried no obituary. Ferris was buried, beside Frances and four of their children, in the little cemetery by Ash Creek. He had written his own irreverent epitaph:

> When I am dead
> Remember I said
> I am no more
> As I was before
> From the world
> I am hurled
> To someone that's new
> Always bright and true
> Or with devils to range
> In fire and in chains[87]

Joshua Lovejoy outlived his half-brother, and it is with him that the family correspondence concludes. Fortunes in Buffalo soured. Between 1866 and 1874, property belonging to Mary and Joshua Lovejoy was seized for nonpayment of taxes and lots were sold at sheriff's auction for $11 and $15 each. The Lovejoys returned to Texas in 1882 where Joshua farmed a rented place on the edge of the Big Thicket and taught at a Negro school near Colita in Polk County. Never having found the easy wealth or fame for which he had longed, Lovejoy became increasingly contentious in old age. Writing to his married daughter Florence Britton in Buffalo, he complained of the "old humdrum southern country" and hard times in Texas. Florence was asked to send money to tide her parents

---

86. Ferris memoranda book, Davis Collection. Jim Ferris married Martha J. Stanford in 1870 and their son was born Jan. 18, 1873. Charley Ferris married Susan Ogle in 1871 but was divorced the next year. In 1873, Charley married Jane Sutton.

87. Ferris memoranda book, Davis Collection.

over until the cotton crop was sold. Mary needed quinine and Josh required eyeglasses. He had to go slow since he suffered a sunstroke.[88]

After years of scheming, Josh spent his last days as a struggling tenant farmer. In 1887, Joshua and Mary moved to live with their son Walter who had a school on Kickapoo Creek about fourteen miles west of Livingston. It was Walter Lovejoy who wrote to his sister of the death of their father on November 11, 1889. Joshua had been taken ill with dysentery, exposed himself too soon to a cold wind, and suffered a stroke.[89] He was buried next to Mary, who had died two years earlier, in Buleah Cemetery, about one hundred yards from Walter's schoolyard door.[90]

Thus died the last of two brothers who hated and feared each other for nearly forty years. Neither forgot or forgave, and their bitter acrimony was to poison the family for generations.

---

88. Joshua Lovejoy to Florence A. Britton, Apr. 19, 1882, Dec. 20, 1883, Oct. 12, 1885, and Oct. 4, 1888, FLC, Box II, Folder 13.

89. Walter Lovejoy to Florence Britton, July 6, 1890, ibid.

90. Mrs. Elzo (Fannie) Been to Homer DeGolyer, Nov. 1941, Davis Collection. Fannie Cannon Been visited the cemetery and talked to a ninety-year-old neighbor Henry Tommie, who remembered the Lovejoys. Walter Lovejoy lived with Tommie until Walter married. Tommie said that Joshua Clarence Lovejoy was short and spare, wore a small beard, and was a "loner." He recalled the Lovejoys as "Yankee Republicans" who "refused to vote with the niggers in Texas."

CONCLUSION

How shall we judge the life of Warren Angus Ferris and what does his experience say to larger questions on the nature of America's frontier experience? Ferris was surely a man of his time. Born early in the nineteenth century on the Niagara frontier, Ferris participated in the heyday of the westward movement. As a youth in the Yellowstone Country, he saw the decline of the beaver trade, the recession of the buffalo, and the demoralization of the American Indian. Ferris's writings described and publicized the trails, mountain passes, and fertile valleys of the Rocky Mountain West, contributing to westward migration. His long career coincided with the canal-building craze, the age of the steamboat, and the coming of the railroad.

Warren Ferris matured on the reckless, unfailingly optimistic Texas frontier where, as a surveyor, he again played a significant role in western settlement. During the freewheeling years of the Republic of Texas, Ferris was as acquisitive as the next man, grabbing what land he could for his friends and family. At last, settling down as a Texas farmer, he experimented with old crops in the new climate and soil and generously shared his knowledge. Thus, mirrored in Ferris's personal experience, we see exploitation and speculation give way to husbandry, cultivation, and community building.

Ferris reflects each of the three stereotypes of that mythic figure, the Mountain Man.[1] He *was* America's "romantic hero" as described by Washington Irving—the rugged individual on the wild frontier— daring physical hardship, risking constant danger, reveling in unrestrained freedom. Warren Ferris also exemplified something of the unprincipled "delinquent," as witness his behavior at the death of Vanderburg, his switch to employ by the rival Hudson's Bay Company, his evasion of the law in Texas when he indulged in speculative activities. Ferris's fiery temper and pride, his slippery loyalties, and questionable business activities might cause some to judge him a rebellious nonconformist. Yet here is

---

1. Every study of the Mountain Man takes its cue from William H. Goetzmann's 1963 essay, "The Mountain Man As Jacksonian Man," which examines subsequent careers of 446 men in the beaver trade to prove them not deviants or social misfits but followers of the American dream. A decade later, Harvey L. Carter and Marcia C. Spencer challenged Goetzmann's conclusions and re-evaluated all three stereotypes. See "Stereotypes of the Mountain Man," *Western Historical Quarterly*, 6 (Jan., 1975), 17–32. Goetzmann responded in the same publication, "A Note on Stereotypes of the Mountain Man," *Western Historical Quarterly*, 6 (July, 1975), 295–302.

no uncouth drifter, no crude savage. Ferris's sensitive and thoughtful nature is made clear in the captivating poetry and prose that he produced throughout his life. A strong sense of mutual dependency and social responsibility was essential to Ferris's success as a leader of trapping and surveying expeditions.

Perhaps Warren Ferris best reflects the image of the "expectant capitalist," a man of enterprise who, though he lived on the roughest frontier, shared the dream of upward mobility held by all Americans.[2] He treated the fur trade as a business in which, as a young man, he might accumulate capital for a Missouri plantation. In Texas, he expected to reap the promise of free land that would bring respectability and status both to him and his family. One suspects that, had it not been for family responsibilities, Ferris might have been content to roam the woods, hunting and fishing. But Warren Ferris was no loner. For his most complete happiness, he required the surroundings of hearth and home.

He was essentially a family man. As revealed in his letter to Melinda, Ferris was strongly motivated by his loved ones. His very coming to Texas was instigated by his brother Charles, the desperate quest for land in Texas was aimed at providing security for the Buffalo family, his second marriage was designed to provide a home for Melinda's infant, the last thirty years of guarding the land on White Rock Creek were driven by his fears that Joshua Lovejoy would wrest the hard-won land from Frances and the children. Warren Ferris's story is necessarily the story of the Ferris/Lovejoy family who, despite barriers of distance and unreliable mails, sustained a close relationship through their remarkable correspondence. The tragedy of the story lies in the estrangement between Ferris and his half-brother Joshua Lovejoy; their lives came to be ruled by personal vendetta.

Warren Ferris apparently held no political ambitions, no thirst for personal power. His only goal was to own land enough for himself and his family. Land was the symbol of status and wealth for every independent man of the era. Like most Texians of the Republic, Ferris was a speculator who gambled on the easy availability of large chunks of cheap land which would soon increase in value. Much of Ferris's life was spent in the measuring and management of land. His early dreams of wealth were dashed by the economic collapse of the 1840s, and his personal ambitions were crushed by the death of his first wife Melinda. With a second wife, Ferris settled for the sober life of a Texas farmer and the slow, steady pattern of the seasons. His later years were devoted to guarding and preserving his holdings, which ironically were lost after his death. As was so often the case, the land passed through the hands of the first generation of settlers and into the hands of merchant-bankers.

---

2. Goetzmann uses the term "Jacksonian Man" to describe the average American who shared the egalitarianism and capitalist values of the Age of Jackson.

For the most part, Warren Ferris was content to remain out of the public eye; he was only drawn into controversy when some contemporary challenged his strongly held opinions. At such times, he could be hot-tempered and outspoken, even profane. While he was a man of action, pursuing occupations which kept him outdoors in the worst of weather, Warren Ferris was also a contemplative man. Like many men of the Romantic period, he studied nature and found joy in experiencing its beauty. Often a risk-taker, Ferris was never foolhardy. He had a healthy respect for danger and observed caution in the proper circumstances. In his personal relationships, Ferris exhibited a family trait of suspicion verging on paranoia. He was easily offended, often expected the worst of people, warned his family of the motives of outsiders.

Warren Ferris studied his world with the precise eye of a surveyor. His impatient curiosity and keen powers of observation made him a careful witness of his times. Although he was well-read in the opinions of others,[3] Ferris based his theories on practical experience. He always looked for a scientific explanation for the phenomena he observed, anchoring his speculations in things he knew. Although he had little formal education, no degrees or licenses, he took on wide responsibilities with energy and competency.

Ferris's attitude toward the natural world reflected a certain ambivalence. He was typical of those frontiersmen who loved the land, but loved to exploit it. He relished nature for its sheer beauty and wisdom, but he also felt free to utilize the land and profit from it. Although he trapped and hunted his share, Ferris was one of the first westerners to note destruction of the natural environment and deplore the loss of a way of life. Regrettably, an early admiration of American Indians gave way to the spirit of his times which resented and despised them. Although a Yankee by birth, his views on slavery and the Civil War matched Southern conservatism.

Warren Angus Ferris ended his life with little material wealth, but he was motivated by that "hope of success" which is so much a part of the American dream. His career is a mirror of Manifest Destiny; his personal ambitions coincided with the nation's drive for Oregon and Texas. Indirectly, he was an agent of American imperialism. Ferris's journal, map, and newspaper articles along with his family's careful retention of his letters evidence an awareness of his pivotal role. In Texas, Ferris as a scout and surveyor opened new land for settlement. Roadbuilder and townbuilder, the surveyor occupied a key position in the development of the West. As a Dallas County farmer, judging the soil and weather, experimenting with new crops, and sharing his knowledge, Ferris contributed to the agricultural development of the Blackland Prairie.

---

3. Ferris stated in the Dallas *Herald*, July 15, 1871, that he had been a reader of the *Scientific American* for fifteen years.

Modern students of the American West suggest that our frontier experience is far more complex than we may have recognized. It is a tale of failure as well as success, of villainy as well as bravery, of greed and exploitation as much as cooperation and progress.[4] Acted out on the stage of the Rocky Mountains in the 1830s and Texas frontier of the 1840s were the clash of convergent cultures—Indian, Hispanic, and Anglo. Patterns of racial ugliness, violence, descriminatory land policy, and irresponsible waste of natural resources were repeated. The life experience of Warren Ferris allows us to look beyond simplistic versions of western history to see the conflicts that rocked entire families. As men and women strived to impose their vision on a hostile environment, many were broken in the struggle.

Texas did not live up to the lofty expectations of the Ferris family. Charles Ferris collapsed under the burden of family responsibilities and failed hopes. Joshua Lovejoy's romantic dreams were crushed. Warren Ferris, saddened by the deaths of two wives and several children and ruled by a corrosive fear of his half-brother, was left with only the memories of his uncommon adventures. Ferris died with little material wealth. His family scattered and their property was lost.

From the editor of the Dallas *Herald*, who failed to note Ferris's death in the 1870s, to the 1970s, when the Dallas City Council allowed his family cemetery to be bulldozed, the memory of Warren A. Ferris was obliterated from the popular history of the area. No landmark bears his name. No public square, no street, no school, no stream perpetuates his memory.[5] It might be said of Ferris, as he wrote of his hero William H. Vanderburgh, "He explored a great deal of country but little known, yet his modesty did not permit him to apply his own name to any pass, valley, or stream." Perhaps Warren Angus Ferris will yet achieve his rightful prominence as a founder of Dallas County, an important player in the opening of North Texas to white settlement, and a quintessential figure in the epic of America's westward movement.

---

4. Elliott West, "A Longer, Grimmer, But More Interesting Story," in Patricia N. Limerick, Clyde A. Milner II, and Charles E. Rankin (eds.), *Trails: Toward a New Western History* (Lawrence: University of Kansas Press, 1991), 105.

5. W. A. Ferris, Dallas *Herald*, Dec. 1, 1866. Ferris, Texas, in Ellis County south of Dallas and Ferris Plaza across from Union Station in the City of Dallas are named for the family of Justus and Royal A. Ferris, not related to Warren A. Ferris. Homer DeGolyer thought that Ferris Street in south Dallas might be named for W. A. Ferris, but this is uncertain.

EPILOGUE

Henry Lovejoy, Warren A. Ferris's stepbrother, died in Buffalo in 1872, the year before Ferris died in Dallas. Minor players in the story, L. A. Cook, Ferris's father-in-law, and Benjamin Rathbun, New York City hotelier, died the same year as Ferris, 1873. Fugitive Lyman Rathbun, living in Texas under the name of "Brewster," ran the ferry across the Sabine River at Brewsters Bluff until his death. A. G. Walker moved on to Tarrant County where he was involved in another bitter county seat fight before reentering politics and serving again in the Texas Senate. John Neely Bryan, after much restless wandering, returned to Dallas, separated from his wife, drank up his money, and died in 1877 at the Texas State Lunatic Asylum in Austin.

In Buffalo, Hester Ferris lived until 1895 when she died at the age of eighty. George W. Ferris, Charles's only surviving son, followed in his father's footsteps, becoming a newspaperman, long in the employ of the Buffalo *Courier*. The youngest child of Charles and Hester Ferris, Sarah Louise, married Arthur Austin of Buffalo. They had no children. Around 1900, Sarah Louise compiled a valuable history of the Ferris/Lovejoy family.

Hester and her children are buried in the Ferris plot of historic old Forest Lawn Cemetery in Buffalo. A most impressive family marker in Forest Lawn is that of the Lovejoys, where Joshua Lovejoy Sr., his first wife Sarah Johnson Lovejoy, son Henry, and his wife Eliza O. Lovejoy are interred. Lars Sellstedt is buried beside his second wife Caroline Scott and her parents, Dr. and Mrs. William K. Scott, in a third area of Forest Lawn Cemetery.

Joshua Lovejoy's daughter Florence, wife of William H. Britton, had four children. The Britton family moved to Colorado, but descendants returned to Buffalo where they retained the Ferris/Lovejoy correspondence, family Bible, and Warren Ferris's map of the Yellowstone County. Another of Lovejoy's daughters, Alice, married a Conrey and moved to California. Son Walter Lovejoy, in Texas, married a widow, Elizabeth "Lizzie" Martin Chambers; they had two daughters.

When Warren A. Ferris died in Dallas in 1873, he had nine living children; three were grown and married, four were teenagers, and two were infants. Although his wife's will (1869) required that the family live at the homeplace for at least five years, after their father died in February 1873 it was no longer possible for the family to stay together. The two oldest sons, Jim and Charley, and one daughter, Mary Catherine, had already married and left home.

James M. "Jim" Ferris, Warren's eldest son, married Martha J. Stanford in 1870 when he was twenty-one years of age. Rev. Amon McCommas, elder of the Christian Church in Dallas County, performed the ceremony, as he did for Jim's sister Mary Catherine. In the 1880s, Jim Ferris moved to Greer County, Oklahoma, where he remarried and started a second family. According to Ferris family stories, Jim took most of his father's personal effects, including his surveying tools, with him to Oklahoma.

Charles D. "Charley" Ferris married Susan Ogle in 1871, but that marriage lasted only one year. In 1873, Charley married Jane Sutton by whom he had four children. He and his family drifted southwest into the Texas Hill Country. In 1876, Charley and his brother Henry were living in Bosque County. Later, Charley Ferris settled in Llano County, west of Austin, where he became a deputy U.S. marshal.

Mary Catherine Ferris, "Kate," another of the older children, married George W. Dozier in early 1873. "Aunt Kate" as she was called, outlived her first husband, married Hardy B. Greenwood, and lived to a ripe old age in Kilgore, Texas, where she was interviewed by historians interested in her father's career.

The youngest children, Sarah Ellen, who was three years of age when her mother died and seven at the death of her father, and Frances Laura, the baby who was only four when Warren Ferris died, were sent to their mother's sister Emily Moore Ellison in Smith County, Texas. Frances Laura died just two years later and was buried at Mt. Carmel Cemetery. Sarah Ellen "Ellie" Ferris recalled that the Ellisons were "very aristocratic." One of the Ellison daughters always stayed dressed to receive callers; visitors in the Ellison home were served wine and small cakes. When her Aunt Emily died in 1879, Ellie lived for a time with their cousin Molly Ellison, who had married a local schoolteacher, John Scarborough. The Scarboroughs were parents of Dorothy Scarborough, a noted Texas novelist.

Ellie later moved to Tarrant County to be with her brother Robert and his family. There she met and married George W. Cannon. On one occasion, Ellie asked Robert Ferris if she might keep some of the brittle, yellowed letters from her father's old trunk. These letters of Warren A. Ferris were her only link with the parents who had died when she was so young. A packet of letters and the memoranda book containing Ferris's poetry were treasured by Sarah Ellen Ferris Cannon over the years. She lived into the 1950s and was a valuable source of family history.

Henry Ferris, age nineteen at his father's death, married Frances Smith. They had no children. Henry lived until 1940. Robert E. "Bob" Ferris, seventeen at Warren's death, married Texana Stanford, sister of

Jim's wife Martha. Robert settled in Arlington, Texas, where many of his descendants still live. Louisa Jane or "Lula," fifteen at the death of her father, married George W. Rutledge and moved to Spur in West Texas. Edward, age thirteen, lived with his brother Robert in Tarrant County. He married a Miss Youngblood in 1884 but tragically died of typhoid only a few months after his marriage.[1]

Ferris's homeplace on White Rock Creek was deserted by 1875. The estate of Frances Ferris was divided nine ways, with one portion going to Walter and William Caruth in payment for "supplies furnished by Caruth & Bros. to W. A. Ferris for the use of the family of said Frances Ferris deceased."[2] Land was sold at public auction in 1876 to pay off claims against the estate; the Caruths bought some of this land and received around $600 in payment for debts incurred by Warren Ferris. Between 1874 and 1877, the Ferris children sold their remaining interest in the White Rock farm to the Caruths for about $400 each.[3] The old log cabin near the cemetery became a stopover for drifters, as did the vacant Ferris farmhouse. Some said that the James boys stayed there and that Sam Bass and his gang holed up in the farmhouse prior to their robbery of the Texas and Pacific train in Mesquite in 1878. The house was destroyed by fire around 1909.

Charley and Jim Ferris, after "rough-and-tumble" boyhoods, jumped on the right side of the law. Both shared their father's love of the outdoors and a life of adventure. In 1885, Charley Ferris was credited with the capture of the Pitts-Yeager band of outlaws. Associates of the Younger and James gangs, these notorious desperados drifted south into Indian Territory, then to West Texas. U.S. Marshal Ferris tracked them into the Texas Hill Country. According to the tabloid press, the daring little ranger rode into their camp, challenged the outlaws, and captured them single-handedly. He was wounded in the encounter and ever after, the press reported, walked in a lop-sided fashion, carrying more lead in one side than the other.[4] With his third wife, Anna Vogel, Charley moved on farther west. A fourth wife, Lizzie Pieland, shared his last years, which were spent on a ranch near the Capitan Mountains in Lincoln County, New Mexico. There, having outlived four wives, too old to enjoy the hunting and trapping he loved, Charley Ferris died in 1919. Some of his descendants

---

1. The Cannon Papers (Davis Collection) trace the history of the children of W. A. Ferris. Nine living children in 1873 were by nickname, from eldest to youngest: Jim, Charley, Kate, Henry, Lula, Bob, Edward, Ellie, and Fannie.

2. Estate of Frances Ferris, Thomas J. Nash, executor. Dallas Co. Probate Records (DPL). An inventory showed 469 acres of land, two horses, twelve head of cattle, one wagon, a sugar mill and fixtures—appraised at a value of $7,000. Claims against the estate included a debt to the Caruths, taxes, and court costs.

3. Caruth Papers.

4. From Pennsylvania *Grit*, Sept. 11, 1904, sent to McCausland by Rena D'Arcy, Apr. 30, 1951, FLC, Box IX, Folder 3.

moved to Arizona and California. One of Charley Ferris's daughters, Mrs. Rena D'Arcy of Wink, Texas, and later Long Beach, California, lived into the 1960s and was interviewed by historians interested in W. A. Ferris.

As deputy sheriff at Altus, Oklahoma, Jim Ferris also had an exciting career chasing outlaws in what was then Indian Territory. One story tells how after being shot in the calf by an outlaw of the Red Buck gang, Jim rode home, cleaned the wound, bound it with a silk handkerchief, remounted, and hunted down the outlaw.[5] Jim Ferris's descendants still live in western Oklahoma; son Eugene Ferris ran the ranch on the old homeplace near the Navaho Mountains on the north fork of the Red River; another son, namesake of his famous ancestor Warren A. Ferris, became tax assessor; and a grandson, Weldon Ferris, was county attorney, later judge, of Jackson County, Oklahoma.

Descendants of Warren A. Ferris scattered from Texas west to New Mexico, Utah, Arizona, and California, but few were left in the Dallas area. Robert Ferris, who lived closest, just across the county line in Tarrant County, came to help neighbors clean the family cemetery in the 1890s. The cemetery, donated by Ferris in 1852 as a community burial place, was the last physical evidence of the homestead. Here were the graves of Frances and Warren Ferris and four of the children, also the neighbor families' dead: the Dyes, the Sages, the Chenaults, the Herndons, the Pembertons. The last burial was in the Negro section; Rev. R. T. Taylor, buried in 1906. The cemetery was still well kept and maintained in 1924, when a housing development, Forest Hills, was initiated. During development, a road (St. Francis) was bulldozed through the Ferris Cemetery. In the 1950s, despite objections by neighbor Robert Cole, the cemetery was further threatened. The graves were disturbed and tombstones vandalized.[6] Although the Ferris family was scattered, they had family reunions and retained the belief that their ancestor was important, even famous. Lucy Pounds Smith of Dallas, granddaughter of Jim Ferris, led an effort in the 1960s to save what was left of the cemetery and to name a neighborhood school[7] for Warren A. Ferris. Both efforts failed.

---

5. Lucy Mae Pounds Smith to Walter McCausland, Jan. 25, 1959, ibid., Box VI, Folder 8. S. W. Harman, *Hell on the Border: A History of the Great United States Criminal Court at Ft. Smith* . . . (Ft. Smith, Ark.: Hell on the Border Publishing Co., 1953), 252–258, relates the case of the infamous Buck Gang, on a thirteen-day rampage of rape and murder in the Creek Nation in July, 1895.

6. Dallas *Morning News*, Feb. 21, 23, 1958. Robert Cole, who had grown up in the neighborhood, was then seventy-eight years of age. He kept records on the cemetery for fifty-eight of those years and tried to get the city of Dallas to maintain it. Cole also provided a sketch of the Ferris Cemetery and homeplace (DHS). Willie Flowers Carlisle in her *Old Cemeteries of Dallas County* (n.p., 1948), 71, also described the cemetery and listed those interred there (DPL).

7. The elementary school across from the Ferris Cemetery was named instead for Alex Sanger, early Dallas merchant. See Smith Papers, in possession of Leland Smith of Mesquite.

Controversy raged over the "lost" cemetery which, like its founder, had been neglected and forgotten by Dallasites. In 1970, the Dallas city council declared the Ferris Cemetery a "public nuisance" and ordered the graves to be excavated and bones re-interred elsewhere. Although no re-interment occurred, the cemetery was abandoned and the land sold for development. Contrary to state law, five houses of the Forest Heights Addition went up on the cemetery grounds. In 1985, the Dallas County Historical Commission began to take an interest in the controversy. Frances James, marker chairperson of the commission, and Rita Barnes, who had researched the cemetery, drew attention to the situation and a series of articles in Dallas newspapers highlighted the "error that haunts the city."[8] Finally, in 1988, the Warren Angus Ferris Cemetery received a Texas Historical Marker, drawing long-overdue attention to the accomplishments of this pioneer Dallas settler.[9] The marker was placed on high ground overlooking the Ferris cemetery; it reads, in part:

> New York native Warren Angus Ferris (1810–1873) spent six years as a trapper and chronicler of the American West before moving to the Republic of Texas in late 1836. As official surveyor for Nacogdoches County he surveyed the Three Forks of the Trinity area and helped set the boundaries for Dallas and other nearby counties. He wrote many articles for early Dallas newspapers.

---

8. Dallas *Morning News*, Nov. 20, 23, 1985, and Dallas *Times Herald*, Nov. 24, 1985.

9. Horace Cannon, grandson of Warren A. Ferris, Nell Davis, great-granddaughter, and Truett Been, great-grandson, were present at the dedication of the marker on December 10, 1988. Also present were descendants of other Dallas County pioneers buried in the Ferris Cemetery. Due to rain, the ceremony was held in the home of architect Bill Dickson which was built on the cemetery grounds. The marker is located on St. Francis at San Leandro in a "commons" of open ground donated and maintained by the homeowners.

Henry Ferris, son of Warren A. and Frances Ferris. *Courtesy Photographic Archives, Harold B. Lee Library, Brigham Young University.*

Charles Drake "Charley" Ferris, son of Warren A. and Frances Ferris. Relatives stated that Charley most closely resembled his father in physical appearance. *Courtesy Photographic Archives, Harold B. Lee Library, Brigham Young University.*

Deputy U.S. Marshal Charley
Ferris (on right with rifle) and part-
ner. *Courtesy Photographic
Archives, Harold B. Lee Library,
Brigham Young University.*

Sarah Ellen "Ellie" Ferris, daughter
of Warren A. and Frances Ferris.
*Courtesy Photographic Archives,
Harold B. Lee Library, Brigham
Young University.*

Three children of Warren A. and Frances Ferris. Standing, left to right: Lousia Jane Ferris, Sarah Ellen Ferris; seated, left to right: a friend, Edward "Ed" Ferris. *Courtesy Photographic Archives, Harold B. Lee Library, Brigham Young University.*

★ A p p e n d i x A ★

P O E M S O F W A R R E N A . F E R R I S

The following lines were composed on a dreary winter day during a surveying excursion remote from habitation or other indications of civilized life whilst the author lay in camp alone and lame where great danger existed.

Lament

Very forlorn and weary here
    Alone I rest my frame
Far far from friends and Kindred dear
    I lie a cripple lame

A streamlet flows beside my lair
    Sheltered by lofty cane
Sought to arrest the chilling air
    And turn the wintry rain

A thousand warblers cheer the wood
    With ever changing lay
But still my mind in irksome mood
    Is cheerful as this day

Which like the forests aspect drear
    Imparts the unwelcome truth
That Autumn hastening year by year
    Succeeds the way of youth

My Comrades gone and I alone
    With anxious care opprest
I hear the forrests hollow moan
    And start ah! fear exprest

But better reason checks the fault
    A fault I blush to own
Tho' sterner spirits often halt
    By sudden terror thrown

From reasons cheek when danger's near
    As pallid cheeks declare
Get this to him is short lived fear
    Who seeks a warriors fare

With thoughts like these I sink to rest
    Morpheus drowns my care
My soul with fleeting visions blest
    I dream of fortune rare

Warren A. Ferris
(memoranda book)

The poems of Warren A. Ferris trace his grief, anguish, gloom, and melancholy following the death of his beloved Melinda, his return to society and optimism, and his courtships seeking a new wife and mother for his young son.

"Far beyond the hours of youth," Warren Ferris was thirty-four years of age, widowed and lonely, when he directed this prayer for wisdom, virtue, truth, and honor—not to a Christian deity—but to a classical goddess.

Invocation to Minerva
Goddess of Wisdom and War

Oh thou celestial goddess hear
A suppliant mortal's fervent prayer
And grant, that I with wisdom may
The laws of honor justly weight
And far beyond the hours of youth
That I may value sterling truth
Where e're I rove, where e're I bide
Let virtue be my constant guide.

Warren A. Ferris
January 1845
(memoranda book)

Only a few months after the death of his first wife, Warren A. Ferris pled for escape from the pains of grief, "teach me how to flee this earthly sphere . . . take my soul to thee . . . "

Invocation

Melinda dear; look from the realms of light
Upon my anguished soul my darkened sight
Oh! let they gentle spirit hover near
And teach me how to flee this earthly sphere
That I, with thee, may pierce my native sky
And with my souls delight enraptured fly
From sun to sun, to be the constant guide
Of my dear wife, my own immortal bride
Oh haste dear shade and take my soul to thee
Be thou the bearer of that blest decree
That joined my soul to thine in endless love
And wafts us on to blissful worlds above.

Warren A. Ferris
January 1845
(memoranda book)

As he watched the spring of 1845 come to Texas, Ferris slowly relinquished his sadness and personal loss, admitting, "beauty like the rose must surely fade." Following "Nature's law," he vowed to choose a new mate.

Ode to Spring

Hear how the wanton birds so sweetly sing
In wildest notes the gay return of Spring
The zephyrs gliding o'er yon laughing dale
With hawthorn blossoms shed the landscape veil
The smiling season decorated the glade
Yet beauty like the rose must surely fade

Each bud expanding and each opening flower
Distill their native sweets in every bower
The bees with unremitting care pursue
Their daily toil and sip nectorious dew
Yet autumn will these lovely scenes invade
And beauty like the rose must surely fade

The stream that flows along so soft and still
The whistling breeze the solitary rill
In murmurs whisper to the anxious heart
That all we love from these gay scenes must part
Then let not care from joy our Souls persuade
Tho' beauty like the rose must surely fade

The bounding doe skims lightly o'er the plain
No anxious cares his blissful joys restrain
Unconscious he that short lived summer past
Yields to the empire of the wintry blast
Yet no reflections sad should joy invade
Tho' beauty like the rose must surely fade

The rising sun in burnished gold displays
His orient bed and sheds his genial rays
O'er all the world dispensing life and light
Celestial rays that charm its ravished sight
With scenes like these a life of care is paid
Tho' beauty like the rose must surely fade

In this fair season when the hills and dales
In brightest verdure clad the whispering gales
In softest murmurs speak and seem to say
That smiling nature bids all things be gay
Yet is this truth to thinking minds display'd
That beauty like the rose must surely fade

This is the season when the warblers pair
The forest tenants leave their wintry lair
And just to nature's laws by instinct known
Choose each his mate and softer passions own
May we like them by natures laws be swayed
Tho' beauty like the rose must early fade

Then dearest girl whilst wisdom points the way
Lets choose the course (and natures laws obey)
That leads to hymns good the brightest throne
To fondest hearts and purest passions Known
Then Constant joy this truth will deeply shade
That beauty like the rose must surely fade.

W.A. Ferris
(memoranda book)

Leander and Laura

Warren A. Ferris wrote in his Memoranda Book that the following exchange of poems was "suggested by a remark from a female friend that abstract science when rigidly studied tended to estrange the mind from domestic peace and to impart a twist of Melancholy." They indicate Ferris's immersion in scientific and philosophic reading, and his friends' urgings that he return to society after a period of isolation.

Laura

Oh say Leander why dost thou pursue
That phantom learning still Oh why will you
Neglect your dearest friends for useless love
That wins respect alone and nothing more
Do cast those mouldering tomes of science far
Nor let hard words and abstract studies mar
Domestic peace accept a sisters care
Oh be my guide my love and pleasures share
Let other prospects chase your gloom away
And Lauras love shall shed a brighter ray
From those dark studies that allure the heart
from dearest friend, and love Leander part
Oh do return and banish from your mind
That impious love that renders you unkind
If you regret I'll strive to love you more
And while away the charm that learning more

Leander

Dear Laura cease you moldering . . . known
I'd not exchange for Alexander's throne
Here in this dark and musty Volume lies
The hidden mysteries of Yon Spangled Skies
Here do we learn that all those twinkling lights
And Worlds immense that cheer our lonely nights
Like phantom here we guide the orb of day
we transits course and mark its devious way
Yes here we learn the worlds extent and trace

Unseeing laws that guide from place to place
The weary stranger onward who may roam
And still pursue his course and distant home
Here too are Laws that guide the Stately Ship
From clime to clime on each successive trip
That bears us Knowledge - wealth from every shore
And freighted back returns with more and more
These laws deduced from Astronomic light
We owe to Newtons almost Second Sight
This Knowledge Laura own is worthy such
As an ambitious stile of Knowing Much

Laura

Leander dear that learning I approve
That does not win away friendship or love
I would not give for all your mystic lore
The kindlier feelings you for Laura bore
Before my Philosophic rival came
And won your heart to seek the bubble fame
Once you were Kind and smiles your features graced
But now how changed alas what gloom Misplaced
Set on that brow so generous frank and Kind
To cloud an ardent and ingeneous mind
But come Leander you will sure forego
A pleasure that becomes your Lauras woe
Let dearest friends your first attention claim
Then if you will the rest devote to fame
And Laura will her heartfelt pleasure show
By every act that love and duty owe
To a dear brother's Sacrifice a flame
That beckoned on to ever lasting fame

Warren A. Ferris
(memoranda book)

Two undated acrostics addressed to the Sims sisters—the first to Miss Elizabeth M. Sims, the second to Miss Martha S. Sims. An acrostic is verse in which letters, in this case the first letter of each line, taken in order, form the name of the person to whom the poem is dedicated.

An Acrostic

Enduring maid allow a friend sincere
License to pay his homely homage here
Indulge his error and his faults approve
Zephyrs at times with noxious vaporing move
And sweetest flow'rets scattered ore the Vale
Bear fullest poison to the willing gale
E're beauty oft' with imperfection joined

The heart attracts but not the loftin mind
How oft we see tho life's so brief and vain
Man Kind Urge impetious to attain
Some latent good some phantom of the heart
Ideal good that can but woe impart
May mine be virtue still, I'll still pursue
Such as I deem preeminent in you

W. A. Ferris

An Acrostic

My plaintive music dart, as my mind
A willing slave to flattery blind
Reluctant when by beauty prest
To trace a falsehood stand confest
Here on this emblem of your heart
A liar, neer; Sooner past
Soul body life yes sooner may
Sweet dreams of hope be *cast away*
I'd sooner brave the terror death
My future hopes consign to lethe
Sooner than Venus' charms confess
    brighter than those of Martha S.

W.A. Ferris
(memoranda book)

Three poems addressed to Miss Mary A. McCommas, written in 1845 when Warren Ferris was courting his neighbor's daughter. Note the first where he tries out the name "Mary Ann Ferris" in an acrostic comprised of the first letter of each line. In the third poem, Ferris speaks directly of marriage to Miss McCommas.

To Summer

Mark how yon streamlets softly glide
Along the enchanting valley wide
Returning summer hails the morn
Yon budding blossoms decked the thorn
A thousand vernal warblers sing
Nought but the blest approach of spring
Nature arrayed in living green
Forever gilds the charming scene
Each lovely flower in every glade
Rich in their native charms display'd
Roses and lillies here and there
In native wildness scent the air
Smiling like Mary fair

W. A. Ferris

To Mary

I've wandered on from clime to clime
    Impatient of delay
As free as flows my simple rhyme
    I've still pursued my way

I've been where blushing flow'rets grow
When all was blissful still
Where all that's lovely to the view
    Expands remote from ill

I've seen them too at blush of dawn
    In native bowers apart
Diffuse their fragrance o'er the lawn
    And fill the raptured heart

Yet have I never seen a rose
    In honey such sweets distill
As the fond kiss of her who knows
    For whom I warble still

Warren A. Ferris
Spring, 1845

To Miss McCommas

Ode to Beauty

Arouse my muse let beauty be the theme
Of highest praise; no visionary dream

Of peerless beauty sing in softest strains
And wake with matchless art the neighboring swains
Let sighs and tears attest thy potent sway
And dying swains thy just decrees obey

As Sol arising in his burnished car
Sheds his effluence o'er the world afar
So all admit the power of beauty's blaze
That far and wide sheds forth its smiling rays

As the smooth stream in placid stillness glides
Among the hosts of flowers that deck its sides
Soft zephyrs scour along the verdant dale
And steal the scents the wanton flowers exhale

So beauty conscious of its matchless power
Sheds its exhaustless scents in every bower
And placid as the stream that glides so still
Soothes every woe and softens every ill

Go then my muse and sing with matchless art
The praise of her who holds my captive heart
Her lovely charm beguiles my soul of rest
And left my anxious heart with care opprest

Oh teach her how to mitigate my pain

To ease my woe and all my cares restrain
Oh bid her yield to love her beauty rare
To be my wife my love and fortunes share

Then will the Gods that bless the minstrels art
Grant every wish that wells my M.A.'s heart
And beauty still triumphant bear the praise
Due to thy loving art thy poets lays

W. A. Ferris
January 7, 1845
(memoranda book)

As the Republic survived its trials and joined the Union—

The Texian Star

Oh say what pale and twinkling star
Like glowworm flitting faint afar
Shed feeble light and transit ray
Like moonbeams melting into day
The Texian Star

When first existant it arose
Too dull to rout our haughty foes
But as small rills to torrents glide
So rose and shed its brillance wide
The Texian Star

But with increasing light and size
Our foemen saw and with surprise
Gazed on its low and progressive way
They in their anger sought to stay
The Texian Star

Their gathering hordes in furious mood
Came charging like a swelling flood
Like night overwhelming gentle day
The whirlwind came to scare away
The Texian Star

Twas there I saw with anguish filled
The coming storm my bosom chilled
And God! My frenzy fevered brain
Saw indistinct but surely wane
The Texian Star

Alas I cried our guardian light
No longer augurs visions bright
But sinking in nights Sable pall
Dire thunders herald now its fall
The Texian Star

But soon triumphant shouts of war

Burst from the impending gloom afar
Chill horror slowly passed away
While Martial spirits hailed that day
The Texian Star

Now gazing where our waning light
Had flickered shone and sank to sight
I saw fair Liberty on high
Point to the polar Star and cry
The Texian Star

W.A. Ferris
(memoranda book)

ABBREVIATED GENEALOGY OF THE FERRIS/LOVEJOY FAMILY

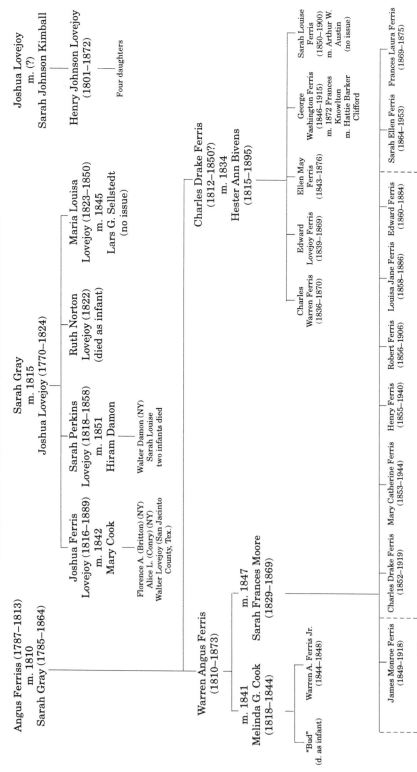

SOME DESCENDANTS OF WARREN ANGUS FERRIS

Warren Angus Ferris m. 1847 Sarah Frances Moore

"Jim" (1849–1918)
- James Monroe m. 1870 Martha J. Stanford later Lizzie L. Rutledge
  - Warren Ferris and Eugene Ferris
    - Weldon Ferris (Okla.)
      - Lucy Mae Pounds Smith (Dallas)
        - Leland Smith (Mesquite, Tex.)

"Charley" (1852–1919)
- Charles Drake m. 1871 Susan Ogle m. 1873 Jane Sutton later Anna Vogel (Bosque Co., Tex.) later Lizzie Pieland (N. Mex.)
  - Robert E. Ferris
    - Rena Belle D'Arcy (Calif.)

"Kate" (1853–1944)
- Mary Catherine m. 1873 Geo. W. Dozier later Hardy B. Greenwood
  - Britt Dozier (Kilgore)
  - Felix Dozier

Henry (1855–1940)
- Henry m. 1875 Sarah Frances Smith (Arlington, Tex.)
  - Carl Ferris
  - Frances (Ferris) McDonald (Rotan, Tex.)

"Bob" (1856–1906)
- Robert m. Texana O. Stanford (Arlington) later m. Cynthia Fuller
  - Ethel Fuller (Dallas)
  - Betty McKool (Dallas)

"Lula" (1858–1886)
- Louisa Jane m. 1876 Geo. W. Rutledge (Spur, Tex.) son George married a Ferris cousin

Edward (1860–1884)
- Edward m. 1884 Ms. Youngblood buried Euless, Tex, (no issue)

"Ellie" (1864–1953)
- Sarah Ellen m. 1879 Geo. W. Cannon
  - Nellie Cled Wright (Mrs. Ed Green, Cisco, Tex.)
  - Fannie P. (Cannon) Been (Eastland Co., Tex.)
  - Horace L. Cannon (San Antonio)
    - Ruby Nell (Been) Davis (Elgin, Tex.)

"Fannie" (1869–1875)
- Frances Laura lived with Ellisons (Smith Co., Tex.) (no issue)

Three living children of W. A. Ferris in 1930s: Mary Catherine, Henry, and Sarah Ellen

INDEX

(Illustrations are indicated by boldfaced page numbers)

"Invocation to Minerva Goddess of Wisdom and War" (W. Ferris): 220
Ionie Indians: 100
Irion, Robert: 61n.9, 72
Ironclad oath: 190
Iroquois Indians: 4, 25
Irrigation: 201
Irving, Washington: 23n.21, 69, 207

★ J ★

Jack County: 168n.6
Jackson, Andrew: 32, 53, 88, 89n.54
Jackson, James: 198
Jackson, W. Turrentine: 36n.64
Jackson, William Henry: 203
Jackson Hole: 29, 33
Jacksonian Man: 208n.2
James, Frances: 215
James, Frank: 196, 213
James, Jesse: 196, 213
Jefferson, Texas: 176
Jefferson River: 26, 29
Jewish City of Refuge: 8
Johnson, Frank W.: 45n.28
Johnson, Henry A.: 187
Johnson, James: 5
Johnston, A. S.: 91, 91n.64
Jones, Anson: 141
Jordan, John: 60n.7

★ K ★

Kaufman County: 115, 124, 129, 158
Keechie Indians: 85, 100, 118
Keene, A. M.: 154n.30
Kemp, Louis W.: 51n.46
Kickapoo Crossing: 121, 122, 124
Kickapoo Indians: 96, 100, 118
Kickapoo Trace: 100, 105, 160
Kickapootown: 85–86
Killough family: 89
Killough Massacre: 89, 96
Kimbro, William: 50n.42
King Block: 105–106, 106n.23, 113, 115, 149
King Philip's War: 1
King, William P.: background of, 99n.2; and Dallas County, ix; death of, 123, 123n.83, 124; and Warren Ferris's assets, 111; and Kingsboro, 112; and settlement preparation, 122, 122n.80; Southern Land Company of, 97, 99, 103–104, 104n.15; and survey expedition, 105; and Trinity River navigation, 133
King's Fort: 111, 112, 112n.57, 119
Kingsboro: 112, 112n.57
Kipp's Rope Walk: 7
Kirtland, Widow: 161
Knight, Obadiah W.: 140–141
Knox/Albright Art Museum: xiv

★ L ★

"La Reunion": 174, 174n.27

Labor (land measurement): 78
Lacy, George: 121
Lacy, Martin: and Board of Land Commissioners, 79n.12; and Burton, 60; and Cherokee Indians, 90, 90n.60; and Ferris, 81, 81n.24; fort of, 60n.5, 89
Lacy, William Young: and Bean, 60; as Ferris's deputy surveyor, 75n.4, 79n.13; Joshua Lovejoy's selling land scrip to, 131n.20; and Reagan, 103n.13, 106n.27
Lacy's Fort: 60n.5, 89
Lafayette, Marie Joseph Paul Yves Roch Gilbert du Motier: 7
Lagow, Thomas: 118, 119, 126
Lamar, Mirabeau B.: and Burton, 76n.5, 83; and Cherokee Treaty, 69; Indian policy of, 88–90, 89n.54, 94; presidential race of 1840, 105n.19; and Rusk, 86n.42
"Lament" (W. Ferris): 219
Land Bill: 75n.2, 80n.16, 83, 84
Land grants: Anglo-American headright grant, 78–80, 80n.18; boundaries of Spanish and Mexican grants, 76; and empresario system, 127; for Peters Company, 122; and Texas Revolution, 42, 42n.14
Land laws: Cherokee Land Bill, 94, 94n.69; and Cherokee Reserve, 78, 94; and land speculation, 79; and surveyor's services, 78–79; transition in, 78
Land speculation: in Cherokee Reserve, 94; and empresario system, 127, 149; and Warren Ferris, 97, 99, 104, 111, 125, 207, 208; and Hedgcoxe War, 169n.11, 171n.18; and Houston, 94, 128n.9; and Indians' rights, 87, 88, 89; and King, 97n.81, 104; and land laws, 79
Land titles: and Bryan, 155n.36; in Dallas County, 152n.24; Warren Ferris's bounty land titles, 73; and Mexican rule, 70, 70n.52; and Peters Colony, 147, 149–150, 167–168, 171, 171n.19; Texas General Land Office litigation in Dallas County, 149
Lanier Crossing: 160
Laramie Range: 19, 19n.9
Latimer, James W.: 174, 174n.26
"Laura" (W. Ferris): 137n.43
LaVaca County: 176
Laytham, William: 147, 147n.5
League: 78
"Leander and Laura" (W. Ferris): 222–223
Lee, Jason: 37
Lemhi Pass: 25, 26
Lewis, Meriwether: 11, 17, 18, 26
Lewis River: 31
Liberty, Texas: 49n.39
Life in the Rocky Mountains (Ferris): Battle of Pierre's Hole in, 28n.38; and Ferris' fame, ix; Charles Ferris's editing of, 53, 128n.12; Ferris's reclaiming of, 137; Ferris's writing of, 43–44; map of, xiii,

career of, 171, 171n.20; during
Reconstruction, 189–190, 190n.35; and
Throckmorton Compromise, 168–169,
169n.12
Throckmorton Compromise: 168–169,
169n.12
Throckmorton County: 168n.6
"To Mary" (W. Ferris): 225
"To My Absent Louisa" (Sellstadt): 162n.53
"To Summer" (W. Ferris): 224
Todd, Jackson: 81n.24
Towash Indians: 100
Town sites: 124n.86
Townsend, John Kirk: 37
Trexler, Harrison A.: xiv
Trinity River: bridge across, 176, 202; and
Dallas County, 149; as garden spot,
99, 99n.1; and Houston, 49; naviga-
tion of, 133, 134, 175–176, 176n.33,
196; Nelson's survey on, 155; settle-
ments along, 89, 133, 134; tributaries
of, 161
Trois Tetons: 25, 36
Troup, G. M.: 89n.54
Turner, Frederick Jackson: x
Turtle Creek: 100
"Twin Sisters": 50
Tyler, John: 141
Typhoid: 146, 195n.57

★ U ★

Under the Bridge (Greenslet): 1
Unicorn: 164–165, 165n.61, 178
Union Army: 188, 190, 192n.44, 194,
194n.55
Union sentiment: of Caroline Cook Henry,
192; in North Texas, 182n.6, 189n.34;
during Reconstruction, 190, 190n.36;
and secession vote, 183n.8, 189
Upper Canada Rebellion of 1838: 82
Urrea, José de: 46
Ute Indians: 22n.18, 37

★ V ★

Van Benthuysen, A. B.: 99n.1
Van Sickle, Benjamin A.: 75n.4, 79n.13
Van Zandt County: 78, 124
Vance, John: 161
Vanderburgh, William H.: 27, 29–31,
201n.77, 207, 210
Vara: 78, 78n.10
Veasey, Thomas: 181–182, 182n.4

Vehlein, Joseph: 70
Velasco, Texas: 51, 52, 59
Velasco, Treaty of: 125n.1
Vernier Compass: **77**
Veterans: and Bird's Fort, 124; and bounty
land grants, 79, 119n.70
Victoria, Texas: 51, 52
Village Creek: 100, 118, 121, 124
Voelker, Fred: xiv

★ W ★

Waco Indians: 118, 133
Walker, Albert G.: and Dallas County
boundaries, 150–152, 150n.14, 152n.21,
155, 158; and Dallas County commis-
sioners, 151n.16; divorce of, 149,
149n.10; as surveyor, 149–150, 149n.9,
152, 153, 154–155, 154n.30, 158; and
Texas Senate, 153, 169n.12, 211
Walker, Joseph: 31, 31n.46, 32
Walker, Louisa Cole: 151
Walker family: 161
Wallace, Jefferson "Big Foot": 118n.69
War of 1812: 2–3
Ward, Thomas W. "Peg Leg": 116n.62, 155,
167, 167n.2
Warner, George: 186, 187
Warren, Abel: 112
Warwick City: 97, 99, 105, 111, 123
Washington County: 177, 178
Washington-on-the-Brazos, Texas: 46, 125
Wasp, The: 129
Wassau Exchange Company: 103n.14
Watchman: 52
Watson, Riley: 161
Weather: drought conditions, 105, 177, 178,
202; and farming, 175; Ferris's knowl-
edge of, 202, 202n.80; immigrants'
adjustment to, 63; and surveying, 102,
115, 116, 158–159; winter weather,
86–87
Weaver, A. C.: 104n.15
Webb, Alexander: 118n.69, 124n.84
Webster, Daniel: 41
Weed, Thurlow: 9n.26
West, John R.: 200–201
West, Robert H.: 160n.49
West Fork of the Trinity: 100, 102, 102n.8
Western Literary and Scientific Academy: 6
Western Literary Messenger: Charles Ferris's
editing of, 51, 128–129; and grizzly bear
essay, 27n.35; *Life in the Rocky
Mountains* in, 17, 33n.52; Rosenstock's